1 5 SEP

TONS FOR TEMPELHOF

The Berlin Airlift

10 TONS FOR TEMPELHOF
The Berlin Airlift

Bob Clarke

TEMPUS

This book is dedicated to Christine and John Clarke.

First published 2007

Tempus Publishing Limited
The Mill, Brimscombe Port,
Stroud, Gloucestershire, GL5 2QG
www.tempus-publishing.com

British Library Cataloguing in Publication Data.
A catalogue record for this book is available from the British Library.

ISBN 978 0 7524 4092 7

Typesetting and origination by Tempus Publishing Limited
Printed in Great Britain

Contents

Acknowledgements

I have to thank many people who have helped me through the last eighteen months, without them this investigation would not have reached fruition. One group of individuals stand head and shoulders above the rest: that band who experienced the war and lived through the aftermath of a devastated Europe – the veterans. These people were a little surprised that I was interested in a brief period some had almost forgotten. To learn something of their daily life and experiences was a privilege. They are Guy Kenney, Allyne Conner, Heinz Johannsen, Ernie Jessen, W.C. (Dub) Southers, John Collier, John Beavin, Roy Smith, Val Spaven, Joe Gyulavics, Sam Pover, John Beauchamp, Richard E. Wilson, Christine Clarke (*née* Bulmer), William Ball, John Dury, Neville Cox, Bella of WAAF, Harlan Senior, Les Haines, Len Guyatt and Dieter Hesse (now Pete McCoy). A special mention goes to the late Edward Newman who helped me with the Bomber Command aspects of the first chapter and inspired so many young people through his work with the Air Training Corps. Thanks are also due to Francis Adam Watt who enlightened me in many ways and trusted me with his superb photograph album.

Others can also step into the limelight. Barry Huntingford, who has, yet again, made sense of madness. Amy Rigg at Tempus, who made this book possible. The staff of the Allied Museum in Berlin, Royal Air Force Museums at Cosford and Hendon, MOD Boscombe Down Record Centre, Pete James, Malcolm Holland, Adrian Robins and Kevin Taylor for their viewpoints, and all those people who have nodded with interest and offered support. Nick Wotherspoon of the Lancashire Aircraft Investigation Team who supplied me with information about the Burtonwood C-54 crash in advance of his own publication. And finally, my beautiful wife Sarah who has come to the conclusion that she will never get the spare bedroom back! To them all I say thank you. Any errors are naturally of my own making.

Preface

Flying into Berlin today is no different to visiting any other major European city. Low-cost airlines funnel weekend tourists to regional airports across the continent, many of them in former Eastern Bloc countries. New routes are constantly opened up; benefits of the 'Peace Dividend' and the continent's new found super club – the European Union. How short memories are: only sixty years ago the entire Northern Hemisphere had been touched by the most devastating war the world had ever seen. Berlin became the last bastion of the Third Reich and, during the last three years of the conflict, large areas were summarily devastated by waves of British and American bombers. This destruction later became total as, throughout April and the beginning of May 1945, the Red Army smashed its way, street by street, to the Reichstag, the cultural centre of Berlin and Hitler's *gross deutches Reich*.

Sixty years on, some public buildings still wear the scars of those fateful days. However, the interested tourist has to search them out as, since the collapse of communism and reunification of the country, Berlin has become one large building site. Tower cranes dominate the skyline as the city, especially in the Eastern sector, finally rises from the ashes of its past. However, Berlin is different to any other European city. It became the focus for a potentially far more dangerous conflict – the Cold War. The uneasy alliance forged through necessity in the face of fascist domination did not last long beyond the unconditional surrender of the Reich and by 1948 the first major crisis had unfolded – the Berlin Blockade. This was the first time the new superpowers stood toe to toe, the direction of European politics over the next forty years were to be decided by who blinked first.

The origin of the Berlin Blockade, like so many other European conflicts, is hard to determine when considered alone. Clearly, two events stand out: the German invasion of the Soviet Union in 1941, and the bombing campaign of the Royal Air Force and United States Army Air Corps from 1942. By this campaign the heart of the country was systematically smashed out in an attempt to bring German war production to a standstill. This almost total devastation was what the occupying forces inherited in 1945. It seems right then to start this account with the destruction of Germany from the air. I trust the reader agrees.

The Battle for Berlin left a devastated landscape populated mainly by women and children. They were soon to be on the front line of the major test to peace in the Cold War.

Here then, is an account of the opening shots of the Cold War. It is a story of changing values, political will, humanity and compassion. It is a story that has probably only been rivalled recently by such events as Live Aid and the Asian Tsunami Disaster Relief effort. It is a story of how East and West divided Europe into two superpower camps. A story of the construction of the Iron Curtain and a conflict that was to dominate Western culture for nearly fifty years. This, then, is the story of the Berlin Airlift.

One

Devastation and Defeat

Bomber offensive

On 30 May 1942 Germany, or more accurately Cologne, suffered the heaviest air raid of the war so far. Air Marshal Arthur T. Harris, Commander-in-Chief, Bomber Command, in the post from February, had been planning 'Millennium' for over a month and was convinced a decisive blow would shake the enemy's resolve. Harris argued with Churchill that month that small raids were ineffective against industrial targets and that 'the cumulative effect of hundreds of them would be needed before the enemy felt the pinch'. Churchill agreed and planning for the first 1,000-bomber raid in history was underway.

As 1,047 aircraft took off from bases all over England the weather started to close in and the trip across the North Sea became decidedly unpleasant. However, over Holland the skies cleared and remained so right on to the target. Almost 900 of the force reached the city and within two hours had dropped 1,455 tons of ordnance. High-explosive bombs blasted roofs open and incendiaries, two thirds of the total bomb load, rained in, setting the buildings ablaze. Later reconnaissance flights showed that 600 acres of the ancient city centre had been almost completely destroyed, only the ancient gothic cathedral, scarred and blackened, appeared to stand reticently defiant. 480 civilians were killed and around 45,000 were 'de-housed'; the war on morale had begun. Harris was convinced that breaking German morale would break the industrial heart of the country and reduce the will to fight. The legacy of this train of thought was to sow the seeds of European post-war division and, ultimately, the Cold War.

The raid on Cologne had widespread implications for both sides. Harris argued that this 'irrefutable demonstration of the power of what was to all intents and purposes a new untried weapon' was now the way forward. Cologne also changed the role of the Luftwaffe. Since the Spanish Civil War the majority of aircraft had been used in support of the army as part of the Blitzkrieg. Now home defence became a priority. Aircraft used in close ground support were reduced to 20 per cent of pre-Cologne levels and the production of single-engine fighters was increased at the expense of bombers. The flak force was also reorganised, bringing upwards of 1 million new recruits, many from the Hitler Youth and League of German Maidens, into uniform, operating searchlights, flak batteries and rudimentary radar units.

A Blenheim of RAF Bomber Command carrying out a daylight attack on the Fortuna Power Station near Cologne on 12 August 1941. Localised raids such as these were little more than an inconvenience to the German war machine. A year later the picture would be completely different.

Attacks continued throughout 1942 on the German mainland but with limited success. The USAAF flew its first strategic bombing mission in Europe on 17 August 1942, destroying rail marshalling yards at Rouen. The twelve B-17E Fortresses were escorted by nine Spitfire squadrons and unsurprisingly none were lost. The 8th Army Air Force had, since arrival in Britain, been preparing for daylight raids over Europe. The Royal Air Force considered large bomber formations in daylight as suicide; however, the USAAF had trained all their crews for just such operations. They argued that daylight precision attacks on strategic targets would reduce the enemies' ability to wage war rather than his will to wage war (as the RAF considered more likely).

At the Casablanca conference in January 1943 the British and American Combined Chiefs of Staff Committee adopted round-the-clock area bombardment. The United States Eighth Air Force and RAF Bomber Command now combined their efforts for the destruction and dislocation of German economic, military, and industrial infrastructure. In support of the Atlantic campaign U-boat construction yards and pens on the occupied west coast of France were high on the initial lists of targets. However, factory complexes within the Reich itself were also targeted. On 5 March aircraft attacked Essen, home of Krupps steel works, in the opening shots of the 'Battle of the Ruhr', principally to slow down arms production. By now Stalin was incessantly demanding that the Western Allies open a second front and attacking German production was seen as a way to prove the Allies' intention to eventually do so, but, in the event, production was only reduced by an estimated 10 per cent. However, Düsseldorf, Aachen, Duisburg, Barmen-Wuppertal and many smaller settlements were heavily damaged in the process. Some attacks were audacious to say the least, the best known was undoubtedly the Dambusters' Raid of 16 May; the military effectiveness of this morale-raising exploit is still discussed today. The Ruhr was well defended by effective radio-controlled flack and searchlights, very quickly being christened 'happy valley' due to the losses British crews suffered. Between March and July 1943 the Battle of the Ruhr cost the lives of 5,600 aircrew; civilian losses are unknown.

By July 1943 American and British aircraft were bombing some targets round the clock, culminating that month with an attack on the port of Hamburg. Operation Gomorrah started on the evening of 24 July when the RAF deployed 'window', tons of aluminium strips or chaff cut to a specific length. Within minutes ground defence and night fighter radars were completely saturated with false 'echoes', subsequently 721 aircraft reached the target area, and ominous fires started. On 26 July 235 Flying Fortresses bombed strategic targets around the docks area of the city, and the following evening 722 RAF aircraft revisited. After this attack large numbers of civilians, mostly women and children, were evacuated. British and American aircraft visited the city a further four times, the final one on the night of 2–3 August. Harris later noted that the 2,353 sorties by Bomber Command, dropping 7,196 bombs, had left 'a scene of unimaginable devastation'. Among that 'scene' were the remains of nearly 45,000 people, many suffocated and incinerated by the ensuing firestorm. Hamburg, Germany's second largest city, had effectively been destroyed in three nights and along with it the Luftwaffe's ability to mount a credible aerial defence. The devastation of Germany was now inevitable.

On 17 August two major targets were hit. During the day over 300 American aircraft bombed the aircraft factory at Regensburg and the ball-bearing factory at Schweinfurt. That night the Royal Air Force bombed Peenemünde on the Baltic coast in an attempt to stop the development of the V2. Mosquitoes drew off most of the German fighter cover due to a diversionary raid on Berlin. This was not the first time the city had been hit but it signalled the start of what was to become 'The Battle of Berlin'.

'Berlin Next'

It was only a matter of time before Bomber Command had the expertise, equipment and ability to punch Berlin hard and now, as the nights grew steadily longer, that time had come. Berlin was the third largest city in the world at the outbreak of war. As the Reich had expanded, so had the government departments located in the city, furthermore Berlin was now the central hub for many major communications networks. The city covered hundreds of square kilometres and had a pre-war population of around 4 million. Five raids in early 1943 killed around 650 Berliners but had little effect beyond morale-boosting headlines in the British press. However, the RAF did help 'celebrate' the tenth anniversary of the Nazi Party coming to power by attacking specific buildings on 30 January using Mosquitoes. Generally though, Hamburg had much more effect on the German Authorities. Evacuation had until then been voluntary, but now Dr. Goebbels – incidentally Berlin's *Gauleiter* (govenor) – ordered the immediate removal of children and young mothers. This initial de-population of the city was so severe that in some suburbs, schools were left empty and were requisitioned as shelters for the soon to be homeless or identified as field hospitals. As the nights became shorter the attacks were reduced until, at the end of March, major operations were switched to the Ruhr. The total number of Berliners killed in this period was about 1,800.

The Battle of Berlin began on the evening of 23 August 1943. In all, sixteen major raids were carried out by the Royal Air Force. A number of factors hampered the bombing campaign, not least the weather. Conditions were so bad that the bomber crews were completely reliant on the markers dropped by the Pathfinder force, it also meant no reconnaissance photographs after raids, so planning was hampered for follow-up attacks. Berlin was, by direct flight, over 600 miles from British airfields and so planners needed the long winter nights if they were to try to limit the losses. The first raid, comprising 727 aircraft, met with limited success. The pathfinder markers were dropped on the wrong area and there was no concentration of bomb effect. However, much damage was done to property and 854 people lost their lives. The second raid caused little damage, but resulted in the third, an all-Lancaster force on 3–4 September, succeeded in dropping 583 tons of high explosive and 382 incendiaries and major damage. The factories of Siemens and AEG were hit, along with the Opera House, several water and electricity works and a brewery.

'From End to End'

Harris, in a letter to Churchill on 3 November 1943, stated, 'We must get the USAAF to wade in with greater force… We can wreck Berlin from end to end if the USAAF will come in on it. It will cost between us 400–500 aircraft. It will cost Germany the war'. However, Harris had to wait until March 1944 for USAAF assistance. RAF raids restarted on 18 November, involving 444 aircraft over Berlin; however, 395 aircraft also bombed Mannheim and Ludwigshafen. Mannheim had been bombed several times already and was now used as a diversion to the attack on the capital. Mosquitoes also visited Essen, Aachen and Frankfurt whilst sixteen Wellingtons laid mines in the St Nazaire area. On 22–23 November Berlin suffered its heaviest raid to date and lost some major buildings in the process. Housing for around 175,000 people was lost along with the Kaiser-Wilhelm-Gedächtniskirche, Charlottenburg Castle and parts of Berlin Zoo, along with several embassies and official buildings. Firestorm conditions killed around 2,000, 500 of those in a shelter in Wilmersdorf. The following night 383 aircraft streamed towards the city. They found the weather as unforgiving as ever, however, major fires were still burning from the night before. Many crews, remembering the consequences of an uncontrollable fire, re-bombed those areas. An estimated 1,800 died that night. Six Mosquitoes kept up the pressure the following night, whilst a major raid took place on Frankfurt by 262 aircraft, on 26–27 November Stuttgart was used as a diversion raid whilst Berlin was again attacked. This time suburbs of the city were destroyed along with parts of the zoo, the majority of whose animals had already been evacuated, although, some of the big cats remained and had to be hunted down as they escaped into the city.

December saw no let-up for the city as major raids occurred on 2nd–3rd (458 aircraft) and 16th–17th (498 aircraft). On this latter attack the National Theatre and military and political archives were destroyed. Major damage was done to the rail system causing supplies travelling to the Eastern Front to be held up. This was further exacerbated by the number of refugees in the city, now in the thousands, all of who knew that a large firestorm was a real possibility. Up to now over a quarter of Berlin's housing had been destroyed. Aircraft again

Berliners pick their way through burning streets after a night raid by British aircraft, September 1943.

A small boy is pulled from the wreckage of his home by a German civil defence team. Goebbels was to evacuate many children from the city – unless they were Hitler Youth.

attacked on the nights of 23rd–24th (379 aircraft) and 29th–30th (712 aircraft); this time southern and eastern districts bore the brunt of the bombing, again reducing housing and civilian facilities. There was no reduction for January 1944. Aircraft attacked on the nights of 1st–2nd (421 aircraft) and 2nd–3rd (383 aircraft). Mosquitoes on small raids kept up the pressure until the night of 20–21 when a force of 769 flew to the once again cloud-covered city. This was quickly followed by raids on 28th–29th (677 aircraft), which hit a number of public buildings including the Reich Chancellery, and 30th–31st (534 aircraft), when over 1,000 were killed and a number of party buildings, including the Propaganda Ministry, were hit. Then, on 15–16 February the largest Royal Air Force formation yet to attack the city was launched, when 891 aircraft took part. Central and south-western districts were heavily damaged; this was to be the last major Bomber Command involvement over the city for a month, although Mosquitoes did fly in on occasion. The final major raid occurred on the night of 24–25 March when 811 aircraft dropped devices over a wide area, causing major damage to housing and the barracks of *Leibstandarte* – Adolf Hitler.

Discussion as to how effective the Royal Air Force raids were during the Battle of Berlin has been constant ever since the end of the Second World War. The campaign was costly in terms of both aircrew and aircraft. 2,938 died during the battle and nearly 500 aircraft were lost. Of course the Battle of Berlin did not stop there, neither did the wholesale destruction of industrial, communication, transport or population centres across Germany. In fact, the USAAF had only just got into their stride, and along with attacks on strategic targets came the adoption of, albeit in daylight, area bombardment. Berlin again became the centre of attention. From March 1944 sporadic Mosquito and B-17 raids kept the pressure on the population. There was a lull in major bombing flights as the Allies dedicated the majority of their air support to the beaches of northern France. Strategic targets were hit, primarily war industries, however it was after Christmas before the air assaults restarted against Berlin. On Monday 26 February 1945 a pathfinder force marked out the city, as usual for Berlin, in thick cloud. Behind them was the biggest force the Allies had yet mustered against the city. Over 1,000 USAF B-17 and B-24 bombers plus an escort of P-51 Mustangs dropped nearly 3,000 tons of bombs in the central district. By now fighter cover was low and the flack batteries were simply overwhelmed by the sheer weight of numbers. Alexanderplatz and Frankfurter Allee were severely damaged, as were a number of museums and numerous residential buildings. Three weeks later a similar force dropped 3,276 tons. The final major air offensive took place to 'celebrate' Hitler's fifty-sixth and last birthday, destroying rail targets around the city. Mosquito raids of between ten and a hundred aircraft were to continue right up until the Soviet forces entered the city.

European Advisory Committee and the Allied Control Council

By 1943 it had become clear Germany could no longer sustain war on two fronts, accordingly, political moves were initiated to manage the country in defeat. One of the most influential organisations regarding German and Berlin, post-war, was the European Advisory Committee (EAC). This was tasked with studying the political problems that were anticipated once Germany had been defeated. The first formal EAC meeting convened on 14 January 1944 at Lancaster House, London. The initial members were Sir William Strang (representing Britain), John Winant (United States Ambassador to Britain) and Feodor Gousev (Russian Ambassador to Britain). In November 1944 René Massigli, representing the French at Churchill's request, joined.

Strang maintained a level of autonomy, enjoying the backing of both the Cabinet and Foreign Office, giving him the authority to push through British proposals. The other members were not so lucky. Any proposal had to be passed back to their respective governments and, not surprisingly, progress was slow. However, when an item under discussion was of interest to the Russians replies could be very quick indeed. At the first meeting Strang tabled a draft surrender document and suggested boundaries for zones of Allied occupation, Winant asked for clarification and guidance from Washington on the subject, and yet he heard nothing for weeks. The Russians then agreed to the proposal just four days later, something of a revelation in Soviet politics! In fact, such was the speed of Russia's acceptance the Americans thought that they had been in private discussion with the British. It was not until 8 March that Winant finally received suggestions on a possible surrender document and zone layout. Washington's proposal was considered unworkable and eventually it was discarded in favour of the original British plan. Germany in defeat was to be temporarily partitioned. By the end of 1944 the EAC had drafted plans to partition Austria into three zones, divide Berlin and Vienna into three sectors, and had created the instruction for the unconditional surrender of Germany. One major recommendation was the formation of the Allied Control Council (ACC).

The primary function of the ACC would be to organise the central administration of Germany, with extra responsibility for ensuring military administration was carried out uniformly across all occupation zones. Military governors were to exercise full powers within each respective zone, but they were expected to act collectively within the ACC. The ACC brief was enormous, including disbanding the German army, the de-Nazification of the population, the generation of a peacetime economy and the organisation of reparations based on a 'democratic principle'. Furthermore, it was required that all ACC decisions be unanimous. The fact that each member held a veto a serious flaw in the system and one the Soviets would exploit in full over subsequent years. The ACC was to have its seat in Berlin but would not administer the city; the 'Kommandatura' would oversee this. The four military commandants, chairing the committee in rotation, would lead this smaller group. This too had a veto system, rendering it ineffective before it even got off the ground.

The end of the fascist yoke

The last major Soviet offensive in the West commenced on 16 April 1945. It was to bring about the final destruction of Berlin, the Third Reich and ultimately end the war in Europe. The Red Army had been amassing troops and equipment on the Oder-Neisse river line since January. Around 2.5 million Red Army soldiers organised into three Army groups, the first Byelorussian, second Byelorussian and first Ukrainian front now stood ready. Facing them were the remnants of Hitler's eastern campaign armies, totalling around 1 million. On the day Hitler proclaimed 'Berlin stays German' Soviet leaders told their front-line troops:

> The time has come to free our fathers, mothers, brothers, sisters, wives, and children still languishing under the fascist yoke in Germany. The time has come to draw up the balance sheet of the abominable crimes perpetrated on our soil by the Hitlerite cannibals and to punish those responsible for those atrocities. The time has come to inflict the final defeat on the enemy and to draw this war to a victorious conclusion.

Stalin expected the operation to be concluded by the May Day holiday, a major date in the Soviet calendar. In a classic example of Stalinist political intrigue he allowed his commanders in the field to think that the Western Allies intended to take the city. In reality Eisenhower had rejected Montgomery's suggestion, why lose troops fighting through built-up areas just to hand back hard-won territory to the Russians? he argued. And so Marshals Zhukov and Koniev were tasked with taking the city, and more importantly the Reichstag, perceived centre of the Nazi empire.

Hitler, a virtual prisoner within the bunker at the Reich Chancellery, now presided over the last moments of his empire. He made sweeping gestures over the map predicting a crushing defeat for the Red Army at the gates of Berlin. As the situation steadily worsened Hitler assumed personal responsibility for the defence of the city, ordering spearhead attacks by panzerkorp battalions no longer in existence. And those who considered fleeing the city prior to the Soviet onslaught now ran a new risk, as Goebbels explained in a radio broadcast on 18 April:

> Any man found not doing his duty will be hanged on a lamppost after a summary judgement. Moreover, placards will be attached to the corpses stating: 'I have been hanged here because I am too cowardly to defend the capital of the Reich'–'I have been hanged because I did not believe in the Führer' – 'I am a deserter and for this reason I shall not see this turning-point of destiny.'

For those who survived the ensuing battle for Berlin 'destiny' was to be forced hard labour in Russia on rebuilding programmes, rape by Soviet soldiers, humiliation, starvation and years of uncertainty as to whether the West would pull out of Berlin and leave the population to the communists.

Combined bombardment from over 25,000 artillery pieces now hit the city, delivering an estimated 25,600 tons of shells on to the city centre in less than a week. The devastation in Berlin was almost total by now. There were no services left to speak of, collapsed buildings blocked streets and the population cowered in makeshift cellar refuges or large public shelters including the Flak towers. Less than 90,000 defenders were now recognisable, the majority of whom were *Volkssturm* (People's Army) comprising invalids and old men or Hitler Youth, who were, in most cases, fanatical fighters. As Soviet troops fought their way into the city the conditions for the civilian population worsened. Fighting was house-to-house, often using artillery at point blank range or demolition charges to bring down

British troops meet with their Soviet allies on 3 May 1945. This scene, photographed at Wismar, was echoed up and down Germany.

Social infrastructure had all but collapsed by April 1945, leaving many to fend for themselves. Here a train at Eschinege is being looted. (US Army Signal Corps)

buildings housing suspected snipers. Many perished due to being trapped under tons of rubble or roasted alive as flame-thrower squads 'cleared areas'. On 30 April, after marrying Eva Braun, Hitler committed suicide. He, like his dream of world domination, ended in flames as he was unceremoniously cremated in the Chancellery garden. The defenders fought on for a further two days before, on 2 May, General Wielding surrendered to the Soviet army.

Large numbers of ground troops now considered surrender to the Western Allies the better option and fled westward. General Busse of the 9th Army ordered his men to make a desperate break-out. The American forces, by now stationed on the far bank of the Elbe, tried in vain to stop the flow of refugees across the river away from the Soviets. However, over 400,000 troops and civilians made it across. The collapse of German forces now picked up speed and the surrender of the army in north-west Germany, Holland and Denmark to Field-Marshal Montgomery took place on 4 May, quickly followed by troops in Austria to Soviet forces.

On 6 May General-Admiral von Friedeburg was dispatched to the Supreme Headquarters Allied Expeditionary Force (SHAEF) at Reims to broker the final instrument of surrender. Whilst there he was authorised to attempt a partial surrender allowing troops trapped in the east to escape the Soviet forces. Eisenhower flatly rejected this and ordered the unconditional surrender to be effective as of midnight on 8 May. Unfortunately, it was a draft document von Friedeburg signed at Reims on 7 May as incredibly, no one had remembered to bring the official surrender document that the European Advisory Council had taken six months to draw up. Subsequently Stalin demanded that the document be re-signed, this time in Berlin, and at 12.43 a.m. on 9 May the war in Europe officially came to an end.

The destruction of Berlin had been almost total. Electricity was for the most part a distant memory, as was the domestic gas supply. The water was unsafe as most of the sewage system was shattered and contamination had spread far and wide. The stench of death was everywhere. Those who had sought refuge from the Soviet onslaught had done so in cellars or public shelters. The flak towers were almost impervious to artillery fire, but unfortunately the same could not be said for the basements of apartment blocks. Many people had perished as the structures came down, or were murdered by Soviet troops on their way through the city. This, coupled with those buried under the rubble or just left out in the streets, brought the horror of war to the heart of Germany.

Reparations

Whilst fires were still burning in Berlin special Soviet units were deployed throughout the city, their aim was to systematically strip the capital of any usable industrial asset. What started as machinery quickly became Soviet property, whether it was nailed down or not. Within a few days the entire city was the scene of frenzied looting. Works of art, beds, tyres, light bulbs, taps and toilets, all were either dismantled or smashed before being loaded onto trucks and sent east. This was not just the fate of Berlin – all areas now under Soviet occupation were treated the same, although the city was singled out for special attention.

The devastation of the capital was almost complete. The Allies inherited a country in ruins, it was the perfect breeding-ground for communism. Interestingly, the wrecked vehicle is probably a Lend-Lease GMC used by the Red Army.

Reparation was no new concept; throughout European history the victor had exacted a price on the aggressor. After the First World War Germany was required to pay £6.6 billion to France, Britain and a host of other devastated nations under Article 231 of the Treaty of Versailles. This had included a large proportion of its steel production, agricultural output and coal from the Ruhr region. The system proved unworkable due to the economic climate of the 1920s, so much so that France reoccupied the Ruhr in an attempt to force the German Government to pay. However, when the stock market crashed in 1929, foreign investment in Germany ceased and deaths through poverty reached a record high in 1932, Hitler later 'cancelled' the debt.

'Make them pay'

The issue of reparations was first raised in a remarkable telegram to Churchill from the Soviet Premier on 15 September 1941. With Operation Barbarossa two months old and looking unstoppable, the British Government had requested that:

> If the Soviet Government would be compelled to destroy its naval vessels at Leningrad
> in order to prevent their falling into the enemy hands, His Majesty's Government would

recognise after the war claims of the Soviet Government to a certain compensation from His Majesty's Government for the restoration of the vessels destroyed.[1]

The reply hinted ominously as to Germany's fate in defeat:

The Soviet Government understands and appreciates the readiness of the British Government to make partial compensation for the damage sustained by the Soviet Union in case the Soviet vessels at Leningrad would actually be destroyed. There could be no doubt that such a course will be adopted should the necessity arise. However, the responsibility for this damage would be not Britain's but Germany's. I think therefore that the damage after the war should be made good at the expense of Germany.[2]

At the Yalta Conference early in 1945 the Russians set out their reparations demands, claiming $10 billion, culminating in the creation of the Allied Reparations Council with its seat in Moscow. No actual figure was agreed; however, the Soviets in true style, argued that their figure had been accepted 'in principle' and so should stand. Basically Germany would be 'obliged to the greatest extent possible to make reparations'. And at Potsdam the level was formalised, obviously in the Soviets favour as they had indeed suffered the most in terms of physical loss. The Potsdam Protocol cited the following:

III. REPARATIONS FROM GERMANY

1. Reparation claims of the U. S. S. R. shall be met by removals from the zone of Germany occupied by the U. S. S. R., and from appropriate German external assets.

2. The U. S. S. R. undertakes to settle the reparation claims of Poland from its own share of reparations.

3. The reparation claims of the United States, the United Kingdom and other countries entitled to reparations shall be met from the Western Zones and from appropriate German external assets.

4. In addition to the reparations to be taken by the U. S. S. R. from its own zone of occupation, the U. S. S. R. shall receive additionally from the Western Zones:

(a) 15 per cent of such usable and complete industrial capital equipment, in the first place from the metallurgical, chemical and machine manufacturing industries as is unnecessary for the German peace economy and should be removed from the Western Zones of Germany, in exchange for an equivalent value of food, coal, potash, zinc, timber, clay products, petroleum products, and such other commodities as may be agreed upon.

(b) 10 per cent of such industrial capital equipment as is unnecessary for the German peace economy and should be removed from the Western Zones, to be transferred to the

---

[1] Memorandum delivered to Molotov by British Ambassador, Sir Stafford Cripps 12/9/41. (Third paragraph after sub-heading 'make them pay'.)
[2] Memorandum from Stalin to Churchill 15/9/41. (Sixth paragraph after 'make them pay'.)

Soviet Government on reparations account without payment or exchange of any kind
in return.

Removals of equipment as provided in (a) and (b) above shall be made simultaneously.

As far as the Soviets were concerned the floodgates were now open. Not only could
they legally remove equipment from their sector, they also demanded equipment and
goods from the Western side. Furthermore, Russia had no intention of removing just
surplus or war machinery. The Allied Reparations Council collapsed by the end of 1945
leaving the monitoring of the reparation programme to the Control Council. So the
Soviets throughout 1945, and certainly in the two months before the three Western Allies
took over their sectors, systematically stripped the city of anything they could lay their
hands on.

'Frau Kommen'

When, on 22 June 1941, Hitler launched Operation Barbarossa (the invasion of the Soviet
Union), he unleashed savagery unparalleled in modern history. Fuelled by Nazi racist
ideology, the Slavic races were considered *Untermenschen* (sub-humans) and were to be

Right: Lt General Lucius D. Clay. Eisenhower's Deputy and eventually United States Military Governor of Germany.

Opposite: Yalta, February 1945, the last time the 'Big Three' met. Yalta, political commentators noted, was the West's betrayal of Eastern Europe as Stalin ran rings around the gravely ill US President Roosevelt.

treated accordingly. This was not to be a war of conquest, more one of extermination. No accurate figure is available for the total deaths caused by the eastern campaign but conservative estimates put it at around 20 million in the Soviet Union alone. Atrocities were widespread and pardonable by officers in charge. But the Soviets too were capable of mass murder.

Before Barbarossa, Germany and the Soviet Union had divided Poland between them. Naturally, large numbers of Polish troops fell into Russian hands and were interned. After Germany turned on Russia the Polish Government in exile requested that the Soviet authorities release the prisoners. Unfortunately, according to Moscow, they had all managed to escape to Manchuria. When the Wehrmacht reached Katyn near Smolensk in 1941 the truth was uncovered. A Red Cross team excavated the site at the request of the Nazi regime and, desperate to portray the Soviets in a bad light, they discovered nearly 15,000 Polish officers mostly shot through the neck, a Soviet police practice. This was not an isolated incident, Stalin had been murdering his own people since he had come to power in 1922, again no accurate figure remains but an estimated 15 million appears likely. Many peasants stripped of the means to support themselves were left to starve whilst ethnic groups were eradicated at the stroke of a pen.

As the German war machine rolled steadily across the Russian Plains throughout 1941–42, the Soviet authorities dismantled large parts of their industrial infrastructure and moved it beyond the Ural Mountains. Anything left behind was destroyed or rendered unusable, this included the harvest and food-producing network the population relied upon for survival. Once the Germans were in retreat they systematically destroyed everything that was left. By 1944 the Soviet Army was liberating a country, quite literally, in ashes.

Clearly, then, the Germans had a lot to fear from the Russians; no compassion could be expected, and in most cases none was forthcoming. As the Soviet armies closed in on Berlin, Hitler prophesied the condition that would befall the population in defeat:

> For the last time, the deadly Jewish-Bolshevik enemy has started a mass attack. He is trying to reduce Germany to rubble and to exterminate our people. Soldiers of the East! You are already fully aware now of the fate that threatens German women and children. Whilst men, children, and older people will be murdered, women and girls will be reduced to the role of barrack-room whores, The rest will be marched off to Siberia.

British Historian Anthony Beever later described the situation:

> By the time the Russians reached Berlin, soldiers were regarding women almost as carnal booty; they felt because they were liberating Europe they could behave as they pleased. Orgies of violence and rape soon gripped the region, often fuelled by alcohol, so much so that the first few months became known as the 'Russian Time' in eastern-occupied Germany.

Ernst Reuter, post-war mayor of Berlin, put the number of victims in the city at around 90,000. Beever later suggested the figures for East Germany between 1945 and 1948 may have been as high as 2 million per year. In fact, the spread of sexually transmitted diseases had reached epidemic proportions by 1946, prompting Soviet officials to impose serious penalties for fraternising with Germans in the Eastern zone.

Prisoner

As the two fronts moved closer across the continent thousands of Germans were taken prisoner by the Allies. In fact, 400,000 were still held in Britain in 1946, mostly used as labour on farms and in factories, but increasingly tolerated by the local population. By Christmas 1946 many were invited into the homes of ordinary people to celebrate the festive period. Unfortunately, the same could not be said of those captured by the Red Army.

Prisoner numbers increased dramatically after the 'Battle of the Bulge' (the Ardennes Offensive) in December 1944. Clearly, the end was near and most German troops now considered internment in a Western prisoner of war (POW) camp preferable to transfer onto the Russian front. For those that fell into Soviet hands the future was far less certain. At the fall of Stalingrad in 1943, 90,000 troops were captured from an estimated force of 280,000, fewer than 5,000 were to see their homeland again. Once Germany capitulated, POWs were loaded onto trains, trucks or simply marched east, viewed as part of the reparations due to the Soviet Union. The remnants of the Berlin defenders, around 130,000, were marched to a mass collection point just outside the city and then transported to the Soviet Union. Many were later employed on big civil engineering projects such as Moscow University, one of Stalin's 'wedding cake' buildings that dominate the Moscow skyline.

And so, by the end of the Second World War, Germany, and to a lesser degree Central Europe, was a scene of total devastation. Nearly 5 million prisoners of war were spread across the Western world and possibly the same number were now in the charge of the Red Army. More than 2 million displaced persons, many of them ethnic Germans removed by the Soviets or slave labourers, were in the American zone alone, and this was to swell by several million more. The machinery of Government had completely collapsed; there were no services in the majority of towns and cities. And the banking system had been replaced with a commodity-based economy centring on the black market. General Lucius Clay arrived in Berlin on 5 June as General Dwight Eisenhower's Deputy Governor. He later recorded his first impressions as he travelled through the devastation from Tempelhof airfield:

> Apparently the Germans along the route, which was lined with Soviet soldiers, had been ordered to remain indoors, and it was only at the intersections that a few could be seen on the streets which crossed our route. They seemed weak, cowed, and furtive and not yet recovered from the shock of the Battle of Berlin. It was like a city of the dead. I had seen nothing quite comparable in Western Germany, and I must confess that my exultation in victory was diminished as I witnessed this degradation of man. I decided then and there never to forget that we were responsible for the government of human beings.[3]

Clay was to go on to be the pivotal figure in the regeneration of Germany and earned the affectionate title *Vater der Luftbrücke* (father of the airlift) from the grateful city population.

---

[3] *Decision in Germany*, Lucius Clay, 1950. (Second to last paragraph of chapter one.)

Two

The Grand Alliance Crumbles

Occupation

On 5 June 1945 a delegation headed by Generals Montgomery, Eisenhower and de Lattre travelled to Berlin to issue the three proclamations on the control of Germany. The European Advisory Commission (EAC) had been working on the document since November 1944 and it comprised three main elements:

(1) Declaration Regarding the Defeat of Germany and the Assumption of Supreme Authority with respect to Germany by the Governments of the UK, the USA, the USSR, and the Provisional Government of the French Republic.
(2) Statement by the Governments of the UK, the USA, the USSR and the Provisional Government of the France Republic on Control Machinery in Germany.
(3) Statement by the Governments of the UK, the USA, the USSR and the Provisional Government of the French Republic on zones of occupation in Germany.

Nowhere did any of the documents contain a guarantee to a right of way into Berlin. This was not an oversight; US Ambassador Winant thought the Soviets would simply accept right of passage as part of a new mutual friendship, 'in which differences would disappear'. This was a serious miscalculation; from the outset the Soviet Military Authority made it known that the Western Allies were in Berlin on sufferance.

The West was convinced that once the proclamations had been issued the Allied Control Council (ACC) would have legal status and the four-power governance of Berlin would commence. Subsequently, a large entourage accompanied the generals to the signings, however, from the outset proceedings did not run smoothly. It was several hours before the Soviet delegation was happy with the documents, even though they had been instrumental in their design within the EAC. After a swift signing ceremony Zhukov invited the delegates to a specially prepared banquet. Eisenhower declined, explaining he would like to leave staff in the city to arrange the entry of the three Western powers. Zhukov suggested that this 'would not be useful' as such arrangements could only be made once all the occupying troops were in their respective zones. The staff were flown home again.

When Germany collapsed Western troops had advanced further east than had at first been thought possible. Now, with the US army well inside the proposed Soviet zone, Churchill was calling for the troops to stay, at least for the time being. Truman, in office for only two months, listened to his advisors and told Churchill that American troops were not going to be used as bargaining chips for other issues. If the Soviets wanted soldiers out of their zone before access to Berlin was granted, then that was the way it would be. Whilst this debate raged Soviet troops were systematically stripping the city of everything, including, by now, a complete power station.

By 29 June British and American representatives were back at Zhukov's headquarters discussing access and deployment to Berlin. This was the first engagement of Lieutenant General Sir Ronald Weeks, new British Deputy Military Governor, accompanied by William Strang, architect of the three German Proclamations and chief designer of the zonal structure. The Russians, awkward as ever, chose not to deal with the French delegation as no firm sector in Berlin had yet been decided for them. Agreement was eventually reached on troop withdrawal allowing, from 1 July, four days to complete the movements; however, there was to be no formal hand-over of territory. Zhukov wanted Allied troops clear as fast as possible but with no contact with his own men. Soviet occupying forces would follow Western withdrawal at no less than 1km. Russian reconnaissance units were allowed to enter areas prior to occupation, but Britain and the United States only agreed to this when their reconnaissance parties were allowed into the city.

Generals Weeks and Clay were also to discuss the thornier subject of access into Berlin. By now Moscow had recognised that this was a major weakness in the whole agreement and was eager to exploit it. Britain and the US proposed that they would require three rail links, two autobahns and as much air access as was deemed necessary to move in their administration garrisons. Zhukov vigorously protested, saying his troops needed those routes during the demobilisation of his forces. Eventually he agreed to the temporary use of one rail link, one autobahn and two air corridors. The situation could then be properly discussed at the Allied Control Council (ACC) at a later date. The Soviets readily agreed, having meticulously combed through the terms of reference for the ACC they detected a major flaw, one that would ultimately bring about the Council's collapse. Every agreement had to be unanimous, yet every member had a veto; clearly no agreement need ever be reached again that was not in Moscow's interests.

Quadripartite

Over the next four days the Soviets were busy. Troops were now encouraged to remove anything they considered of value, especially within the sectors the British, French and US were about to occupy. Anything that could not be moved was smashed. Machinery was cut up haphazardly, whilst gangs of forced German labourers loaded the remnants onto trucks. And as the trains moved east the track was ripped up behind them. Rail in the Western sectors was reduced down to a single line where possible. Bizarrely, the removal of rail track was later to aid the construction of Tegel Airfield during the blockade.

Whilst the Soviet Army systematically stripped the city, ordinary Germans were struggling to survive.

Entrance to the city was not going to be easy either. After initially agreeing to the British and Americans taking up their sectors on 4 July, the Soviets went all-out to make sure they missed the deadline. For the British this was no more than a minor inconvenience. Naturally, for the Americans it was a source of national pride, a fact not wasted on Moscow. Advanced parties moved in two days before to identify buildings suitable to accommodate upwards of 50,000 troops. The task would have been difficult enough without any Soviet involvement. Finding any structure habitable within the city proved difficult. Most of the surviving buildings had been occupied in the immediate post-war months by combat troops and were now in a worse state than the bombing had left them. The 2nd Armoured Division of the United States made a quick start through the Soviet zone, reaching the outskirts of the city on 1 July. By 4 July the Americans had occupied the old Leibstandarte – Adolf Hitler Barracks. The British fared little better.

No sooner had the 7th Armoured Division (7th Armoured Brigade, Desert Rats) crossed into the Soviet zone than they were stopped by Russian troops. In the first of a series of hold-ups they were informed that they had no right to access and would have to return to barracks. When this didn't work the Soviets warned of dangerous bridges. Indignantly the Desert Rats pressed on. Eventually, buildings spread across the Spandau district became the British headquarters in Berlin. For the 7th AB it was the end of a campaign that had started in the deserts of North Africa; on 6 July 1945 they celebrated by parading before the Siegessaüle in the drizzle.

The same day Generals Weeks and Clay met with the Soviet Military Authority to discuss the establishment of a quadripartite government for the city, the French were still without a foothold. Some pressing items quickly made their way onto the agenda. Most critical was the question of food and coal for the three Western sectors. General Zhukov warned the delegation that they would have to supply their own food and fuel, as there was a major shortage in both the Eastern zone and Russia itself. The problem was, he pointed out, fighting in the east had gone on for longer, destroying many crops and food production areas, and whilst traditionally the German capital had relied on the surrounding area for the majority of food, it could no longer do that. Especially since large areas of the former eastern territories now fell inside Polish and Soviet spheres of influence. The same was true of coal production, since the area concerned, Silesia, had been given to the Poles as the country's border had moved westwards. Zhukov suggested that coal be made available from the Ruhr. Weeks retorted that some stocks must be made available from the east as most of the Ruhr's supplies were needed for the rest of Germany. Eventually brown coal did arrive from Silesia supplementing Ruhr supplies. To reduce the amount of city coal supplies burnt for electrical power some current would, in times of peak demand, be supplied from generating stations outside the city. Naturally the Russians were all in favour as they could easily switch that off.

Kommandatura

As the city was divided into three, the French were still an occupier in waiting; an understanding of co-operation was needed to allow all districts to function as one. To govern Berlin along the same lines as Germany an organisation known as the 'Inter-Allied Military Kommandatura' was formed. The chairmanship rotated once a month, giving each occupying power the opportunity to be host. The group was formally initiated on 11 July 1945, delivering Order No. 1, announcing that the Allied Kommandatura had now assumed control over the city. Up until this point the Soviets had been working very hard. Not only had they been removing equipment and labour from Berlin they had also positioned many German communists in places of authority. Before the war many German communists had fled to the east and Moscow and, convinced of eventual victory, the Russians had trained up a number. Under the direction of Walter Ulbricht, pupil of the Lenin School in Moscow and veteran of the Spanish Civil War, the new communists were to prepare Germany for 'democracy'.

On 30 April, whilst the battle for Berlin still raged, Ulbricht and his colleagues were transported into the city. As the fighting subsided small number of survivors naturally banded together to form support and self-help groups. Ulbricht's Central Committee rapidly broke these up. All reconstruction must be, just like the Soviet Union, controlled from a centralised position, he argued. But it didn't stop there, the 'battle for hearts and minds' started in earnest. Shops were soon reopened, often selling fresh produce, and hospitals were restocked with life-saving drugs, usually at the expense of other Russian zone towns. People sympathetic to the communist cause were also earmarked for roles in local government. On 17 May Berlin's post-war civil administration – the Magistrat – was instituted. The Soviet Military Authorities appointed Dr Werner, a political neutral as mayor, but seven out of the sixteen departments were headed by communists, as was the deputy mayor's position. Moscow had been keen to ensure the new administrations were not obviously communist led, hoping instead that the Allies would accept the administrations without change. On 11 July the Kommandatura issued its first communiqué, stating that, 'all existing regulations and ordinances issued by the Commander of the Soviet Army Garrison shall remain'. For the time being the Soviets would have their way. The Red Army did impose one rather bizarre point, the city was to work to Moscow time, two hours ahead of Europe.

The following day British representatives took over responsibility for the six districts in their sector. At the head of each was a *Bürgermeister*, Soviet-appointed of course, who although not outwardly communist was controlled by a committee who were. The British quickly set about removing the disproportionate elements of the districts, however, many officials who were left still sought Soviet approval before obeying any British orders. Above this was the Kommandatura ultimately controlling the city Magistrat. Unfortunately, a flaw had again been built into the system. Action could only be taken on those subjects on which a decision was reached unanimously. In their eagerness to retain parity, the architects of the Kommandatura gave each member a veto. Again the Russian representatives had a way of manipulating the system legally.

All change at Potsdam

On 12 April 1945 Theodore Roosevelt died leaving his Vice President, Harry S. Truman, to preside over the 'peace of Europe' and the defeat of Japan. Eager to influence the

Potsdam, July–August 1945. Here the framework was established for the future control of Germany. It also introduced Harry S. Truman and Clement Attlee to the world.

new incumbent, Churchill commenced a telegram campaign urging the inexperienced leader to delay the withdrawal of US troops from areas allotted to the USSR. Truman had other ideas and initially stuck to the EAC plan for occupation zones. Roosevelt had been working on the principle that, 'we can do business with the Russians' and for the sake of the alliance Truman continued along that path. They might, after all, be needed in the fight against Japan, so the President did not want to upset Stalin and lose his support.

As US troops began their withdrawal to the West, Churchill became increasingly desperate. Britain had gone to war to prevent Central European domination by a single regime, by letting the Red Army move into their allotted Eastern zone, a different but no less sinister regime would be doing just that. Unfortunately, Truman reminded Churchill, the zones were almost totally the design of the British element at the EAC so he really had no cause for complaint. Churchill quietly fumed.

The last Tripartite meeting of the European war opened at Potsdam on 17 July 1945. The conference was to discuss the continuing struggle with the Japanese and how control over Germany was to be managed. Potsdam was, politically, a dynamic meeting in which the lines were drawn for the final 'world peace' that so many hoped for.

Unfortunately, Potsdam actually achieved very little. In Britain the first general election for nearly a decade took place on 5 July, but the results were not announced until 26 July, well into the conference, as many votes were cast overseas. Dramatically, Winston Churchill, the country's stoic leader, resigned after his party was convincingly defeated in a Labour landslide. Clement Attlee and Ernest Bevin, Anthony Eden's replacement as Foreign Secretary, subsequently represented British interests for the last few days of the conference.

It was now that the three main powers agreed to divide Germany into four zones for the duration of the occupation. Also, Germany was to have no central government, the Allied Control Council (ACC) would instead govern it. The ACC would exercise authority on all matters affecting Germany as a whole, unfortunately each member, and by now this included the French, had a veto. Normally this wouldn't have been too much of a problem; however, as the ACC needed to reach unanimous decisions it was, like the Kommandatura, doomed to failure from the outset.

All sides agreed to a declaration of economic unity as a basic principle, however, it was increasingly apparent by this stage that Stalin was unlikely to keep to it. He had after all demanded $10 billion in reparations at the Yalta conference and was now arguing that the figure had been agreed on. The Allied Reparations Committee formed at Yalta to investigate Russian claims made little progress throughout its eight months of existence. In fact, over thirty meetings produced nothing more than a protest against Russia's $10 billion demands. In the West's view, the priorities had now shifted from reparations and then recovery to immediate feeding and rebuilding. It was now clear that a pastoral Germany was not in Europe's best economic interests. Eventually the West compromised in an attempt to move forward. Rather than concede to Stalin's $10 billion bill, he would be given reparations from the West. Up to 15 per cent of goods from manufacturing, mining or agriculture in the Western zones would be shipped to the Soviet Union. Also, 10 per cent of all industrial machinery identified as removable in the Western zone would be railroaded east. Typically the majority of this was to stand out in all weathers at Russian-controlled marshalling yards around occupied Eastern Europe, rendering the majority scrap. It was to be some time before the West put a stop to the Soviets 'bleeding Germany white'.

France

The issue of France's right to occupation were also re-discussed at Potsdam. When the initial agreement to divide Germany into zones was signed it only covered Britain, America and the Soviet Union. By the time of the Yalta conference in January 1945 Churchill had convinced Roosevelt and Stalin that France should be included as an occupying force. Churchill, naturally, had an ulterior motive. Top of the list was the fact that Britain was bankrupt; the prospect of administering and re-building large parts of a shattered Europe was extremely unpalatable to the British Government. If some of that responsibility could be laid-off to the French then so much the better. Stalin agreed, but only if the French territories were carved out of those allotted to Britain and America. At Potsdam, Truman argued that all three powers should give up land for France; Stalin disagreed. Eventually France was given territory as agreed at Yalta. The matter of French occupation in Berlin had to wait until Attlee returned as the victorious Prime Minister. It was finally proposed that the French sector would comprise two former British boroughs. Both Truman and Stalin quickly agreed to this, the only problem was the French were not at the meeting, or any other for that matter at Potsdam. This would become a bone of contention over the coming years.

When the conference wound up on 2 August very little had actually been achieved. Potsdam did authorise the Allied Control Council, allowing it to finally get underway on 10 August. What it did not do was prevent the Soviet Union's expansion into Central Europe. What Potsdam did mean was that very soon hundreds of thousands of Germans living in the eastern provinces would be reduced to 'exile' status and forcibly removed from their homeland. In allowing the redefinition of the Polish border the Western Allies profligately ceded control of Germany's major coal producing area and its richest agricultural land, whilst simultaneously increasing their refugee problem ten-fold. The Potsdam Declaration also called, for the final time, for the unconditional surrender of Japan, with the dire warning that, 'The alternative for Japan is prompt and utter destruction'. Another component of the Cold War, the nuclear weapon, was just around the corner.

DPs

Potsdam, viewed by many as the new beginning, in fact did just the opposite. Germany after the war was once likened to 'an ant's nest someone had kicked over'. Everywhere was a scene of devastation and despair. As the Red Army had surged ever further westward, a bow-wave of refugees was created desperate to escape the fate of so many Russian prisoners. This had been partially intended as the sight of large groups fleeing the Soviets reinforced the panic that had already set in to the German population. It also served to slow down the movement of troops to the front, something the Wehrmacht had encouraged during its successful campaigns of 1939–42. But it was not just refugees that now filled every corner of Germany. Throughout the twelve years of the Third Reich millions had been forcibly removed from their homeland and set to work on vast civil engineering projects or war-related industries. Added to this were millions of prisoners of war and newly liberated occupants of the many Concentration camps and their subsidiary sites.

With such conditions tempting disease on an epidemic scale the Western Allies first priority was to repatriate as many Displaced Persons (DPs), as they officially became known, as possible. Over 6 million had been identified by May 1945, and an incredible 80 per cent had been repatriated by November that year. This went a long way to easing the pressure on the food distribution system that was being propped up with the release of military rations. In the Russian zone DPs were not such a problem. Many simply starved to death or were included in the mass marches to the shattered cities of Stalingrad, Leningrad and other industrial cities to work on the building of the Soviet economy. A measure of how DPs expected the Soviet authorities to treat them came as troops on all sides withdrew into their pre-determined zones on occupation. General Clay noted that anyone who wished to stay could do so, with two days' food supply. However, 'few if any displaced persons failed to leave'. To make matters worse the British and American zones were almost overwhelmed in the next twelve months as over 7.5 million men, women and children were forcibly driven into occupied Germany.

Politics damn politics

The first truly free elections held in Germany for over thirteen years commenced on 20 January 1946 at Wurttemberg-Baden in the American zone. The election was a small step on the way to real democracy. In a demonstration of enthusiasm over 86 per cent turned out to elect the local council. Occupation forces were kept off the streets during the polls, the only real interference was to ensure former Nazis neither registered for candidacy nor voted. Slowly the other zones followed suit, and by September 1946 local councils at the very least were being elected to office across Germany. Unfortunately voters in the Soviet zone had nowhere near the choice of candidates their Western zone counterparts had. The Soviets ensured ballot papers comprised mainly communist-orientated candidates, the only officially recognised party of the Soviet Military Authority.

Groups in the British zone soon represented the whole political spectrum. From the German Party (DP), a nationalistic group on the right through to the aptly named Centre Party (Zentrum), who became the Christian Democratic Union (CDU), and on to the Communist Party of Germany (KPD). Political parties sprung up, quite literally everywhere. General Clay found this encouraging, noting that, 'The growth of these political parties indicates to me that there is considerable vigour left in German political life'. However, he pointed out that 'it is regrettable that there are so many' and indeed political fragmentation was of concern to many. Of these 'many' a few were destined to become entrenched in the political fight for Berlin.

The Soviet Military Authority had managed, by late 1945, to place Communist Party members in practically all Berlin's municipal offices. These were not all in the top positions, in Russian eyes it was acceptable for Social Democrats to hold them, but certainly communists were in a deputising capacity, the position that often held true power. Not taking the top job also prevented the Western Allies pointing towards an immediate takeover of the city. However, even when almost total subjugation had been achieved, Walter Ulbricht, leader of the communists, knew that to win elections under a true communist banner would be nigh on impossible. Clearly a more acceptable face was required.

When the Communist Party re-formed in Germany, the uniting of all worker parties had been at the core of its policy. From the outset the German communists were convinced that it was in their best interests to merge with the Social Democratic Party. Subsequently, moves to combine the two groups were well under way by Christmas 1945. Throughout January the following year the communists, backed by the Soviet Military Authority and especially Marshal Zhukov, increased the pressure on the socialists. Opposition to the merger was immense with demonstrations throughout the Soviet zone, whilst in Berlin a members meeting was held on 1 March. Over 1,500 representatives

'Eight pretty lasses dressed in bright red skirts – and with large letters on each reading WALHT SED (Vote SED), march in a parade of the SED party in recent election campaigns.' (Acme Newspapers Inc.)

packed the Admiralpalast Hall that morning. Otto Grotewohl, leader of the SDP, trying to make himself heard over the noise, announced that the executive committee had endorsed the proposals and the two parties were to merge. The delegates disagreed, demanding a strike ballot which was immediately passed, they argued that every member should be balloted before such a monumental decision was taken and even then only on the approval of the Kommandatura. As the political situation steadily worsened, especially in Berlin, the Western Allies kept their distance; this was after all an internal German matter, one that, by the terms of the Potsdam conference, should be encouraged.

The Soviets needed no encouragement in Berlin. They immediately set about spreading rumours, suggesting that the Western Allies would soon be leaving the city. And anyone who opposed the merger, or had voted against it, would suffer once they had gone. Pro-Soviet municipal workers, those who had been placed in office, threatened other

'Russian Communist propaganda is now going "all out" to convince and sway the German people in the upcoming elections.' (Acme Newspapers Inc.)

staff with job losses. And two district party leaders who dared to voice their opposition were summarily dismissed by the Soviet Military Authority. The dismantling of factories slowed and families of prisoners of war began to receive mail from the East; 'maybe the Soviets were benevolent after all' reasoned some of the population. Eventually, Russian manipulation became so obvious that a new Social Democratic newspaper was sanctioned in the British sector in an attempt to counter the propaganda. British troops were instructed to arrest communist agitators who had travelled into their zone and were threatening SDP members with violence and kidnap. They arrested twelve in one night alone. Voting on the merger was held on 31 March 1946 and even though the Soviets closed most of their polling stations due to a 'technicality' the majority of party members visited the booths. Nearly 80 per cent of the votes cast were against the merger. This did not stop the merger going ahead in the Soviet zone and the SDP was effectively snuffed out. The SED was subsequently recognised as the only Socialist party in the Eastern zone. For Berlin the issues were different. The SDP disappeared from the Eastern sector of the city, however, the party remained in the British, American and French areas, and would become a major source of opposition to the Russians throughout the blockade.

Just three days before the merger vote the Kommandatura had issued an order that a new city constitution be drawn up. This would necessitate the election of a city council and ultimately cause the return of Ernst Reuter, a major voice of Soviet opposition. In October 1946 the elections finally took place. The run-up to the momentous day saw some of the most vigorous campaigning yet. Floats festooned with posters and occupied by well-dressed singing, smiling children made a bizarre sight against the backdrop of the ruined city. Crushed coal briquettes and children's books were distributed by SED officials in an attempt to win the welfare vote, whilst other scarce goods such as children's shoes and clothing, free from ration restrictions, suddenly appeared. And just in case this was not sufficient encouragement, members of other parties were roughed up or threatened with violence for good measure. In one glaring attempt to influence the vote the SMA announced that it would, due to shortages, be supplying only the Soviet sector of Berlin with fresh fruit and vegetables. The SED then petitioned the SMA, asking for the restoration of produce deliveries to all sectors, the idea being that the SED would appear to have the population's health at heart. Colonel Howley raised the issue at a bad tempered session of the Kommandatura, accusing the Soviets of clear voter manipulation. After lengthy discussion, fruit and vegetable deliveries were once again distributed throughout all four sectors. But Moscow didn't stop there: alcohol and cigarettes were distributed free throughout the city. These commodities had a major impact as they were both the currency of defeat, making their way quickly onto the black market.

And, as if bribery and threats were not enough, the Soviet Military Authority also ensured that rallies by opposing parties were at the very least disrupted. Halls booked for meetings by rival groups were occupied at the last minute or the venue was suddenly required by the military, cancelling the meeting. The texts of any speeches to be made at political meetings were also required to be submitted to the SMA in Russian for approval, whilst the Soviet-controlled radio pumped out ever increasing examples of good deeds by SED members or produced lists of names of German POWs due for release. These lists also made their way into the Soviet-sponsored press, very effectively clogging up campaign information from other parties, as families were more interested in tracing loved ones than reading even more propaganda.

When the Red Army had taken the city, one of its main objectives was the control of Radio Berlin. Throughout the post-surrender months the SMA consistently refused to relinquish total control of the station situated in the British-controlled sector of Berlin. Throughout the merger campaign of 1946 the British and American governors had attempted to secure more airtime for other political parties, but to no avail. So, on 7 February, the United States started broadcasting seven hours a day using the Schöneberg telephone exchange. The system was not ideal, reception was poor and only a few thousand were able to receive the station; however, it did signal the beginning of a fragmented radio network for the city. Then, on 5 September 1946, a new station, Radio in the American Sector (RIAS), using an old US Army psychological warfare Mobile 1,000 W transmitter, came on air. RIAS was destined to become one of the iconic organisations of the Cold War.

But the West need not have worried. The city's population were still raw from the treatment of soldiers and subsequent devastating 'Russian time' as it had become known.

The population also bore witness to thirteen years of intense propaganda as directed by Goebbels. As General Clay put it later, 'they had seen his promises fail, one by one, until they were surrounded by their own ruin'. The propaganda now delivered by the Soviet-controlled media had little effect; Berliners have long memories. Even with an aggressive campaign such as the SED had mounted, they only returned 19.8 per cent of the vote. The Social Democrats achieved 48.7 per cent and the Christian Democrats 22 per cent. The SED were soundly defeated whilst Soviet policies received a resounding thumbs down from the city's population. The atmosphere at the Kommandatura now rapidly worsened, as did the situation of many skilled workers across Berlin. In retribution for the lack of SED support, thousands of key scientists, engineers and designers were rounded up and transported, often with their families, to the East. This was all the fault of the West argued the SMA, they had clearly been promoting the return of right-wing militaristic tendencies and this unfair result was the logical outcome. Not only had Berlin voted 'fascist' in the eyes of the Soviets, the British and American zones were now to merge, clearly increasing their militaristic strength.

Ernst Reuter

Ernst Reuter first came into contact with communism whilst a POW in a Russian camp during the latter stages of the First World War. After becoming a pupil of Lenin and serving under Stalin as a commissar he travelled back to Germany. In the political turmoil of post-war Germany he became Secretary of the National Communist Party. By 1921 he had become disillusioned by the often violent tactics of the party and left to join the SPD. He served on the Berlin city assembly until 1933 when he was interned by the National Socialists. He was surprisingly released in 1935, in part due to the efforts of the London City Council, but was forced to leave the country. Reuter spent the next eleven years in exile in Turkey. On his return to Berlin he was elected to the Magistrat, taking up his old position of transport secretary.

By June 1947 Reuter had been elected *Oberbürgermeister* (Lord Mayor) of Berlin, replacing the ineffectual Otto Ostrowski who had been voted into the post after the October elections. Ostrowski saw his primary task as being that of overseeing the rebuilding of the devastated city before winter. To ensure this ran smoothly he sat on the fence, rarely siding with either the left or the right. This didn't last long as the Soviets soon found a way to manipulate him. He had divorced his wife during the war under dubious circumstances (she was Jewish). When Ostrowski first applied for office this situation was investigated by a British team, but no evidence of wrongdoing was discovered and he was allowed to stand. The Soviets now capitalised on this, holding meetings with the Mayor three to four times a week. Eventually Ostrowski, losing the support of the SDP members, tried to resign. The Soviet Military Authority thought otherwise and blocked his resignation: it was a lot better to have someone weak in office than someone who would outwardly oppose their plans. The situation was taken to the Kommandatura and eventually onto the Allied Control Council where, surprisingly, General Clay supported the Russians. If Ostrowski were to leave office his successor would have to receive prior

Ernst Reuter was elected *Oberbürgermeister* of Berlin in June 1947. The Soviets would block his inauguration using the (extremely flawed) veto system in the Kommandatura.

Soviet approval. To the population of Berlin this was a bitter blow as it seemed the Western Allies were now allowing the Soviets to dictate the political landscape in the city.

As far as the SDP was concerned Ernst Reuter was the natural successor to the post of *Oberbürgermeister*, a view not shared by either the SED or the Soviets. Reuter was elected into office on 24 June 1947, receiving eighty-nine out of the available 108 votes from the municipal deputies. The Soviets immediately objected to the appointment at the Kommandatura, as was now expected, and the decision to block Reuter taking office was upheld by the Allied Control Council. Moscow, fearful of Reuter, had clearly won the day. But this was not to be the last word; the Magistrat decided not to name a successor, instead instructing the Deputy Mayor, Louise Schroeder to act on his behalf. Reuter would become the mayor-in-waiting, taking his rightful place once the Russians finally sealed the city. Until then the city was in the hands of the formidable Frau Schroeder, who it turned out was completely impervious to Soviet threats. Naturally they claimed that she, too, was an illegal appointment and should not be recognised. This was slapped down in the Kommandatura; the West was finally recognising how to deal with Moscow.

Zonal fusion

When the Council of Foreign Ministers met in Paris in April 1946 the political landscape had already deteriorated to the point of collapse. The conference took the usual format, the West would put forward proposals and the Soviets would shout them down. Molotov not only renewed his demands for excessive reparations, he now argued that the Ruhr should not be governed by Britain alone. The raw materials and manufacturing capacity of the area should be under 'four-power' control, he demanded. Naturally, if the Russians had been allowed entry to the Ruhr, even more materials would make their way east, further crippling any chance of European recovery. Bevin now took the bull by the horns. There would be no Soviet involvement in any British or Western interest, especially since there was already a steady flow of reparations and materials to the East whilst only refugees and displaced persons moved to the West. On 11 July American Secretary of State James Byron offered all the Berlin zones the chance to join with the Americans in an administrative and economic venture to alleviate the city's problems. The British, mindful of the problems encountered throughout the 1945–46 winter, agreed in principle to the proposals two weeks later. The French, however, saw reunification, no matter how small, as one step too far and opposed the moves. Obviously the Soviets denounced the proposal, and now suggested that the Western Allies were prepared to divide Germany into spheres of influence, the subtext being that only they could be seen as the true upholders of democracy wishing to see a unified Germany. Moscow clearly recognised that to control the country as they hoped needed Germany to be in one piece; with division this would become increasingly unlikely.

By the spring of 1946 the civilian population within the British and American zones were suffering some of the worst conditions in continental Europe. To make matters worse the Western zones were steadily filling up with 'expelled' ethnic Germans. Over 7 million flooded into the area, primarily from Czechoslovakia, Hungary and the recently acquired Polish-administered territory in Eastern Germany. In an episode that would be recognised today as ethnic cleansing, the remnants of German territorialism were systematically de-housed and dumped in the Western zones. Surprisingly, the Allied Control Council condoned the movements:

> The Three Governments, having considered the question in all its aspects, recognize that the transfer to Germany of German populations, or elements thereof, remaining in Poland, Czechoslovakia and Hungary, will have to be undertaken. They agree that any transfers that take place should be effected in an orderly and humane manner.

Unfortunately, expulsions, especially in Czechoslovakia, were anything but humane. In the last few days of the conflict ethnic Germans actively assisted the retreating German Army in destroying villages and towns. And now the Czech authorities made it their business to root out and expel all Germans, both migrant and ethnic.

Eduard Beneš, on his return from London to assume the presidency of Czechoslovakia, declared it:

A Hungarian Swabian Peasant with his wife and baby share the long trip from Hungary to the American Zone in Germany. The shipment of the Swabians – the German minority – was authorised but not made mandatory by the Potsdam agreement. (World Wide Photo)

… necessary … to liquidate out especially uncompromisingly the Germans in the Czech lands, let our motto be: to definitively de-Germanise our homeland, culturally, economically, politically.

Germans were forced to wear white armbands and walk in the road rather than on the footpath and were only served in shops after all others had finished. By 1950 Czechoslovakia's German population had been reduced from 25 per cent down to 1.6 per cent; over 3 million were to eventually move west. And it didn't stop at Germans. Property owned by Hungarians, an ally of Hitler's, was to be confiscated and the people expelled from the country. Of course Hungary, by now under the influence of a Soviet administration, did not want them either so they too trudged west into Bavaria and other southern German states. Hungary also followed a similar programme of expulsion. German-speaking minorities were systematically removed from their traditional homelands and sent west. In just one example, between January and November 1946, 104,200 Swabian peasants had been uprooted and 'shipped' across Central

Europe to the American zone. How to feed this influx, even at a basic subsistence level, rapidly became the number one priority.

Public health had reached emergency proportions during the course of the year. Only 20 per cent of the nation's children were near to the standard weight for their age, whilst malnutrition was encouraging major disease to reach epedemic proportions. Of course this could, in some part, be avoided if the level of nutrition could be increased. The ration set by the United Nations' Relief and Rehabilitation Administration recommended a normal daily intake of 2,650 calories, but the Allies were nowhere near achieving that recommendation. Those in the Ruhr, especially in physically demanding jobs such as steel production and mining, began to feel the brunt of the poor conditions. And as the health of workers deteriorated so did the production levels the British and Americans were placing so many hopes on. As the Soviets held most of the food producing regions Britain and America were having to import a large proportion of the required food into their respective zones. Added to this was the huge cost of administering the zones separately, often duplicating offices. So the offer to merge was readily taken up by Bevin and agreed in Parliament just two weeks later. Naturally Moscow protested, but the facts were plain to see. Whilst Germany remained a political vacuum, progress in rebuilding both the country and Europe was going to be at best slow. This, coupled with the obstructiveness of the Soviets, would eventually produce the perfect breeding ground for revolution. Churchill warned, with the support of President Truman, about this during his 'Iron Curtain' speech at Fulton. Of course others were also thinking along similar lines by now. Truman had himself told Secretary Byrnes that he was 'tired of babying the Soviets'. Secretary of State George Marshall was also concerned. He recognised that Moscow intended to dominate a united Germany in the very near future and thus the stability of Europe was at risk. Worried by the lack of progress in the proposed 'Bizone', as it had become known, Washington now pushed the proposals forward. It was clear that there were only two choices left to the West, allow the Soviets to dominate an eventually unified Germany or set up a separate administration. By the end of 1947 the latter seemed inevitable.

Marshall Plan

Whilst the fight over the Reuter's post was in progress, back in America, George C. Marshall, US Secretary of State, was sowing the first seeds of the European Recovery Programme, soon to become known as 'The Marshall Plan'. He announced to a Harvard audience, on 5 July 1947, that any chance of a full European recovery must be on a cooperative basis and ideally all nations of the old world must be involved. Britain signed up immediately and France just a week later. This was no surprise as both countries were near to bankruptcy and, after the termination of lend-lease, this was clearly the lifeline Bevin had hoped for. Marshall outlined the plan further when he said, 'Our policy is directed not against any country or doctrine but against hunger, poverty, desperation and chaos'. A clear invitation to those countries in the east currently under Soviet control. However, Marshall also warned, 'any government which manoeuvres to block the recovery of other countries cannot expect help from us'. This reference to Russian influence over

The Marshall Plan would ultimately be the catalyst for the division of Germany and Europe.

Eastern Europe garnered a swift response from some of those directly affected, the Polish ambassador to the United States, Josef Winiewicz, indicated that there was great public interest in the scheme but he had received no 'official' direction as yet. *Pravda* issued far clearer direction, denouncing the speech as 'a new stage in Washington's campaign against the forces of world democracy and progress'.

By 26 June Foreign Ministers meeting in Paris learned that Moscow would not entertain any assistance in either the Soviet Union nor in satellite states. Clearly the Marshall Plan would eradicate the conditions Moscow needed for communism to spread across Western Europe and so Stalin denounced the idea. If aid was allowed into Poland, Hungary and Czechoslovakia, then control would most probably be lost and Russia could

'The cleanup starts.' It would take more that the removal of rubble to build Berlin again, and the Soviets knew it.

eventually lose its grip on Eastern Europe altogether. Washington held a different view. Involving Germany in the plan had quite a psychological impact. The ostracised German people were participating in an international endeavour and as such confidence could only grow, as did industrial output, thus aiding the nations recovery. Molotov finally collapsed the meeting on 2 July and instructed all Eastern European countries to ignore the 'imperialistic' offer. The Czech government had planned to discuss the offer further until a brief audience with Stalin changed the Premier's mind.

The division of Europe into East and West was now assured. The 'Iron Curtain' Churchill had warned the world about so graphically was finally being drawn across Europe. But there was a sticking point: a line across a map was one thing, a political divide could be respected up to a point, but what of Berlin? The city, deep within the Soviet zone, suddenly took on a whole new importance. It had become a capitalist oasis in the desert of communism. This assured conflict at some stage in the future, although no one at the time could have predicted that the conflict would be fought with statistics rather than soldiers.

Three

'This is an ugly and dangerous situation.'

1948 did not start well. The combination of millions of displaced persons, a poor food ration which only just made 1,000 calories for manual workers and a rapidly depreciating Reichsmark were testing the Bizone Administration to the limit. Dissent amongst manual workers was now so bad that a number of strikes were called across many industrial sites. Workers walked out for twenty-four hours in the Ruhr in mid-January and the following month there were strikes right across the Bizone. The possibility of food riots was also causing major concern by February. Financially, Britain was in a very poor state. Suffering from crippling payment deficits and a fuel shortage which cost the country 30 per cent of its industrial output, the Government knew they were close to bankruptcy. Washington had not helped the situation. Shortly after the defeat of Japan the Truman administration cancelled the lend–lease agreement. The Attlee Government effectively had the financial rug pulled from under them. Robert Nixon, an International News Service correspondent of the era, interviewed in 1970 later noted that:

> … he [Truman] almost cut the jugular vein of Britain by the termination of lend-lease. If lend-lease had been carried on, it would have cost only a dime a dollar of what the Marshall plan later cost. The Marshall plan started off with a seventeen billion dollar whack.[1]

London was now required to pay back massive loans for equipment still in Britain, adding to the financial misery. Incidentally, the annual payment to the US government was not completed until 2006. All this was a backdrop to the social reforms the Labour Government had been pushing through. This included a policy of selective nationalisation including the Bank of England, rail, coal and the airlines. But without doubt their crowning achievement was the creation of the Welfare State. Successes aside, it was clear that Britain could not now maintain the position it had held on the world stage. Trading rivals had been defeated in war, however, a new global power, America, had taken their place. Britain effectively mortgaged itself to the United States through a $3,700 million loan. It was clear that the

---

[1] Robert Nixon, 28 October 1970. (Second paragraph of chapter three.)

sooner Germany could economically support itself the quicker the financial pressure would be reduced on the UK, pressure that was keenly felt by the population.

On the ration

Britain throughout the war had been exposed to the full force of Government propaganda in an attempt to support rationing. Characters such as 'Doctor Carrot' and 'Potato Pete' were recruited to get the message across. Pete, incidentally, had his own nursery rhyme:

> *There was an old woman who lived in a shoe.*
> *She had so many children she didn't know what to do.*
> *She gave them potatoes instead of some bread,*
> *And the children were happy and very well fed.*

However, by the end of the war the population had by and large accepted that 'Digging for Victory' and food shortages were likely to be the norm for a few years into the peace. Unfortunately, 1945 proved to be one of the poorest international wheat harvests on record, forcing the Government to announce bread rationing from 21 July 1946, something unheard of even in the depths of the war. Churchill immediately described the Food Minister's announcement as, 'one of the gravest I have ever heard in peace time'. Interestingly, the bread ration was removed on 25 July 1948, one month after the first flights into Berlin. Of course, who you knew was a definite bonus. Christine Clarke was a young girl living in the East Yorkshire village of Hunmanby in 1948. She remembered:

> Bread was not much of a problem as Bob [Dad] was a Master Baker at the time and used to make sure we were ok. Other things were a bit rarer. Sweets were in short supply, sugar as well, but gelatine cubes weren't so we used to eat them as sweets. We had a lot of relations who lived in Canada, one had even visited during the war, and they used to send over food parcels. They had lots of dried fruit, Demerara sugar and chocolate!

Bread was to be baked in Berlin as it was more weight effective to fly in ingredients and fuel than the loaves themselves. The continuing British ration conditions led to some surprising situations, not least the 'Ration Book Olympics' held in London in August 1948. It would be another year before the Marshall Plan effect kicked in. Even so, some rationing lasted well into the 1950s.

A dangerous conflict?

Secretary Marshall wrote, in February 1948, that Eastern Germany was now being shaped by the Soviets in a similar way to those countries already occupied. And it would not be long before they had designs on the Western areas, dragging Central Europe into a very dangerous conflict. The time had now come to act. The British Government had long argued that a divided Germany, whilst not ideal, may become a reality. Similar thoughts had started to permeate Washington during the latter part of 1947 and Marshall concluded it was time to bring them to a head. The 'Truman Doctrine', of which the 'Marshall Plan' became an obvious and important component, was utilised to the full. Free people were now to receive the support of the United States, and the tide of communism was finally to be checked. Not only had the battle plans been drawn for the Berlin Blockade but the world now plunged headlong into the Cold War, with Berlin becoming the cultural centre of the struggle.

The Soviet Military Authority took the opportunity to welcome in the New Year with a further round of travel restrictions. Land access was Berlin's weak spot, one that Moscow was eager to exploit. The Soviets began spreading rumours that Berlin would soon become part of the Eastern zone, especially if the Allies were intent on pushing forward currency reform. On 24 January a British train travelling from Berlin to the West was stopped at the border. The two sealed carriages carrying 120 Germans was unhitched and after a day's delay directed back to the city. This clearly had the desired effect. When the Allies raised the issue at the Allied Control Council the Soviets immediately stopped a further train, this time an American one, and searched all German passengers. And it did not stop at trains; cars and trucks were also forbidden to use the autobahns and were liable to stop searches every mile or so. That was if they actually managed to cross from west to east as the SMA demanded large amounts of paperwork and permits to even enter the Eastern zone, and in classic fashion they changed the format every week to making it virtually impossible to have the right credentials when requested to produce them. In Berlin itself the Soviet authority also started to restrict travel between the sectors. A number of routes were blocked, tramlines pulled up and roads made impassable, all making the division of the city more realistic. By late February the traditional shortages winter brought were noticeably worse due to travel restrictions, and in Berlin the shortages were becoming acute.

Allied Control Council crumbles

The European Foreign Ministers met in London on 6 March to investigate the formation of a West German Government. Critically, the Soviets were not invited and argued that as the meeting was a clear violation of the Potsdam accord no decision could be considered legal. In reality, they realised that any opportunity to influence Germany as a whole was rapidly slipping between their fingers. And this was no usual victors' conference; the Benelux countries (Belgium, Netherlands and Luxemburg) were also present. Much to the Soviets' displeasure the Marshall Plan was also on the agenda. If the delegates had any reservations as to whether the Soviets should have been invited they were quickly dispelled. Whilst in session the conference learned of a Red Army coup in Czechoslovakia and Stalin's political advances towards Finland and Norway. With the dangers now apparently obvious, Secretary of State Marshall announced that the United States was ready 'to proceed at once in the joint discussions on the establishment of an Atlantic security system.' The seeds of an iconic Cold War organisation – NATO – were sown and by 17 March the Treaty of Brussels had been signed. An attack on one was now an attack on all.

The Allied Control Council building. This was also home to the Berlin Air Safety Centre, one of the only Quadrapartite organisations to stay intact throughout the blockade.

On 20 March the Allied Control Council met in Berlin for what was to be the last time. Marshal Sokolovsky immediately set about attacking Robertson and Clay, arguing that between them they had informed the Soviets of neither the meeting in London nor the outcome. Further to this line, Sokolovsky argued that the United Kingdom, America and France were using the ACC meetings as a screen behind which they plotted the division of Germany. Clearly, the Western Allies were not about to discuss the London conference nor allow the Soviets to use the ACC as a platform of propaganda. Unfortunately, this was just what Moscow had hoped would happen. Sokolovsky produced a prepared statement, and, reading from it declared the ACC dead. With that the Soviet delegates and their entourage upped and left leaving Clay, Robertson and Koenig speechless. Clay later commented:

> We knew that day as we left the conference room that quadripartite government had broken up and that the split in Germany which in view of Soviet intransigence had seemed inevitable for some months had taken place.

Word spread fast across the city as the storm clouds began to gather.

The Soviets clamp down

It was not long before the Soviets stepped up their interference of land traffic. By 26 March Russian officials were accusing the West of allowing 'illegal' traffic into the city, suggesting that measures would be put into place to 'protect' Berlin's inhabitants from 'terrorist elements'. This 'protection' proved to be draconian in the extreme. From 1 April all Western nationals travelling by rail or autobahn would be required to present their identity papers at control points and have their luggage and personal effects searched. Furthermore, no freight would now be allowed to leave Berlin by rail unless it had orders granting permission by the Russian Kommandatura. The British and American authorities subsequently limited the transport of military and civil freight to the journey into the city, each train leaving for the West was subsequently empty. Waterway traffic was also affected as barge companies were told that they needed new customs papers to travel through the Soviet zone from Berlin. The Western Allies now accused the Soviet authorities of illegally denying their right to unrestricted access to Berlin, but the Soviets thought otherwise. They argued that no such agreement existed and to a certain extent they were right: access through the Soviet zone had been no more than a gentleman's agreement in 1945 and had never been properly formalised. General Clay tested Russian resolve by sending through a train with a few armed guards on board. The Soviets allowed the train over the border and then shunted it off the mainline into a siding using electrically operated points. The train's occupants waited two days before it was clear they were not going to be allowed to continue to Berlin. The train was subsequently withdrawn to the American zone.

And it was not just rail traffic that was disrupted. On 2 April the Soviets requested that the Western Allies close down their emergency aid stations which had been built on the international highway leading from Berlin into the British zone. The stations had been built at around 25-mile intervals along the autobahn to aid drivers who found themselves in difficulty. Initially, the West ignored the request and continued to man the stations. Subsequently any supply vehicles to the stations were stopped, forcing the staff to abandon the sites. An order was also given to deny all communications staff from the West access to telephone repeater stations between Berlin and the Western zones. It appeared that Berlin would soon lose its telephone link with the outside world.

Little lift

The day after the Soviet restrictions came into force the Americans decided to exploit the one unrestricted route into Berlin – air. Berlin had two airfields available to the Western sectors, Gatow and Tempelhof, and they already had a daily service. Now the Americans stepped up the number of flights into the city in an attempt to compensate for the surface transport harassment. In the first day alone thirty-one aircraft from the 61st Troop Carrier Wing had flown into Tempelhof from Frankfurt with a mixture of civilian passengers and freight. The aircraft used was the workhorse of the Second World War, the Douglas

More than 100 tons of freight were shipped without incident by air from Rhine-Main airfield to the Tempelhof air base in the American sector of Berlin, after Soviet officials announced the new travel restrictions on all American, British and French travel to and from the city. (US Army Signal Corps)

C47 Skytrain. Britain too increased their flights into the city although correspondents in Berlin 'expressed doubt whether the three sectors could be long maintained by this means alone'.

General Clay decided that the restrictions might well signal Russian intentions to force the Allies from Berlin. If this was the case he wanted as much military weight as possible behind any subsequent decision he made, including air power. The newly formed United States Air Force (Europe) under the leadership of Lt-Gen. Curtis E. LeMay, was subsequently tasked with building up available forces in Europe. Throughout the years after the Second World War the level of service personnel stationed in theatre had been reduced from just over 2 million to 350,000, as had been agreed at Potsdam. LeMay quickly set about building stock piles of ordnance and equipment; he even re-activated some airfields, placing technical staff on them in readiness for any aircraft that might be deployed from the United States.

As air corridor traffic steadily increased, the Soviets were left with a dilemma. It was quite easy to disrupt trains and barges, or close roads and bridges, but the only way to stop aircraft was to shoot them down. Clearly any action like that would spark a rapid escalation in the already poor relations and probably start a new conflict. Just such an incident took place on 5 April close to the border between the British and Soviet sectors. A scheduled British European Airways Vickers Viking was on its final approach into Gatow, when suddenly a Yak-3 Russian fighter passed close by at speed. The Yak then turned and made another high-speed pass, misjudged the manoeuvre and crashed head-on into the Viking,

The wreckage of British European Airways Vickers Viking lies just inside the Soviet sector after a head-on collision with a Yak-3.

ripping the starboard wing clean-off the aircraft. Both aircraft crashed in flames killing all on board, wreckage coming down on both sides of the sector border. Maj Gen Herbert was immediately on the scene. He discovered that the Yak had come down in the British sector but was already guarded by Russian troops. Unfortunately the Viking fuselage lay just inside the Soviet sector; this too was now surrounded by armed Russians. After some lengthy negotiations Herbert agreed to allow one Russian sentry to remain at the Yak site as long as one British soldier was allowed to stay with the Viking.

The bodies of the four crew, John Ralph, pilot, Norman Merrington, co-pilot, Charles Mamser, radio operator, and Leonard G. Goodman, steward, along with their ten passengers, including two from America and one from Australia, had to be left at the crash site whilst the political wrangling over access to the aircraft dragged on. Robertson was enraged by the situation and immediately ordered fighter escort for all British aircraft using the corridors. Initially the Soviets were very apologetic. Sokolovsky even gave Robertson an assurance that the SMA had no intention of interfering with aircraft using the corridors. However, this attitude did not last for long. When a quadripartite board of inquiry was requested the Soviets blamed the accident on the British, saying no request for the aircraft to be allowed to traverse Soviet airspace had been lodged and in any case the Yak was legally allowed to be there. Eventually a board of enquiry was convened, but it comprised only Russian and British investigators. The Soviets argued that French and American representatives were not required and forbade their inclusion. The board published its findings in two separate reports but both came to similar conclusions, the

Tempelhof, the primary American air base. Three runways were eventually constructed to take airlift traffic.

accident was just that, no malicious intent was intended and the crash was down to an error on the part of the Yak pilot. Above all else it gave the Allies an indication that the Soviets would probably not interfere with Western air traffic in the corridors. Clearly this was, in part, due to the swift decision by Brian Robertson to post fighter escorts for all air traffic into Gatow. Moscow, whilst wanting the Western Allies to leave their sectors of Berlin, were not in a position to launch an all-out attack to obtain it. Certainly they were capable of taking the city, but now realised that any such venture would quickly escalate out of all proportion and, whilst retaining the largest army on the continent, the Red Army was exhausted and poorly equipped. The city would have to be taken by stealth and bluff and the West had just called Moscow's.

The situation was eagerly reported in the British press. Cyril Falls, Chichele Professor of the History of War, Oxford, wrote in the *Illustrated London News* about the worsening climate:

This is an ugly and dangerous situation. The Western Allies hold in their sectors only very small garrisons, which are surrounded by the vast forces still retained in the Russian Zone. From the purely physical point of view the Russians could at any moment force their former

Allies to quit Berlin -provided they were prepared to face the consequences of such an action. Another consideration is that an itching finger on the trigger might cause bloodshed and bring about an international incident of the gravest kind.[2]

Harassment of traffic in the air corridors continued right through to the end of the blockade, but the Soviets were careful not to cause any more fatalities. Flights continued into the city under the 'little lift' banner, primarily delivering supplies for the military garrisons and flying out staff and equipment. The SED made the most of the situation, suggesting that the Western Allies were about to leave and abandon the population to its fate. In reality, the movement of staff was more to do with their requirement elsewhere in the newly formed Bizone than reducing the garrison. The travel restrictions eventually led to the complete suspension of passenger trains throughout April. However, freight was allowed into the city. The West took the opportunity to build on coal reserves in the city throughout April and May. Over 10,000 tons were shipped each month, adding to the stockpile substantially, which was to be a welcome buffer in the ensuing winter crisis that was already looming. Throughout the next few months the Soviets closed bridges, re-routed road traffic, searched or turned back trains, laid-up barges with new paperwork demands and generally increased the political pressure on the city.

If Moscow thought these moves would encourage the Allies to leave Berlin they were mistaken. By 17 April statements in the British press were all talking of staying and Clay described a withdrawal as 'unthinkable'. The 'Little Lift' was a valuable exercise as it demonstrated that the logistics of such a venture needed to be fully integrated if it was to continue to deliver a useful daily payload. LeMay removed the USAF aircraft servicing teams from Tempelhof, relocating them at Frankfurt, whilst at Gatow the finishing touches to the new concrete runway were sped-up. A rudimentary loading system was also implemented, ensuring the aircraft spent the minimum amount of time on the ground. Even so, this supply run was only geared towards keeping the military garrisons supplied.

'We Stay'

June saw yet another round of Soviet restrictions. On Sunday 13 June three buses containing British soldiers and their families were travelling from Berlin to the British zone. Around 200 metres from the border the convoy was stopped, after inspecting all papers and passports the Russian troops ordered everyone off the buses and into the woods. After a lengthy and loud discussion the terrified passengers were eventually allowed back onto the coaches and into the British zone. This was the last traffic to be allowed through; all vehicles behind the three buses were turned round and sent back to Berlin. Two days earlier the British had been informed that no more rail freight traffic

---

[2] The *Illustrated London News*, 17 April 1948. (Sixth paragraph after sub-heading 'little lift'.)

would be allowed into Berlin as the goods yards were already congested. It turned out the reason for the congestion was that the Soviets had removed most of the rail lines under the pretext of reparations payments. Within six hours rail freight ground to a halt, and with it came the prospect of food shortages as this was the primary way to supply the city. It was now clear that Moscow was quite prepared to endanger the lives of the population in an attempt to gain control of Berlin.

To add to the tension a financial crisis was also looming. The constant turning back of freight, especially raw materials from industry, was causing a large trade deficit in the city. To make matters worse, finished goods from the Osram and Blaupunkt factories were building up in warehouses across the city as they could not obtain the export paperwork required to shift them to the West. Those goods that were allowed out of the city had to be fully inspected by Soviet officials before release. This even entailed emptying boxes of light bulbs and the content being counted, all on the pretext that some were making their way onto the black market.

Currency

As the political drive towards a West German state had become more determined, so the fiscal issues affecting recovery increasingly came under scrutiny. During the last year of the war the Allies had printed their own marks, in an attempt to control soldiers' spending and limit the black market. Unfortunately, the Soviets had been given plates so that they might use the same currency. Moscow sanctioned the printing of millions of marks without any controls whatsoever. As the discussion moved to replacing the by now worthless Reichsmark and Rentenmark, naturally the Soviets demanded to be in control of its printing. With the benefit of hindsight the Western Allies refused, paving the way for the Deutschmark and the Ostmark, two Cold War currencies. Of course this was immediately denounced by Moscow as yet more evidence of the West's intention to split Germany up. In reality Whitehall and Washington realised that any successful recovery would have to be based on a currency that held the confidence of internal and external markets. By 1947 confidence was placed fairly and squarely in the cigarette, although anything was reasonably considered to have a value on the black market.

The collapse of the banking infrastructure at the end of the war, in Germany vigorously controlled from a central position, forced the inevitable barter system into being. Initially this was a rather ad hoc affair with transactions covering straight swaps; however, after the Soviets allowed the Western Allies into Berlin the black market became the main way to obtain goods and food. GIs' watches were prized items, but it was the cigarette that became the stable currency. But the financial crisis was much more complex than just the black market effect. Farmers and growers were producing goods in rural areas but hanging on to any surplus. Any pay they received for food was in the rapidly devaluing Reichsmark, further reducing the incentive to sell to the zonal authorities. Subsequently the distribution of food stuffs was either through the black market or, in a large number of cases, not at all. Manufacturing fared little better. Here owners were stockpiling raw materials rather than producing goods that either sold for Reichsmarks or were taken as part of the reparations programme. This meant very few consumer goods were reaching the shops and so the incentive to work was removed and subsequently production took a rapid dive.

General Robertson had long considered with Clay that the need for currency reform had become urgent as far back as 1946. Throughout the Conference of Foreign Ministers meetings in 1947 the drive for four-power acceptance towards reform was blocked by the Soviets. By 1948 it was clear that a West German Administration was to become a reality and therefore a stable currency was needed to underpin its economic well-being. The new currency was announced on 18 June; however, Berlin was for the time being going to be excluded from the reform. Later that day Louise Schroeder, leader of the SDU, was summoned to SMA headquarters. There she was informed that the Russians were to introduce a new Eastern zone currency and it was to be used throughout the city. She refused to accept the ultimatum, saying any such decree had to be ratified by the Magistrat. After initial talks the Magistrat decided to accept both currencies, allowing either to be used. Unfortunately, what was seen as a compromise by the City Council was not by the Russians. The following day at a special meeting of the City Council, the acting Mayor, Ernst Reuter, made the following statement:

> After a week of tension, the reform of currency was proclaimed yesterday in Western Germany by the three occupying powers. We have learned with extreme misgivings that no agreement was possible among all the Allies on a currency reform to the whole of Germany. Berlin was and is powerless to change this fact. What confronts us now, is the necessity of tackling the resulting difficulties. The city government will do everything it can to make life in Berlin function as smoothly as possible. The people of Berlin may also rest assured that food will be supplied them. We learned to our satisfaction that the Western powers as well as the Soviets have announced that freight traffic would continue and thus ensure that supplies the Berlin would be coming in.

That same day General Ganeval, Commandant of the French sector and current chairman of the Kommandatura, called a meeting to discuss the effects of currency reform in Berlin. However, the Soviets refused to attend; four-power governance was now truly at an end and major conflict was now only a breath away. From 20 June the situation spiralled out of control. All road, rail and water traffic suffered another round of permit restrictions and the following day an American military train was stopped in the Russian zone. After a day spent in a railway siding, a Soviet engine was hooked up to the carriages, armed guards were posted on board and the train was unceremoniously driven back to the Western zone.

Posted

As relations rapidly began to deteriorate the British Government decided to build up forces stationed in Germany. One such serviceman was twenty-year-old John Beavin. As the Soviets walked out of the Kommandatura, Beavin was starting his long journey from

Food distribution was, in the early days of the lift, a haphazard affair, often just one step away from looting.

RAF Coltishall in Norfolk to 80 Squadron based at Wunstorf. The route took him to the Hook of Holland on board the troopship *Empire Pakistan* and from there onto a train through Holland and Germany:

> … this journey was an eye-opener for me, first all the Dutch kids lining the track, to whom we threw oranges and sweets etc, they were still starving in the Netherlands. And then there were all the wrecked locomotives and goods wagons shot up by our fighter-bombers. The train itself was not in a very good condition and nor were the tracks, hence a slow and noisy passage.

Beavin arrived at Wunstorf on the evening of Wednesday 16 June. Thursday was spent arriving on station and on Friday he was allocated a Spitfire to look after. 80 Squadron had recently been re-equipped with the new Mark 24 Spitfire, the last variant of the iconic Second World War fighter, and was to be the last unit to operate the aircraft. That Saturday Beavin and a few mates decided to visit the nearby town of Hannover, and what they discovered there demonstrates the type of conditions to be found across most of Germany three years after defeat:

The local train of three coaches, two reserved for us troops, the third coach crammed full, there were people hanging from the doors and on the roof, they were the starving city people either coming or going out into the countryside to barter for a couple of cabbages or whatever. As the train entered the suburbs of Hannover it slowed to a crawl, due to the utter devastation, there were barely any complete buildings, it was mostly a wall here, a chimney stack there, as I was taking all this in I saw on old lady emerge from under a sheet of corrugated iron to go scavenging amongst the ruins. Two or three miles further on in the city centre it was not much better although the rubble had been cleared from the roads and a few trams were running.

The following Monday Beavin reported for work to be informed that he had been detached, along with his aircraft, to Gatow, and he should pack for departure immediately. The Air Ministry, mindful of the Viking incident a few months earlier, thought a clear message needed to be sent to the Soviet Airforce, and 80 Squadron assumed escort duties. The groundcrews saw the aircraft off to Gatow, and then loaded two Dakotas with their kit and Spitfire spares and followed the fighters into the city. When the squadron arrived they found construction staff frantically finishing the solid runway. The Spitfires were assigned a hangar on the edge of the parade square; unfortunately, as Gatow had been a training establishment the hangar had never contained live aircraft, so the parade square had a flagpole in the middle of it causing rather an obstruction. Beavin and some colleagues were ordered to remove it but on pulling it down they discovered it was needed elsewhere. Unfortunately they hadn't used the crane and the pole was now scrap. Once the entrance was clear the Spitfires were pushed into the hangar and remained there for five weeks, and weren't scrambled once.

The currency reform announcement devastated the Soviets' plans for Germany. With a currency involving only the United Kingdom, United States and France the Russians knew that any probable control of the country would slip through their fingers. They were no closer to participating in the control of the Ruhr, had failed to influence decisions over the creation of a West German state, had lost out on reparations, and now had a rapidly developing capitalist outpost in their midst. In a last-ditch attempt to head off the new currency, Moscow argued that the notes used in Berlin should be the same as those used in the Soviet zone. To their surprise the West agreed; however it would need to be controlled by all four occupying powers. Indignantly the SMA introduced its own currency on 22 June. Now with nothing to lose, the West introduced the Deutschmark into the city the following day. To identify it from the Deutschemarks already issued in West Germany the letter 'B' was stamped centrally on each note. Berlin had become a microcosm of Germany – currency reform had now sealed the city from the outside world and divided it in two.

The City Council met at the Rathaus on 23 June to ratify the two currency proposal of the Magistrat. The meeting, scheduled for 4 p.m., was significantly delayed as members of the SED and officials from the Soviet Military Authority forced their way into the building. After two hours the session was reconvened. Frau Schroeder, Deputy Mayor, argued that both currencies must be allowed to circulate; Reuter had already briefed her over the idea, and above the chaos the assembly agreed to allow both new currencies in

The new Deutschmark was introduced into Berlin on 23 June 1948. The 'B' stamp was to combat profiteering and movement of the notes out of the city.

Brandenburg Gate. Travel restrictions around the city were often no more than a helpful sign. This would cause the allies many headaches in the coming months. (US Army Signals Corps)

the city. Violence then ensued. As council members tried to leave the building the waiting SED mob set about them. Unfortunately the Rathaus was situated in the Soviet sector, and so the SMA-supported police just stood back and 'monitored' the situation. Not all were brave enough to leave and barricaded themselves in the building. It was a further three hours before they too managed to escape with the aid of some sympathetic police officers.

'Technical Difficulties'

Within a few hours the true implications of the decision became clear. On 24 June the Soviet licence news agency ADN carried the following statement:

> Because of technical difficulties on the railroad right of way, the transport division of the Soviet Military Administration in Germany was compelled to stop during the night of 24 June, all passenger and freight traffic in both directions on the line between Berlin and Helmstedt. Major-General Kvashnin has issued all necessary orders for prompt repair work. It is reported that at present it is impossible to re-route traffic in the interest of maintaining rail service, since such measures would unfavourably affect the entire railroad traffic in the Soviet Zone of occupation.

Water traffic was also suspended, and no reason was given. The lights dimmed across the Western sectors as electrical power from the Soviet zone and power plants across the Russian sectors stopped supplying the city. Ironically, a chronic shortage of coal was given as the reason why power had been cut. Motor transport was allowed in and out of the city; however, this was not as straightforward as it sounded. All traffic was forced to make a 25km detour as the bridge over the Elbe was conveniently under repair. The detour took traffic to a ferry and that could only cope with two vehicles at a time. Transport from the West was effectively at a standstill. And worse was to come, the following day the SMA stopped the shipment of brown coal into the Western sectors and refused to honour the agreement over milk for children. Supplying the garrison by air had been possible at a push; now an extra 2 million plus were isolated. That day eight Royal Air Force Dakotas arrived at Wunsdorf with a total lift capacity of 20 tons. The situation looked very bleak indeed.

Four

Constructing the Bridge

The airlift proper has always been identified as starting on 25–26 June 1948. This is not accurate. Flights had continued since the April crisis and plans had been drawn up in London for supplying the British garrison in the middle of May. For their part the Americans had been working on their response over the same period and had continued to fly in supplies for its garrison using, as were the British, the DC-3, work horse of the Second World War. April had demonstrated the city's vulnerability, and ensured a stockpile was amassed just in case. This stockpile, critically including eighteen days' worth of coffee, meant the city had a buffer allowing for some build-up in operations. Further Dakotas of 30 Squadron, based at RAF Waterbeach, had been on standby since early June in case of such an event. The first of two squadron deployments was initiated under Operation Knicker on the evening of 24 June, the second deployment comprising eight Dakotas was on its way on 28 June; destination Wunstorf. This chapter charts the construction of the airbridge until 14 October 1948, the day the effort was combined under one operational headquarters at Wiesbaden, the Combined Airlift Taskforce (CALTF).

Notes

Whilst military operations built up, the political wrangling was also gathering pace. 24 June became a pivotal day in the building crisis. That day the Soviet Military Authority (SMA) announced that they would prohibit the distribution of any supplies from the surrounding Soviet zone to the Western sectors of the city. If the population wanted to eat they would have to register in the Soviet sector. This was in direct contravention of the Potsdam accord and violated the ruling four-power supply agreement covering the supply of the city from a central pool. The West immediately cancelled all distribution of supplies from any allied sector to the Soviets. Tit-for-tat had arrived, a process that was to become commonplace for the entire Cold War. The 24th was also the day General Clay considered using an armed unit of combat engineers along the autobahn to fix the allegedly unsafe bridges. It was clear from intelligence reports that the Soviets were using the bridges as an excuse, and Clay considered the immediate forcing of the blockade to be the correct course of action.

Washington was not convinced and neither was General Brian Robertson, British military commander, who thought war was the likely outcome of any armed incursions into the Soviet zone. Robertson wrote to Marshal Sokolovsky on 26 June protesting that essential freight trains were being interrupted for no real purpose and the interference should stop immediately. The same day Ernest Bevin, British Foreign Secretary, expressed the view that Western withdrawal from Berlin would have serious, if not disastrous, consequences in Western Germany, and throughout Western Europe. He went on to demand that both the British and Americans should make the greatest possible effort to mobilise their air strength as a demonstration to all of Europe of the technical abilities they possessed, any contact with the Soviets should be after this, placing the Western Allies in a strong position.

Sokolovsky's reply came on 29 June. He cited restrictions on interzonal passenger traffic as being connected with currency control; however, he assured Robertson that passenger transport by rail would be re-established soon. Nevertheless, the restrictions on motor traffic would be retained to prevent currency from the Western zones being taken to Berlin. Sokolovsky also requested that freight train movements between the Soviet and British zones be re-established as soon as possible. It has to be remembered that until the blockade the governance of Germany had run as a four-zone country, each reliant on the other to a certain extent. Once it was clear the Soviet Military Authority intended to interfere with rail and road traffic the West had no option but to stop the flow of goods east. Sokolovsky now pinned the blame on the blockade fairly and squarely on the Western Allies, and especially the events following the London conference, to which the Soviets had not been invited. The creation of a Western currency imposed upon Berlin had caused economic disorders in the Soviet zone and this had made it impossible for alternative routes to be provided. 'A typical example of Soviet vague and implied promises' thought British staff in Berlin; clearly the West was getting nowhere. On 30 June an official at the Department of State in Washington noted that the American Embassy in Moscow, 'believes that we should not discount Soviet willingness to starve the German population of Berlin as the price for getting the Western powers out of the city'. By 6 July it was clear that negotiations at city level would be going nowhere. It was now time to deal with the situation country to country. It also confirmed Western suspicions that the civil population of Berlin was to be used as a pawn in the emerging superpower politics.

'Knickers!'

The requirements for Operation Knicker were that a daily cargo lift of at least 58,000kg would be needed to sustain the British Garrison based in the Spandau district of the city. On the return trip families of those trapped in the city were to be repatriated to the United Kingdom. These were estimated to number around 2,000. The problem was that two squadrons of ageing Dakotas were not going to prove effective in the short term, never mind if the lift suddenly outgrew the expected four-week duration. The first true British airlift flight comprised three Dakotas on the evening of 25 June and carried in just over 6 tons of supplies. The following day the RAF managed 13 tons whilst the USAF

The Douglas Dakota was the mainstay of the early Royal Air Force effort. Nearly a hundred were brought out of storage to supplement the lift.

delivered 80. The name 'Operation Knicker' raised quite a few eyebrows, and, during the early days of the lift, many vehicles sported bloomers and underpants from their radio aerials. However, Knickers' days were numbered as a larger, more comprehensive operation would clearly be needed if any dent in the supply requirements of the city were to be made.

ACI Roy Smith had been at his desk in the signals section at HQ 46 Group RAF Abingdon since 7 a.m. on 30 June:

> … when I was summoned to my bosses office, told to go to the mess and get an early tea, and return immediately to the office. This I duly did, and was told to open a Secret File headed 'Operation Cater Paterson'. I then spent a long evening and longer night typing lists of radio spares to be made available at Wunstorf and Gatow needed for the Avro York aircraft.

Operation Cater Paterson was a greatly enhanced effort, 46 Group would be joined by 38 and 47 Groups and the day Smith opened the signal a further thirty-eight aircraft arrived at RAF Wunstorf. Within a week aircraft from 30, 46, 53, 77 and 238 Squadrons plus a detachment from 240 Operational Conversion Unit (OCU) were parked up at the small airbase. Orders given by 46 Group demanded 160 flights by the aging Dakotas per day, leading in 400 tons for three days. This was then to be reduced to 210 tons utilising eighty-four aircraft for the duration of the emergency. To complement the operation 46 Group's Avro Yorks, forty initially, were to operate above a hundred flights per day. Cater Paterson was ambitious and, unfortunately for the Western Allies, a public relations disaster. A well-known removal company in Britain was also called Cater Paterson and it was not long before Moscow was making full capital on the situation. Clearly the Royal Air Force had named their operation thus as they were planning to move out of the city. By mid-July the operation had become known as Plainfare; the code name was used throughout the rest of the airlift. To complement the lift, at least until Gatow's new runway was fully operational, flying boats from Coastal Command were brought into operation. The more unusual part of the British airlift operated between Hamburg and Lake Havel until 14 December; this is fully explored later.

The expected 160 plus flights never materialised. A number of factors conspired against the plans, not least the weather. Rain and low cloud dogged the flight into Berlin, just as it had done during the bombing raids some years earlier. The weather also affected operations at Wunstorf. The airfield was one of Hitler's expansion period fields, designed initially for bomber groups, but throughout the early 1940s it had been used as a training site. It had two concrete runways and limited hard-standing, any additional aircraft parking was on grass. The rain quickly turned these areas into seas of mud; aircraft, fuel tankers, trucks full of equipment and cargo, and groundcrew all struggled through the mire. And the problems did not stop there. Whilst the Dakota was a rugged aircraft, it did suffer in damp weather and a number became unserviceable due to moisture getting into the electrics. Spares were also a problem, as was the amount of first-line equipment such as fuel bowsers and even chocks. But by far the most critical aspect of the whole operation was manning. Since the war the Royal Air Force had been running down its manpower and by 1948 this had reached critical levels. Now both groundcrew and aircrew were in short supply; the only answer was to post men in from other theatres. Eventually London would come up with a radical solution – the use of civilian contractors – but this was, for the moment, some way off. For now RAF serving crews would have to make up the shortfall.

Leading Aircraftman John Beauchamp had been stationed at RAF Pershore when he was posted on short notice to RAF Lyneham. A rigger by trade, this started LAC Beauchamp's long association with tents:

> Lyneham was short of manpower as most had been posted into Germany so men were posted in from all over the place, this included us. We were billeted in tents near the gate which was a long way from the mess. I always remember Master Pike, Warrant Officer in charge of the line, he organised absolutely everything, from manning to aircraft spares, an incredible chap. One day he said 'you four riggers get your small kit you're off to Germany' and so we went back to our tented billet and then took the next available DC-3 to Wunstorf.

Dakotas were arriving at Lyneham from all over the world, there receiving a rudimentary servicing before dispatch to Wunstorf. On completion of set flying hours the aircraft were flown back to Lyneham for major servicing. Any transportable unserviceable components were flown back to the UK at the same time. On completion of the servicing the aircraft was loaded full of first line spares and flown back to Wunstorf.

On arrival at Wunstorf LAC Beauchamp discovered he was back in temporary accommodation again:

Unloading a Transport
Command Dakota at Gatow.
(With thanks to Frank Watt)

We were billeted in tents at Wunstorf, come rain or shine we just got on with it. Then one
day the Royal Engineers laid on running water. It was luxury! The water pipe fed a row of
galvanized basins, of course the water was cold. We were fed at a tented mess. The food was
cooked in some World War Two field Kitchen units, the food was bloody marvellous, it was
incredible what they could cook up, of course nobody asked where the meat came from!

The introduction of Avro Yorks from 47 Group increased dramatically the daily tonnage
and by 18 July nearly 1,000 tons a day were being flown into the city. This said, the
weather continued to make the operation very difficult indeed. On a number of occasions
air traffic control at Gatow closed the airfield completely due to low visibility, driving rain
or, on occasion, snow. When the aircraft could fly into Gatow they were limited to one
every fifteen minutes, primarily to allow collections of water on the runway to be swept
clear. Conditions did not just affect the operation of the aircraft; groundcrew also suffered.
As more staff were brought in to load or service the aircraft, accommodation began to run
out. Eventually all rooms, including loft space, were double bunked and many were left
sleeping in tents on the airfield. The combination of damp conditions and the constant
drone of aircraft engines took their toll, fatigue set in reducing groundcrew's effectiveness
and thus the number of flights. Something clearly had to be done.

Organisation

The assembled aircraft fleet came from all over the United Kingdom. Dakotas flew in from RAF Waterbeach, Oakington, Broadwell, Fairford and Abingdon, whilst the Yorks were provided by Lyneham, Bassingbourn and Abingdon. Such a myriad of squadrons caused inevitable duplications and misunderstandings, so a central HQ was formed to man operations, effectively pooling all aircrew. When the operations had initially commenced the Dakota was the only method of transport; accordingly flight times could be mapped accurately from take-off to landing. Unfortunately, by 10 July this was no longer possible as the Dakota had been joined by Yorks and Sunderlands, each with their own cruising speed and flight time to the city. Normally this would not have caused a problem; however, all aircraft needed to be operated through one of the three narrow air corridors making coordination critical. To overcome this aircraft were dispatched in type waves, so all Dakotas would fly, then all Yorks. The Sunderlands operated at a lower altitude and, as they were landing at Lake Havel, did not dramatically interfere with operations at Gatow; however they still needed to be controlled, placing extra pressure on the system.

Whilst the waved principle alleviated problems for air traffic control, the same could not be said for the unloading crews. It meant that bursts of activity were interspersed with periods of standby. Clearly a steady rate would be more productive, and so the programme was revised; this time each aircraft was paced per hour so an even flow, as long as the weather held out, could be maintained. Steadily the gaps between aircraft were reduced to four minutes at Gatow. Another way of increasing efficiency was to increase the load each aircraft was capable of carrying. In the case of the Dakota, a number of safety equipment items were removed, including dinghies fitted for ditching; the number of fire extinguishers and amount of fuel used was also reduced. By 16 July increases in the all-up weight had given an increase in payload of 2,000lb or almost 30 per cent more capacity.

The increase in flights and weight was desirable but the punishment the aircraft were suffering was not, and very quickly unserviceability went through the roof. Both Yorks and Dakotas were suffering from electrical problems, and this was now compounded by the short flights each aircraft was conducting. Spares became a major issue as reserves were eaten up at an alarming rate. Tyres, brake units and eventually complete undercarriages began to show the stress of repeated landings, often at maximum landing weights. Added to this was the Yorks' dislike of short operations. The aircraft had been designed for long-haul flights around the Empire, not short hops at maximum weight, and now lots of niggly little snags were causing the groundcrew headaches and removing the aircraft from the front line.

LAC Beauchamp was on the line at Wunstorf and remembers the struggle at both ends of the bridge:

Our aircraft were flying in flour and coal, occasionally the aircraft carried flour on the first flight and coal on the second. Of course a lot of the cargos were in Hessian sacks and the dust made an awful sticky mess. When an aircraft landed at Gatow they often kept one engine running as there were no starter trolleys and if the batteries went flat you were stuck. At

The introduction of the Avro York greatly increased the RAF's daily load capability.

Wunstorf we had a dispensation to not 'over service' the aircraft. Unless the crew said they had a problem we didn't fix it. One thing that did take a battering was aircraft tyres. PSP cut them up so bad we were in danger of changing one a flight. We had some stuff called 'tyre doe'. If a tyre had a split in it we could use this, it got forced into the split and then once it had set hard it was knocked into the split with a hammer. We were allowed three repairs. The Civvies soon clicked onto this and were often on the scrounge, Every rigger guarded their doh like the crown jewels.

And the problems did not stop there. An increase in aircraft movements called for an increase in loading staff at both ends of the airbridge. By the middle of June it was clear that the RAF were not coping with the demand and on the 28th the British Army formed the Army Air Transport Organisation (AATO) with headquarters at RAF Wunstorf. This took responsibility for the loading and unloading of freight by operating a Rear Airfield Supply Organisation (RASO) at bases in the British zone and a Forward Airfield Supply Organization (FASO) at Gatow. Also the rapid build-up of the RAF fleet meant that the armada soon outgrew the small base at Wunstorf, and by the end of July some of the aircraft were readied for redeployment to the airbase at Fassberg.

In all the confusion it was inevitable that someone would slip through the net and that is exactly what happened to 80 Fighter Squadron who had flown into Gatow expecting trouble from Russian Yaks. Leading Aircraftman Beavin and his colleagues 'were never given any duties and spent our time down the city, or at the lake watching the Sunderlands', but there were other temptations far beyond sightseeing:

In Berlin we had our photos taken at the Brandenburg Tor, we were warned of the dangers lurking in the Russian Zone so we avoided it like the plague. Most of the time was spent chasing girls, that is when we had any fags to barter, and yes, we were invariably successful. I managed to purchase a camera, not a Leica just a cheap folding one which I used for the next five years.

Cameras became much sought-after items and were easily obtainable on the black market. Of course, no British serviceman could legally hold the new Deutschemark; they were paid in British Armed Forces Special Vouchers know as 'BAFS', and these were no good to the Germans. But other commodities were worth far more than money. AC1 Frank Watt, based at RAF Fassberg, had things sorted: 'I had a scam going, my folks used to send me coffee rolled in a newspaper and declared it as such, coffee was like gold dust for buying things'. The Berliners lived off coffee but unfortunately had had to suffer from the 'ersatz' variety since the early 1940s. Ersatz coffee was a blend of grain, chicory and anything else that would give it colour, the only thing it did not do was taste like coffee, hence the real thing demanded a premium rate of exchange. Newspapers 'exported' to Berlin became big business, so much so that a guard was mounted at the gate of RAF Abingdon and staff leaving the site were liable to be searched. It transpired that when a York flew back to the base it was invariably carrying box loads of cameras, china or expensive clocks for 'customers' back home. All items discovered were confiscated, though strangely no record has been kept explaining what happened to the items after that.

Vittles

Naturally, blockade busting was not just the preserve of the British occupation forces. The Americans had a substantial presence in the city under the command of Colonel Frank Howley and, via the direction of Curtis LeMay, fully intended to supply the garrison by air. General Clay later described the episode as 'one of the most ruthless efforts in modern times to use mass starvation for political coercion'. On 24 June Clay instructed LeMay to remove all transport aircraft in theatre from other duties and put them on the Berlin run. Subsequently around a hundred C-47s were available, many from the 61st troop carrier Group, and they were ferrying food and supplies in to the city by the following day. By 26 June the USAF publicity department was declaring:

> The U.S. Air Forces will continue to step up the air transport of vital goods to Berlin. The airlift which at present is exclusively used in provisioning only U.S. personnel shall henceforth carry a part of the foodstuffs for supplying the German population.

The United States would operate Operation Vittles primarily from two airfields located in their zone. Rhein-Main, near Frankfurt, was a large Luftwaffe base occupied by the United States since the latter stages of the Second World War. Over the years it had become an important central hub for American troops and equipment moving in and out of Germany. Critically, it had good transport links and was soon upgraded to an efficient

A Douglas C-47 Skytrain heads for Tempelhof. The US withdrew the type early in the lift in favour of the C-54 Skymaster.

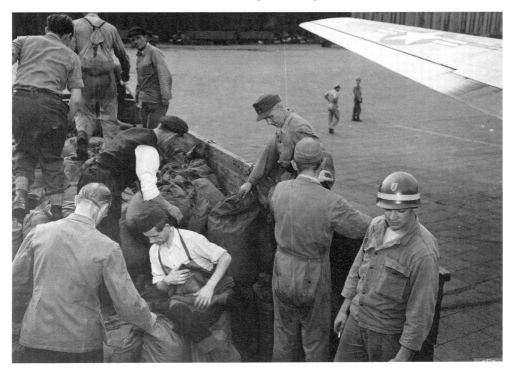

The introduction of the C-54 radically increased the tonnage capacity of Operation Vittles. Here, 10 tons of coal are unloaded by German workers. (US Army Signals Corps)

airfield. The second principal base was located close by at Wiesbaden, again under United States Air Force Europe control. The problem was that both the airfields lay deep in the American zone over 260 miles from Berlin, increasing fatigue on both aircraft and aircrews. Over time Vittles crews would redeploy to British stations; however, like the Royal Air Force effort the first few weeks were very much a hit or miss affair. So much so that Lieutenant General William Tunner, who had just become deputy commander of the Military Air Transport Service (MATS), later wrote, 'the airlift ran more or less by itself until Brigadier General Joseph Smith, commander of the military post at Wiesbaden, was tapped for the job'.

Even with a hundred C-47s, LeMay knew he had reached the limits of his capacity. The United States had numerous examples of the larger C-54 stationed in theatres around the world, critically with a 10-ton payload capability. The US Government had purchased over 1,000 of the Douglas aircraft throughout the war, building up a formidable transport capability in the process. Now, more than ever, that capability was in demand. Four squadrons were directed into Germany on 27 June. Crews were rather surprised to learn of their immediate detachment and dismayed to discover it was open-ended. Aircraft flew in from places as varied as Alaska, the Caribbean and Hawaii. Some, like the 54th Troop Carrier Squadron based at Anchorage, did not even have time to remove their snow shoes from the aircraft.

Armed convoys

Whilst the aircraft that made up the Vittles fleet were being assembled, General Clay and Robert Murphy, his political advisor, were trying to win support for a quick solution. They were eager that the West should force its way into the city by armed convoy to reassert the Allies right of entry. Designated Task Force Trudeau, the convoy was to run straight through the Soviet zone, repairing bridges where necessary, and into the city. To defend itself the convoy would have armour and artillery complemented by around 6,000 troops.

Murphy re-assessed the situation on 10 July, and came to the conclusion that the situation now passed 'into a physical struggle for the maintenance of our position'. In his opinion, 'the only cure now was the use of a guarded truck convoy reinforced by troops if necessary in order to force our established right to the use of service transportation into Berlin'. The National Security Council echoed these sentiments, concluding that by the end of October conditions in Central Europe would be so bad that the United States would have to consider using an armed convoy to break the blockade. Whilst the plans sounded heroic, and the Soviets had probably not prepared themselves for such a venture, the logistics made the possibilities of success somewhat remote. Any convoy would have to travel through at least 110 miles of the Soviet zone, cross numerous bridges and, most importantly, be safe. Other options were even less palatable. All water and rail traffic was under the control of the Soviets and if either was to be used as a route to supply the city, vast numbers of troops would be needed to control marshalling yards, locks and crossing points. A top-secret Department of State document, dated 20 July, demonstrates some of the opinions of the time:

> Ambassador Smith in Moscow expressed the view that any move by the Western powers to supply Berlin with an armed overland convoy would be met by the Soviets with armed force, since the whole position and prestige of the USSR would be at stake and Moscow would not be able to retreat. Smith feels that a 'little shooting' would not necessarily produce a conflict, but he feels that all other possibilities should be exhausted before we attempt anything in the nature of armed convoys.

The British were horrified. The Military Governor told Clay straight, 'If you do that, it will be war – it's a simple as that'. Even so, planning for the convoys did receive some backing from the senate, however, by August it had become apparent that the airlift would sustain the population, albeit at a rudimentary level. And later the Soviets declared that an armed convoy would indeed have been seen as an act of aggression, one that would have attracted an armed response.

'Willy the Whip'

In his book, *Decision in Germany* (1950), General Clay said of the airlift, 'Later, to obtain maximum efficiency, General Robertson agreed to place British air transport in an

'Willy the Whip'. General William H. Tunner, the most experienced 'air mover' of his generation.

integrated command headed by our General William H. Tunner'. This was quite an understatement. Tunner had probably the most experience of any individual available at the time. During the Second World War he had masterminded the air supply operation flying equipment from India over the Himalayas into China. Now, at the start of the main airlift he was Deputy of the Military Air Transport Service (MATS), an organisation specifically designed for such a venture. Unfortunately, MATS was not involved. As Tunner read the news reports it became clear that the airlift was running on borrowed time and would very soon burn itself out. He later noted:

> I read how desk officers took off whenever they got a chance and ran to the flight line to find planes sitting there waiting for them. This was all very exciting, and loads of fun, but successful operations are not built on such methods. If the airlift was going to succeed and Berlin to remain free, there must be less festivity and more attention to dull details, such as good, steady, reliable maintenance.[1]

---

[1] 'Over The Hump', page 160. (Second paragraph after sub-heading: 'Willy the Whip'.)

MATS had nearly 300 C-54s on charge, based around the world, their integration into the airlift would provide a substantial boost and allow for the slower, less efficient C-47s to be reassigned. And on 23 July MATS was ordered to establish an Airlift Task Force Headquarters in Germany. The advanced party, including Tunner, arrived in Wiesbaden on 29 July, initially under the command of LeMay. Throughout August transport squadrons from around the world were redirected to Germany. Soon nine complete squadrons were flying on Operation Vittles, each aircraft having three crews for staff rotation, a far cry from the newspaper reports Tunner had read a month earlier. Statistics aside the American air corridor was becoming dangerously congested as the arriving C-54s were pressed into service.

Airfield chess

As aircraft flooded into Germany usable airfield space rapidly diminished. The RAF had identified their primary base as Wunstorf, and on 24 June Transport Command had, near enough, completely taken the base over. Subsequently the billets vacated by 80 Squadron were nowhere near big enough for the influx of personnel and soon men were being billeted in the loft spaces of any suitable building. However, billets were not the only problem. As the weather deteriorated so the airfields, with little hard standing, became seas of mud. It became so desperate at Wunstorf that the aircraft had to be taxied around on almost full throttle. And when it stopped raining the mud dried into ridges, often so deep that men broke ankles on them. The Station Commander, in desperation, had bulldozers come in and level the ridges off; unfortunately with no grass to hold the soil together the slightest breeze made the airfield look more like a dustbowl site in the mid-west United States than Germany. In an attempt to counter this, the RAF Airfield Construction Wing increased both the loading area and runways by laying Pierced Steel Planking (PSP), but it was quickly realised that the base was at the point of collapse. At this time the site was operating both the Dakota and York. Differences in loads, times for flight readiness, take-off distances, fuel load and speed all added to the confusion at Wunstorf and led to the airfield being cleared for just four-engine aircraft by the middle of July. The slower, less effective Dakotas were relocated to Fassberg to the north-east of the site.

Fassberg, a portrait of combined operations

Fassberg dated from 1936. It had been a Luftwaffe training school until the last few months of the war. Subsequently the base was used as a staging runway for RAF fighter squadrons, however, it was subsequently downgraded in 1947, becoming a transitory home for the RAF Regiment and other support units. This was not to be for long. Wunstorf was almost at breaking point by early July, especially when the number of Yorks started to increase. Fassberg was identified as the ideal base to relocate the Dakotas, close to the air corridor and vacant. In just over a week the Airfield Construction crews had covered an area of 800 by 500 yards with PSP and work on the renovation of barrack blocks and hangar space was moving on a-pace. A railway line was built along with sidings right up to the airfield and on 19 July the first Dakotas flights were undertaken. These were symbolic as they were carrying coal, the black gold that was to be so critical in the coming winter.

AC1 Val Spaven, a 77 Squadron engine mechanic, had just returned from a detachment to the Suez Canal:

Arriving back at RAF Oakington we went through customs then flew back to RAF Waterbeach. I took the chance to have some leave and show my brown knees. When I returned to RAF Waterbeach all the crew were on the Berlin Airlift. It was not long before I was on a DC-3, this DC-3 had the fuselage door removed to make room for a spare propeller. Any plane going to Germany would carry any cargo available.

Conditions at the camp were quite acceptable to the British servicemen as AC Spaven elaborates:

The station was well constructed with two storey barracks, double windows and double doors. I believe the floors were heated but we were not there in winter. Indoor swimming pool, a recreation centre complete with bowling ally, not ten pin but a single plank you had to keep on to get to the pins. Egg and chips was a favourite as we listened to a small musician group with the ex-Luftwaffe Commander on the piano.

As the USAF built up their Skymaster fleet the air corridors they were operating were becoming dangerously congested. Furthermore, the trip to Berlin from Frankfurt or Wiesbaden was nearly twice as far as the British were covering, which meant more hours in the air for less payload delivered. It was not long before Tunner had brokered a deal allowing the USAF to operate C-54s from Fassberg, and so on 22 August the Dakotas were on the move again, this time to Lübeck, just 3km from the Soviet border. AC Spaven remembers 'first contact':

The first we saw of the ground crew Americans was at breakfast when they complained about our food. The next day for breakfast there was a selection of bacon and eggs, fruit juices and cereals in small cartons, which we hadn't seen before. 24th of August we were on our way to RAF Lübeck.

AC1 Frank Watt was Fassberg's dental technician and subsequently remained at the Station Sick Quarters (SSQ) when the British Dakotas flew out:

At first we had the old faithful Dakotas with British crews but as they were too small on tonnage we called in the yanks with their big Skymasters. When the yanks arrived straight from tropical climes they did not think much of this cold limey airbase! Soon the airfield was a hive of Yankee ingenuity rows of planes and lots of German and DP labourers to load the planes. Operation Vittles had begun and there was no sign of plain fare to be seen, all of a sudden Fass was a US base. We had a contingent of army boys, RASC doing guard duties etc, and at the SHQ the RAF ensign and Old Glory flew side by side, two COs to dish out their own brand of discipline.

The hundredth load from Fassberg. The integration of C-54 crews with the British paid off in the long term. (US Army Signals Corps)

Food on combined bases became a major issue. The American servicemen were used to good quality fare and enjoyed nearly twice the rations of their British counterparts. It was not long before air and ground crews were complaining bitterly to their superiors. The diet of fish, tea and egg and chips did not go down well and neither did the state of the accommodation. Lieutenant Colonel H. Mosely, USAF Deputy Air Surgeon, later commented that the lack of latrine facilities and hot water created conditions 'similar to those found in Nazi concentration camps'. However, every cloud has a silver lining, as AC Watt recalled:

One of the good points being run by the yanks was that they took over the catering, and to austerity starved erks it was heaven. They had a Dakota that flew in each day from Denmark fresh meat and steaks delivered to the door. Nothing too good for the blockade busters!! Stacks of pancakes with maple syrup, two eggs lashings of bacon and hash brownies, what a breakfast every day. Slowly we gelled to their ways and had the SSQ running like a clock, one of the bad points was they got choice of accommodation and grabbed all the best billets, you cant win 'em all.

Outside the Malcolm Club, Fassberg. (With thanks to Frank Watt, second right)

Life on the combined bases was colourful to say the least. The lack of facilities meant problems all too often bubbled over in the bars on and around the site. Rivalries were not always nationality-based; traditional arguments between British Services were just as likely to erupt:

> There were a few problems with the squaddys they resented the pay difference and after a few beers they let it be known. I am afraid there was no unions in the forces, we at least had cheap cigarettes and beer in the NAAFI. I had a bit of a do one night when I was with my US equivalent and some squaddys kept making remarks the Malcolm Club (MC) was for British only, like a fool I told them in no uncertain terms that the MC was a RAF club and they were guests sharing also, all of a sudden I was clobbered on the nose with a Guinness bottle which luckily did not break. Next thing I recall was back at SSQ, my yank pal had dragged me out as he made an inglorious exit. I still carry the bump on my nose and I can't stand Guinness.

'The USAFE's giant Globemaster landed at Berlin's Gatow Air Field with 20 tons of flour to help supply the blockaded city of Berlin.' International Tractor units are in attendance. (US Army Signals Corps)

The move to Lübeck

Lübeck was by no means the best site in the world but the accommodation was far better than that at Fassberg; however, it was a bit of a shock to Transport Command personnel. AC Spaven remembers:

> 24th August we were on our way the RAF Lubeck on the Baltic, this was a fighter station for gunnery practice. The fighter station had strict discipline and we were dressed for work not inspection, several 'bods' were put on a charge to overcome this.

Within a few days of arriving the airfield had begun to take shape:

> The airfield set up was done in a few days with 80,000 square metres of PSP laid for aircraft parking, a hangar was converted to Operation Plainfare operations, a counter had been built for pilots to check in and out with their 700's aircraft log books. The counter had sections listed engines, airframes, instruments, wireless, electrical and radar. There was a large dispersal board with the aircraft parking all numbered for easy locating. A lot better than Fassberg.

It was not long before Lubeck became the base for all British C-47s, and this naturally brought in problems with accommodation. For the RAF personnel it was billeting as normal, although the civilian crews had a mixed bag. The civilian Dakotas flew in a few days later and immediately overstretched the situation.

Pierced Steel Planking (PSP) rolled-up prior to removal. It was quickly realised that PSP could not withstand the landing the airlift demanded of it.

Victim of success

As the year marched steadily on the airlift was coming under mounting pressure, not from the Russians or even the European weather, but its own success. The tonnage being flown in to the two Berlin airfields had been steadily increasing as more C-54s were committed by the USAF. This had been complemented by the introduction of first the Avro York and then the civil contract operation (discussed later). Records throughout this period were set and broken with almost monotonous regularity. In 707 flights on 12 August the RAF and US air fleets delivered 4,742 tons, the first time but not the last that an above daily average (4,500 tons) was broken. On 14 August the first Douglas C-74 globe master flew in to Tempelhof direct from the United States carrying eighteen C-54 engines weighing in at an incredible 38,000lb. A few days later the C-74 commenced internal flights carrying 20 tons of flour at a time, twice that of the York and C-54 and nearly seven times that of the ageing Dakota. A clear message had been sent to the Soviets; all the Allies had to do now was keep the flow steady and safe.

By September the maintenance depot at RAF Burtonwood had been reopened, work was gathering pace at the Tegel construction site and work had begun on extending the runway at RAF Celle in the British zone. On the eighteenth of that month United States Air Force Europe celebrated Air Force Day by flying a combine and record load of 6,987.7 tons to Berlin. The gloves were now most definitely off. The following day a York taking off from Wunstorf crashed, killing all five crew. This was the first fatal British crash;

Construction of the second runway at Tempelhof. Crushed brick and debris from the bombed-out city were utilised as foundation levels here at Gatow and during construction of the new airfield at Tegel.

the Americans had lost nine crew in three accidents already. The shortages of RAF crews became critical as training aircraft and personnel had all been committed to Operation Plainfare. Transport Command had removed aircraft from strategic air routes and its own training centres to meet Plainfare commitments. Now it was apparent that unless the training programme resumed then the lift, or at least the RAF involvement in it, could collapse altogether. In direct consequence, by the end of the month twenty Dakotas and at least ten Avro Yorks had been removed from Germany and placed back into Operational Conversion Units in the UK. This had a dramatic effect on the British daily tonnage, one that was only to be made up with the introduction, in November, of the brand-new Handley Page Hastings. Crews were a different matter, and on 21 September a fifty-strong contingent of South African pilots departed to Germany. They were soon to be joined by crews from Australia and New Zealand.

At the end of the month the United States decided that there was no room in their flying programme for the aged C-47. All were removed from Vittles flights into Berlin in favour of the faster, larger, C-54. The RAF could not afford such luxuries; instead the Air Ministry and Foreign Office decided to recruit more civilian operators. The situation rapidly became more confused. It was clearly now time to amalgamate the two operations fully; however, service pride meant the path to cooperation would not, at least initially, run smooth.

Five

Controlling the Flow

October signalled major changes to the air supply of Berlin. Restructuring from command level down saw to it that the airlift rapidly became a well-oiled machine capable of coping with the German winter. If a statement was to be made as to Allied intentions towards the city it would now need to be an extremely bold one. The boldest of all would be to build an air bridge so convincing that the Russians were left in no doubt as to the seriousness of the situation they had placed Central Europe in. Some aspects of this statement, such as the construction of new airfields, had already commenced, however, they came into their own during the winter months.

Combined Air Lift Taskforce (CALTF)

The American takeover of RAF Fassberg in August had demonstrated that closer ties, at least at the airhead, were possible. That same month the Berlin Airlift Task Force (BATF) structured a system whereby United States aircraft could use either Tempelhof or Gatow, depending on which had less traffic at the time. This had worked extremely well with British Air Traffic Controllers working alongside their American counterparts. However, further mergers were not to be so straightforward.

That same month meetings between General Curtis LeMay and the Air Marshal Sir Arthur Sanders were exploring the possibility of a full merger. The British believed that there was no requirement for an overall unified command. The Air Ministry pointed out that the two sovereign services were operating in different parts of Germany and using different flight techniques, especially navigation. The BATF office in Berlin, along with the Berlin Air Safety Centre, already provided integrated control and so there was no need to relinquish command to a single multinational outfit. Furthermore, Transport Command was now taking charge of the RAF effort, including air bases. Technically, they would also assume control of USAF aircraft operating from the British zone. LeMay and Tunner were not impressed. The meetings dragged on whilst Sanders argued the British position. Turner later noted the Air Marshal might as well have been talking to LeMay's cigar as the General never budged an inch. On 14 October a joint directive was signed

The first of many consignments of the dreaded dehydrated potatoes delivered to Gatow by RAF York. To many, this meant conditions worse than those during the war.

by LeMay and Saunders, setting up the Combined Air Lift Task Force (CALTF). The headquarters of CALTF were at the airbase at Wiesbaden in the American zone. General Tunner was placed in command; his deputy was Air Commodore Merer, previously Air Officer Commanding 46 Group.

The third Berlin Airfield

Even with the expansion of Tempelhof and Gatow it was clear a third airfield would radically improve the situation. Subsequently, a large tract of land was identified in the French sector. The site had good, unobstructed approaches, was fairly flat and transport links to the city were, assuming minor improvements were made, ideal. It did have one major obstacle; the Soviet-controlled Radio Berlin transmitter tower. Discussions with the French made rapid headway and agreement was soon reached for the construction and operation of the proposed third Berlin airfield. The French had until this point sat on the sidelines, receiving the majority of their supplies via the UK and US effort. This had caused some consternation among air and ground crews when they discovered they were loading wine for the French garrison. It was eventually pointed out that wine was part of a Frenchman's staple diet and not classed as a luxury. The one aircraft that France had been using came to an ignominious end when, allegedly, a British truck was 'accidentally' backed in to it. Now the US Government was offering the French a new airfield, one that they would maintain and operate; it was just far too tempting.

Col Peterson of the US Engineering Corps, a veteran of the 'Hump' operation during the war, designed the base from scratch with obvious benefits. Taxiways ran direct from runway to unloading bays, which in turn were positioned against a new railway cutting, allowing sacks to be gravity loaded onto trucks or train carriages for delivery into the city. All barrack and administration buildings were positioned close to the aircraft parking area, cutting down on the amount of fuel needed to ferry staff about the base, whilst allowing key personnel to be available at a moment's notice.

Just as had been the case at Gatow, raw materials presented a major problem. Flying in concrete for the 2ft-thick base layer of the runway would have required the entire airlift capacity for at least two months, so an alternative was sought. Brick from devastated residential areas close by was trucked out to the site and laid in 6in layers. The brick was then crushed and compacted using a couple of old steam rollers even the Russians had not wanted. Other equipment, however, was not so easy to come by. The problem was that earth-moving plant and crushers were just too big to transport by air, even with the massive C-74s now available. Clearly, if the cargo hold of an aircraft was smaller than the equipment then there was only one course of action. Construction machinery was shipped into Rhein-Main where teams of engineers marked the units up into sections and then dismantled them. In some cases this required parts to be physically cut before loading. The majority of the equipment was then loaded on to C-82 Packets, the ideal aircraft with its clamshell doors, where it was flown to Tempelhof. There, the same engineers who had dismantled and cut the equipment up reassembled it. The lessons learned at Gatow were now employed at the Tagel construction site. Ballast left when the Russians had ripped up the railway tracks around the city, along with cobbles from already demolished streets, were bound together with bitumen and laid as a top surface for the runway.

Construction workers were the least utilised of all German trades in the city up to this point but an appeal for workers brought forward all manner of help including women and children. The conditions were harsh with no safety clothing provided; in fact, in the September some women wore little more than swimming costumes. Over 18,000 Berliners were employed on the project attracting 120 marks an hour and a hot meal, the meal proving more of an attraction than the pay in most cases. Later accounts proclaimed:

> … this job consumed a million feet of crushed brick or an equivalent of 10 city blocks of brick all of which was handled by German volunteer labour.[1]

The project started on 5 August with a completion deadline of 1 January. This deadline was critical, as the winter drew in the number of aircraft using Gatow and Tempelhof would naturally reduce, also Sunderland operations would have to be suspended over the deepest winter months as the Havel froze-over, making landing impossible. Due to the phenomenal efforts of the people of Berlin the first aircraft landed at the airfield on 5 November 1948. Just one last obstacle remained, the Radio Berlin transmitter, but not

---

[1] A special study of Operation Vittles. (1949)

for long. On 16 December, aircraft descending in to Tegel discovered the flight hazard had been 'removed'. French sappers, in an uncharacteristic act of provocation, had demolished the tower. Formal requests to remove them had been lodged by the station's director, Heinz Schmidt, but the French neglected to inform the real power behind the station, especially since the Soviet Military Authority had announced that control of the station was now formally back in the hands of the Berlin City assembly. General Kotikov fumed down the phone but the damage had been done, to the towers anyway.

The construction of new runways and hard standings was not confined to Berlin. The use of C-54s based at RAF Fassberg demonstrated the obvious benefits of stationing aircraft in the British zone, and it wasn't long before other airfields were being considered for upgrade.

Weather

Berlin is notorious for its bad weather. The unpredictability of rain, mist and cloud dogged the Berlin Airlift just as it had the bombing campaign a few years earlier, but if the Western Allies were to break the blockade then weather predictions had to be accurate. As the airlift continued it became clear that, whilst forecasting for the next day or so aided flying operations, the key to success would be the accurate prediction of weather five to six days in advance. If this could be done it would allow for planning maximum flights during marginal and good conditions, thus acting as a buffer for poor or non-flying days.

Previously, weather reports had been mostly 'theatre critical', a classic example being D-Day, now the situation had changed dramatically. The tonnage flown relied totally on the conditions at both ends of the bridge. This in turn relied on the conditions across the Atlantic as extra supplies were shipped in via surface or air transport. Subsequently, information from many different sources was pooled to gain as accurate a forecast as possible. A network of weather ships spanning the whole of the North Atlantic channelled information into London and on to Frankfurt. This was complemented by air sorties to the south and west of the British Isles. No.202 Squadron Royal Air Force Meteorological Unit based at RAF Aldergrove in Northern Ireland flew continuous daily weather reconnaissance patrols over the North Atlantic. The squadron operated Halifax Mk. VI on the Bismuth missions, something it had done since early in the war. Bismuth was the radio call sign originating from the British Isles Meteorological Office Unit Temperature and Humidity Missions. The aircraft flew out across the air corridor over Donegal and out into the Atlantic, taking readings at heights from several thousand feet down to 300ft off the ocean. This sortie pattern took the aircraft on a round trip taking several hours. Further aircraft headed north-west out into the Atlantic.

Hundreds of observation points across Europe telexed in information about local weather, and balloons were released at set intervals to monitor the upper atmospheric conditions. This was complemented by every seventh American aircraft carrying a radio operator, whose secondary task was to report in conditions at four points during the flight while weather modelling also began to be developed. Meteorological records of the last fifteen years were used to build up a probable number of flight weather days for any one month of the year. This, along with weather trends estimated for each of the airlift airfields, plus the information from the Northern Hemisphere, was used to issue a four-day forecast issued every three days. On top of this a twenty-four-hour forecast was issued, all agreed by telephone conferencing. The forecasters were in almost constant contact with air traffic at every base, and here the Meteorological Officer worked with the planners. This ensured a reduction of aircraft waiting to fly in bad weather, reducing fatigue on air and ground crew alike. However, a full wave could be generated for when conditions improved, ensuring the maximum load was delivered to the city.

Berlin Air Safety Centre (BASC)

The Berlin Air Safety Centre was established on 12 December 1945 by the Allied Control Authority and began operations in February the next year. Under rules of entry the BASC was given the following brief:

> The Berlin Air Safety Centre has been established in the Allied Control Authority Buildings with the object of ensuring safety of flight for all aircraft in the Berlin area. The Safety Centre regulates all flying in the Berlin Control Zone and also in the corridors extending from Berlin to the boundaries of adjacent control zones.[2]

A noble statement indeed. As always, in reality this was not the case. Although the Soviets withdrew from the majority of the Quadrapartite organisations this was not one of them, in fact the BASC was one of the few four-power organisations to survive right up until German reunification. The benefit to the Soviets of their continued involvement was obvious, as this was a legal way of monitoring the West's aircraft movements into the city. Interestingly, this was a well-known situation. When Tunner requested that freight figures be released in the world's press, senior staff in Washington preferred to keep it secret – until it was pointed out that all flights were being processed at the BASC and so the Soviets were well aware of the numbers involved.

Corporal Richard E. Wilson of the 158th Army Airways Communications System (AACS) was posted to Berlin in September 1948:

> I was an air traffic controller; my first job was in something called the Berlin Air Safety Centre, the true function of which remains unknown to me to this day. It did not involve controlling air traffic. What I did was transmit aircraft departure and arrival times to the Rhein-Main and Wiesbaden airports in the American Zone. It was an interesting job, though. I worked in a small room with two other Americans - one was an officer. There were also British, French and Soviet teams working beside us in the same room. Each team included one officer. I don't remember any names, but one of the British officers was a Flight Lieutenant who appeared to me to be about seventy years old!

---

2 Corbett, *Berlin and the British Ally.*

FLIGHT PLAN No.						BERLIN AIR SAFETY CENTRE				
TIME RECEIVED					Z	TIME DELIVERED				Z
B	D	FK	BE	TF	RADIO	RAF	SOV	FRENCH	TOWER	

ADDRESS

A/ IDENT. and C/S	B/ OPERATING AGENCY	C/ TYPE	D/ PILOT	E/ PT. OF DEPT.
F/ PROPO. DEPT. TIME	G/ ACTUAL DEPT. TIME	H/ ALTITUDE and ROUTE		J/ PT. OF DESTN.
K/ AIRSPEED	L/ ETE	M/ ENDURANCE		N/ ET. PT. No RET.
P/ FREQ/S	Q/ NAV. and APP. AIDS	R/ No. ON BOARD		S/ ALTERNATE
T/ REMARKS				

Berlin Air Safety Centre record card. Corporal Richard Wilson maintained these whilst at the centre in late 1948.

Each ally was required to notify the others of all flights entering the corridors. The centre occupied five rooms of the old Appeals Court building which had previously held the Allied Control Council until the Soviet walk-out. Each nationality had a room allocated with a central common room where all met. Each time a flight entered the corridor, the appropriate national representative would hand a card to the Soviet representative. This included basic flight details including timings, altitude and route, airspeed, ETA, number of crew or passengers, destination and departure airfield. The Soviet official looked over it and then ominously stamped it with a warning that he could not ensure the safety of the flight. He then returned it to the appropriate national representative and the strip would be placed on the board for tracking and the flight would continue on at its own risk. Although virtually all cooperation between the Western Allies and the Soviets collapsed during the Berlin Blockade, it was business as usual at the BASC. It became the coordination centre for search and rescue operations for Western aircraft that crashed in the corridors. The Soviet representative notified Soviet commanders in their zone of the last known coordinates of missing aircraft so that they could get assistance to the crash site as quickly as possible. Corporal Wilson remembers the process well:

Whenever there was any kind of international incident involving aircraft, the place would bustle with activity. The officer whose country was involved in the incident would approach the Soviet officer to file a complaint (it always involved the Soviets, of course). Invariably, the Soviet officer would promise to look into the incident, but as far as I remember nothing ever came of any complaints.

Air traffic

Early in the lift one major problem had been the handling of aircraft at the Berlin end of the bridge. It was all too easy for aircraft that missed their landing slot to be placed on hold, often creating large stacks above the city. This procedure came to an abrupt end on the airlift's fiftieth day. The weather that day was extremely bad. There was no possibility of visual air traffic control and the airfield radar was having problems seeing through the driving rain. A C-54 attempted to land on Tempelhof's PSP runway, overshot, and crashed into a ditch at the end of the runway in flames; luckily the crew escaped. The runway was further blocked when the next aircraft landed too far down the runway, braked hard to stop before the wreckage and blew two tyres. As the third aircraft in the wave dropped out of the clouds, construction teams on the ground realised he was about to land on the new concrete runway, the problem being that it was not finished. The undercarriage left the aircraft as the C-54 bounced through construction equipment; in three minutes Tempelhof was closed.

Aircraft on the ground had their take-offs delayed in case they collided with one of the thirty or so planes now stacked above the city, and with further aircraft appearing at the rate of one every three minutes the situation looked likely to get worse. As the stack steadily grew so did the radio calls to air traffic control requesting clarification of the situation. In amongst this stack was General Tunner, on his way to present an award to a USAF pilot; there were hundreds of dignitaries, groundcrew and civilians on the airbase awaiting the ceremony. Tunner literally blew a gasket, demanding all aircraft above and below him return to base; he had been made to look a complete fool in front of the very people who needed to have confidence in the lift. As with many things there was no one defining problem that made the situation a crisis. A series of components had come together that day conspiring to make up the 'circus'. Air traffic had been overwhelmed by a combination of extreme weather conditions and lack of training. The military controllers were simply not used to such high-density flying and further training was needed on the GCA equipment. It was not long before Washington had dispatched air traffic controllers from civil airfields to operate Tempelhof. Military staff were hand-picked and posted out to Germany to bolster the network; this included Corporal Wilson. But not all of them had such a memorable first day in the tower as Wilson remembers:

> I remember my first two hours working in Tempelhof tower. I had been told to just observe; I didn't have to do anything. My training would start the following day. So I was standing behind the Local Controller, the guy who controls the landings and takeoffs. It appeared to me that one of the landing C-54s (I think in British parlance they were called Skymasters) was travelling very fast as it touched down on the runway. I thought that maybe they all landed this way. Soon, someone else noticed and gave a shout – something like, 'Holy Christ!' – and, sure enough, the airplane overran the end of the runway, crossed the street (I think it was Berliner Strasse), and penetrated the facade of a bombed-out building on the other side of the street.

Tunner improved the situation on the ground. Now crews would stay by their aircraft. Here an unloading crew draws up (left), the latest weather and return manifest is delivered (centre), whilst the 'Follow Me' jeep (right) stands by to guide the aircraft back onto the line.

Ground Controlled Approach (GCA)

> The victory over the weather could not have been gained – indeed, the whole airbridge would have been impossible – without the use of radio and radar, and a few other kinds of scientific equipment.[3]

That scientific equipment was Ground Controlled Approach. The system had been introduced at Gatow in 1946 and was an immediate success. So much so that the RAF initiated a training programme for the system which, surprisingly, included the Russians. The aim, at Gatow at least, was to have one A/C movement in any ninety-second period culminating in one landing and one taking off every three minutes, day or night. In bad weather this was extended to five minutes. In fog the GCA controller came into his own and would talk the aircraft down on to the runway, occasionally in zero visibility.

As aircraft flew down the northern corridor they headed for the Frohnau radio beacon. At this point the captain made contact with Gatow Air Traffic Control (ATC). In good visibility the pilot visually controlled the landing with clearance and advice from ATC. However, in poor visibility ATC handed the pilot over to the GCA controller. The set-up comprised two caravans at the end of the runway manned by pilots or navigators.

Approach lights were fitted to both original Berlin bases early in the blockade; however, different systems were employed. The USAF engineers encountered an interesting

---

3 Berlin Air Lift, HMSO 1949.

The benefits of a nose wheel-mounted aircraft are evident when compared with the photograph on page 64. This load of flour would take around eight minutes to move to the truck. The aircraft could be on its way in as little as twenty to twenty-five minutes.

problem when erecting their system. Tempelhof was surrounded by building sites, making the airfield approach difficult at the best of times. The addition of a high-intensity approach light system, it was hoped, would help the planes in low-visibility conditions. Unfortunately, the only suitable place to locate the lights was in the Neukoelin Cemetery. Several graves had to be relocated and many more were disturbed during the laying of high voltage cables. Naturally, the Soviet press gained maximum mileage from the situation, declaring:

> Recently heavy damages were done at Neukoelin Thomas Cemetery caused by hundreds of children chasing after candies dropped into the cemetery by American pilots prior to landing. Now in a reckless manner holes and long cable ducts have been dug and masts with position lights erected. The Americans behave in Berlin like troops engaged in a war in the enemy country.[4]

---

4 *Die Woche in Bild*, 21 November 1948.

Gatow was the first base in the world to use a new lighting aid developed by the Royal Aircraft Establishment. Rather than having lights aligned with either side of the runway and the pilot flying down the middle, the RAE had a single line of sodium lights extending out along the project centre line of the runway. At regular intervals this was crossed by a single line, increasing in length the closer the aircraft got to the runway threshold. Incidentally, this system was implemented at London after it had been extensively 'tested' in the airlift.

The battle for Hastings

In early October the RAF identified another potential airlift airfield, Schleswigland on the Baltic coast. Being the most northern airfield in the British zone it suffered in the winter months from poor weather; however, checks proved that the site was suitable for upgrade before it even became fully operational. This included the construction of additional hangars, and an extension to the existing rail line, increased aircraft loading and unloading facilities on the apron, and refurbishment of most of the existing barrack blocks. Most important was the extension and enlargement of the fuel storage installations. The majority of the British 'wet lift' operations were destined to be launched from Schleswigland over the coming months.

Schleswigland was also to become the home for all Handley Page Hastings, RAF Transport Command's brand new transport aircraft. The Hastings was designed to replace the ageing Yorks and Haltons; both, it has to be remembered, were based on Second World War bomber aircraft, and whilst capable they were not ideal. The Hastings had many benefits, it had a large cross-sectional area fuselage allowing bulky cargo to be carried; in addition it had a large freight door measuring 9ft 5in by 5ft 9in and cruised at over 250mph. It did, however, have one drawback: the Hastings was a 'tail dragger', and because of this it proved difficult to load straight from the back of a truck.

On 1 November the first stream of Hastings departed RAF Dishforth, North Yorkshire, en route to Germany. The eight aircraft left at five-minute intervals, due to low cloud, then went into formation over the North Sea for some PR photographs. On board the 47 Squadron lead aircraft, piloted by Squadron Leader PJS Finlayson, Commanding Officer, was a reporter from *The Aeroplane*, John Fricker. His words illustrate the sensation of flying in an unpressurised aircraft:

> The barn-like interior of our aircraft was devoid of seats or similar luxuries, but the very efficient cabin heating maintained a sub-tropical temperature, until most of the windows were removed for the benefit of the photographers when the formation was at last achieved.

The 47 Squadron Hastings carried forty aircrew and seventy groundcrew on the first wave and the following day they were flying to the city with 8 tons of coal each. Much to the consternation of the crews, proud of their new, low hour aircraft, a month later 297 Squadron, also from Dishforth joined the lift, again carrying mostly coal.

The introduction of the Handley Page Hastings gave Transport Command increased bulky cargo capacity and higher speeds. TG503 is pictured shortly after delivery. This aircraft is now at the Allied Museum in Berlin.

The first detachment of Hastings arrived at RAF Schleswigland on 1 November 1948. TG514 of 47 Squadron taxis onto the keys at Schleswigland in early 1949.

Air operations

By November flight planning had become a very complex process indeed. Problems with aircraft at different speeds and operating heights had been further exacerbated by the introduction of Hastings. Furthermore, there was now a bewildering array of civil aircraft in the fleet. Some idea of the timings required of the controllers can be learned from the following passage:

> The problem is thus to feed aircraft, with different cruising speeds and flying at different heights from widely separated aerodromes, into the funnel of the Northern corridor from Hamburg so that they arrive over the Frohnau Eureka beacon, 16 miles from Berlin, with an accuracy of plus on minus 30 seconds from the estimated time of arrival. The solution has been provided by the use of a system in which each 24-hour period is divided into six blocks of four hours each, during which time each batch of aircraft does the round trip to Berlin.
>
> The type batches are staggered so that a constant stream of aircraft pours through the corridors, which are 20 miles wide and extend from 1000 to 10,000 feet. The northern 'axis' extends over 84 miles of the Russian Zone and very seldom contains fewer than 15 aircraft in its stream. The air corridors now point to Berlin like an arrowhead, with aircraft going in along the north and south 'axis' and coming out along the shaft [the Wunstorf Corridor] before dispersing to their various bases. Each batch of aircraft flies at carefully regulated heights, with the Skymasters at the top at 6,500 feet.[5]

Once the aircraft was on approach, air traffic control expected the aircraft to be touching down at the three minutes' interval, within plus or minus ten seconds of their estimated time of arrival. This tolerance was incredibly fine and had to be strictly adhered to; this meant that pilots only got one shot at the runway. If they had a problem and had to abort the landing or were a fraction outside their landing slot they had to return to their home base fully loaded. Planning had become so critical and margins so fine that one aircraft could effectively wreck the whole process that day. Putting that into perspective, on 17 October Gatow recorded 454 movements. Aircrews did not relish the thought of returning to their home base fully loaded, as by now competition was forming between squadrons and airbases as to the daily tonnage. Unfortunately this sometimes caused very dangerous situations. Captain Sam Pover of the civilian contract Air Transport Charter (CI) remembers one such incident whilst descending into Gatow:

> It was a dark November night, around four in the morning and I was descending from the east into Gatow. I had been the last in a wave of Dakotas from Fuhlsbüttel (Hamburg), behind me was a stream of Yorks. Suddenly over the intercom came:
>
> 'I should be number one, I can see the lights of the airfield and I'm faster.'

---

5 Group Captain R.J. Cohen to J. Fricker, November 1948.

'overshoot,' came the reply from air-traffic.

'why?' responded the York.

'overshoot,' responded air-traffic again.

Again the York pilot demanded to know the reason why.

'this is Gatow tower, overshoot.'

With that the pilot throttled up and prepared to overshoot. Anyone who's been in the Dakota knows how noisy they are and so it was with some alarm that I heard his engines open up and then he passed by the front of my aircraft with about 5 feet clearance. We were all glad to see the NAAFI truck I can tell you!

Tragedy did strike on 18 November when a Royal Air Force Dakota disappeared near Lübeck. The aircraft was returning in bad weather and visibility was around a mile; however the cloud was creeping steadily down. Unfortunately the pilot was the only one of the Dakota wave that was not instrument-rated. Lübeck air traffic control waited for the pilot to radio in once he had broken cloud but the call never came. The second aircraft in the wave reported seeing burning wreckage in the Russian zone as he made his final approach. Three flight crew died on board the aircraft. The tragedy was even more deeply felt when the body of a fourth passenger was located, a soldier who had been given compassionate leave. Losses such as these were deeply felt by service and civilian crews alike and although accidents were rare the airlift was to claim more lives before the blockade was lifted.

Throughout November the airlift battled against the weather. Thick European fogs covered much of Berlin for days at a time stretching the GCA crews to the limit. Gatow and Tempelhof had better navigation facilities whilst the zone bases had a mixture of navigational aids, and in some cases none at all. But now the wisdom of having several bases spread across the American and British zones came into its own. If one base was closed extra flights from another could be laid on, and it did not really matter about the weather in Berlin as the most advanced navigational equipment was laid in there. The monthly record for Gatow shows 1,316 GCA landings for November, and whilst this did lower the tonnage it did not stop a stockpile of nearly a month's worth of food being built. The idea behind the full amalgamation was beginning to bear fruit. This was to be further demonstrated with the opening of the second United States airlift terminal in the British zone on 15 December 1948 – RAF Celle.

Celle

Celle originally opened in 1935 as part of Germany's accelerated airfield expansion during the early years of the Reich; however, it remained a Luftwaffe training base until the final stages of the war. It was briefly occupied by radar operating Junkers 88s, used as guidance and control aircraft for night fighter defence against the increasing Allied bomber formations. Post-1945 Celle was home to various RAF squadrons, before becoming No.1 Barracks Equipment Disposal Unit in the autumn of 1947. By September 1948 Celle had been identified as an airlift base and work set about converting the by now dilapidated RAF site. From the outset Celle was to be the home to USAF C-54s, alleviating congestion around the Frankfurt corridor entrance. Also, the RAF base was very much closer to the Soviet sector border, cutting down on flying time, fuel use and more importantly, fatigue on the aircraft.

RAF construction teams employing thousands of German labourers undertook building work on the airfield. During three months of work over 60,000 tons of earth were moved and a 1,700m runway was constructed along with over 100,000 sq.m of hard-standing. Added to this was new accommodation for nearly 2,500 ground staff, hutting for German labourers, bulk fuel storage sites, rail head facilities and ramp lighting for twenty-four-hour operations. Coupled with this was Celle's location close to the Fhuse Canal and good rail links just a few hundred metres away from the aircraft loading area.

The first operational flights into Berlin started on 16 December. The day before, 317th Troop Carrier Group had deployed to the airfield from Wiesbaden, they continued to fly until 31 July 1949. The Celle flights sounded the death knoll for Sunderland operations to Lake Havel; they were suspended the same day, never to resume. The new facilities at Celle were considered the height of technical planning by the Air Ministry, but to be effective they needed to run efficiently. Luckily the base was one of a number used by the Army Operational Research Group (AORG) to monitor aspects of the army's involvement with Operation Plainfare. What they discovered on visits to Plainfare airfields between 1 and 7 April 1949, subsequently published in a secret report, now gives some idea of the complexities of just one of the operational bases.

Contained within the British sectors were six Rear-Airfield Supply Organisations (RASO) operating under the control of the Army Air Transport Organisation (AATO). The RASO at Celle was divided into a number of units, all with specific tasks to perform. These included four platoons of 79 Company (RASO) Air Freight, two platoons of 10-ton lorries operated by 524 members of the German Civilian Labour Organisation (GCLO). Also part of the force was a platoon of 3-ton lorries operated by 505 members of the GCLO, six GCLO labour groups comprising approximately 1,500 labourers and 279 Civil Mixed Watchman Service members.

79 Company Air Freight were responsible for loading aircraft under the supervision of either USAF or RAF command. This included the reception and clearance of food and coal trains as dictated by AATO, a job which was done in conjunction with staff coordinating reserves of food and coal held on the base. Any backloaded freight from Berlin was also the responsibility of RASO who ensured it was loaded onto the correct transport away from the airfield. Each Saturday a weekly programme that laid down the tonnage and details of commodities to be flown out in the next seven days was issued by AATO. This system was complemented by a signal where required, especially if modifications in civil supplies such as coal were needed.

Transport was at a premium in Berlin. The increase in air traffic placed additional pressure on the few vehicles in the city. Here a group of GMC CCKW 353s line up.

The 10- and 3-ton lorries collected loads from either the railhead or reserve Depot (in the case of Celle just the other side of the canal), and then parked at the Check Point. A twelve-man German labour team plus a single British and American loader accompanied the load. Time was often spent drinking black-market coffee in purpose-built rest huts or the NAAFI, especially in the winter months. Once each aircraft reached the 10-mile point it radioed in stating number, serviceability and whether it contained a backload or not. Once the call was received a pre-arranged load complete with its handlers and checkers was called forward onto the 'ready line'. As the aircraft taxied in the loaded trucks followed the aircraft onto the ramp. By the time Celle was fully operational crews had become very efficient in this process, often the loading trucks backed up to the aircraft whilst the flight crew were still shutting down the engines. The normal backload from Berlin was empty coal sacks, which in turn were removed and taken back to the railhead where they were delivered to the bagging centres.

Loading the aircraft also carried its own responsibilities for RASO personnel. Firstly the weekly programme would be broken down into daily lift loads; this would then be further reduced to single aircraft loads. Next the lorries were called to the aircraft, which were moved out to the specified ramp position. Finally, the load would be moved onto the aircraft correctly stowed and lashed down before the paperwork and manifest was

As part of Operation Santa Claus the Red Cross distributed toys to around 10,000 children in the city.

Christmas card from Fassberg. (With thanks to Frank Watt)

completed. During the inspection period at Celle, loading crews of twelve men were achieving a fifteen-minute time for moving 10 tons of supplies. However, this had been carried out in five minutes forty-five seconds during a record attempt.

Some loads were unfortunately more awkward than others. For instance, one 10-ton lorry could carry the equivalent of one C-54 load of coal, making transportation and coordination simple. However, light and bulky loads such as drums of dried milk or dehydrated vegetables made it necessary for two trucks to be used. This said, such loads did not adversely affect times. Even so, careful coordination ensured that multiple loads were not frequent.

The commitment for Celle was 1,100 tons per day until April, comprising 1,000 tons of coal and 100 tons of food. Between 15 December 1948 and 8 April 1949 13,000 tons of various foods along with 90,000 tons of coal had been flown into Berlin. Of the thirty-eight 317th Troop Carrier Group Skymasters at the base, an average of twenty to twenty-five were serviceable at any one time. Each aircraft carried 9.8 short tons per trip and was expected to carry out six sorties every twenty-four hours. Ground crews were also trained to cope with other aircraft types, as diversions caused by bad weather were frequent during the winter months.

An idea of the tonnage moved within a twenty-four-hour period can be obtained from the AORG report. The daily site report for the twenty-four hours ending at 12 p.m. on 26 February 1949 stated the following:

> Food in the form of lard, 30 tons, fish 114 tons, baby food 20 tons, skimmed milk 35 tons totalling 119 tons was flown in to the city on 19 sorties. Long flame coal 1,409 tons and ordinary coal 110 tons was flown in by 146 sorties and 12 sorties respectively.

These figures clearly exceed the HQ CALTF commitment for the airfield, and it is interesting that the British Army survey team chose one of Celle's busiest periods to record lift progress. The *Task Force Times* from the same day builds on the report's findings, adding them to the other base totals. The combined airlift delivered 7,639 tons in 879 flights, 'striking at the Berlin blockade with the greatest continuous high tonnage streak in its history'.

In the fortnight running-up to Christmas, C-54s from Fassberg, aided by the Red Cross, conducted Operation Santa Claus ensuring that 10,000 Berlin children received gifts over the festive period. Bob Hope arrived with his entourage including the Christmas Caravan troupe to tour the airlift bases. And by New Year's Eve the airlift had completed 100,000 flights into the city. Significantly, 5,000 of those had been conducted by British civilian aircraft.

Six

Sunderland! Sunderland!

On the 15 December 1948 a large group of German children excitedly congregated on the banks of Lake Havel. They had gathered religiously every day for the past six months, ready to watch the arrival of the Sunderland seaplanes. That day they were disappointed. The RAF had been forced to cease operations the previous day due to increasingly poor weather conditions. The West's fear that winter could wreck the airlift was partially realised when the lake threatened to freeze, making landing impossible. Initially it was planned that flights on to the lake would resume in the spring of 1949; however, this intention had been scrapped by mid-February. The part played by the Sunderland Squadrons is one of the lesser-investigated areas of Operation Plainfare; this chapter tells their story.

As the blockade started to bite, the Allies were faced with a dilemma, continue flying into the two operational airfields and be restricted by the number of landings or find an alternative site? Completion of the 2,000-yard concrete runway at Gatow was still some way off. Meanwhile, the project to build a second runway at Tempelhof was still in the planning stages. The Royal Air Force quickly realised they had the ideal 'weapon' in their arsenal – the Short Sunderland. The aircraft could carry an awkward payload, up to 5 tons in weight and more importantly could land on water, something the British and American sectors contained in large quantities.

Plans

Surveys were immediately commissioned on expanses of water in all three Allied sectors and by 28 June one area had been selected. Air Commodore Waite (later Officer Commanding Airlift HQ) and Wing Commander Crosby (Officer Commanding 201 Squadron), confirmed that Lake Havel was indeed 'suitable for flying-boat operations in view of [the] sheltered nature of Lake[,] consider suitable temporary moorings could be laid from local resources'. Gatow, 5km distant, would coordinate all aircraft movements, cover flight briefing and meteorological information. Mindful of the urgency of the situation, it was suggested that operations could probably start within twenty-four hours if rudimentary services were available. An airfield controller (waterborne) would be essential along with a rudimentary radio installation and somewhere to moor the aircraft. Meanwhile the Foreign Office also contacted the Air Ministry and Air Headquarters BAFO with similar thoughts. Clearly, any means of importing food into the city were valuable and Sunderlands should be considered if only because the '… use of heavy flying boats would also have great moral value'.

The Havel was ideally suited to flying-boat operations. The lake had three unhindered landing directions, each over 4,000m in length. The minimum depth in the landing lanes was between 4 and 8m and the proposed mooring area was again 4m. Surprisingly the Havel, unlike many other stretches of waterway in Europe after the war, had very few obstructions, making it relatively easy to find safe moorings for the aircraft. Transport to and from the Sunderlands would not present much of a problem either, as a number of barges had been stranded by the Soviet closure of Greater Berlin's waterways. Adding to this was a number of sailing clubs some run by the Allies, based around the shore, all with motor launches that could be easily pressed into service. Air Headquarters BAFO was initially concerned with the introduction of another aircraft type, bringing with it all the problems of different operating speeds and heights. However, it was soon realised that great value would be gained from using such unusual aircraft, and more importantly 'would provide an additional indication to the Russians that we intend to use all resources to break the blockade'.

If conditions at Lake Havel were good, they were anything but at the proposed detachment base on the Elbe near Hamburg. The landing area had originally formed part of the Blohm & Voss factory complex at Finkenwerder. Naturally this site, along with the majority of the city, had received the attention of the Royal Air Force on a number of occasions throughout the war. Bomb damage and a number of sunken vessels made subsequent landing or taxying a hazardous affair, a situation exacerbated by choppy conditions and keen tides. Even the mooring buoys were those designed for large ships rather than 'delicately skinned' aircraft. Coupled with this was a lack of ways to refuel the aircraft or billet the crews. In fact, conditions were so bad that OC BAFO suggested it may be better to 'fly direct from U.K. carrying token loads, object primarily being morale effect in Berlin'.

Underway

None of this deterred Major General Herbert, commander of the British Troops in Berlin, and he signalled Col Frank Howley on 1 July requesting permission to use the areas of Lake Havel that lay within the US sector. The following day Howley agreed, allowing the British to use a small shipyard on the mainland facing the Schwannen Insel as a base. By 3 July ten temporary moorings were ready to receive aircraft on the Elbe. Conservatively the Air Ministry estimated a capability of ten flights a day uplifting around 75 tons to the beleaguered city.

The sudden burst of activity around the lake attracted much local attention. During the first few rumour-filled weeks of the blockade, it was difficult to keep a lid on anything. With the possibility of a reconnaissance flight on 5 June, AC Waite was eager to warn the

Berliners of what was going on. A hastily prepared statement was issued to Western press and radio stations outlining the proposed addition to the airlift.

Alongside the public release, a top-secret signal circulated around the Air Ministry, Allied Headquarters BAFO, Coastal Command and British Allied Headquarters at Wunstorf, laying out the forthcoming operation. Flying boats of Coastal Command were to be coordinated with other airlift operations into Berlin under the operational control of Wunstorf. Air movements would be controlled via RAF Utersen and RAF Gatow for aircraft control and safety. A total of ten Sunderland flying boats were to be used. Two seaplane tenders fitted with VHF radio, then based at Lübeck, were to be moved to the Hamburg base for aircraft control and ground purposes. Army dispatchers were to provide additional sites for the loading and backloading of freight. An estimated thirty-six officers, seventy senior non-commissioned officers and thirty other ranks would require accommodation at Finkenwerder. At Lake Havel, OC RAF Gatow, Brian Yarde, was made responsible for acquiring motor launches to service the aircraft at the Berlin end. The overall responsibility for technical matters, such as servicing and aircraft repairs remained the domain of the Coastal Command detachment. In addition, the operation would fly only six days a week and then only in daylight. Sundays were to be used as crew rest and maintenance days. On 4 July a signal from RAF Gatow stated simply, 'arrangement for launches complete. Require minimum of two hours warning of flying boats ETA to clear shipping from Havel.' Finally, on 5 July, one of the more unusual episodes of Operation Plainfare got underway.

And so that morning Sunderland VB887, piloted by Wing Commander Crosby and Flying Officer Jack Halt, swooped down on to Lake Havel carrying a load of Spam. The flight had taken just over an hour, attracting interest from many Russian aircraft en route. A flotilla of small boats and launches made their way to greet the aircraft, taking no notice of the orders the river police had issued earlier. Crew members likened it to an arrival in Hawaii. Maj.-Gen. Herbert, AC Waite and Gp Capt. Yarde were also on hand to welcome the aircraft, as was NBC America, who promptly interviewed the crew for 'the folks back home'.

It had been a hectic few days for the Sunderland crew. The Coastal Command detachment comprised elements of 201 and 230 Squadrons, both latterly based at RAF Calshot, Hampshire. Equipped with Short Sunderland Mk5s, the squadrons had led a quiet existence since the end of the war, participating in exercises with the Home Fleet and flying goodwill trips around the world. When the call came to support the airlift, the majority of both squadrons were on detachment at Castle Archdale in Northern Ireland. By the morning of 3 July Jack Halt and other crews were frantically criss-crossing Europe, flying from Archdale down to Calshot, collecting equipment and then the following day flying on to Hamburg. Halt's flying log entry for the fifth simply states: 'Hamburg – Berlin. 1st A/C to alight on Havel Lake. – Ham'. He would pilot eighty flights into the city over the coming months.

Short Sunderland VB887 on Lake Havel. This was the first aircraft to carry in cargo and was to become a major attraction in the coming months.

Visitors

Not all welcomed the Sunderland detachment and it quickly attracted the attention of more than casual local observers. On 8 July Sergeant Kading, in charge of the Water Police on duty that morning, reported that a Russian officer had been making inquiries at the police station. Captain Rabaschnikow, in charge of Waterways in the Soviet zone and Greater Berlin, was then on his way to investigate operations for himself. The 'inspection' was 'to ascertain if there was any interference or danger to commercial traffic using the river'. Captain Rabaschnikow suggested the buoys marking lanes designated for barge traffic should be moved, 'leaving a clear course for the landing seaplanes'. Clearly this would have had the opposite effect with river traffic obstructing any landing attempt. Further to this, he offered to send more police boats to help patrol the Havel, mindful of the chaos this would undoubtedly cause, the offer was 'politely declined'. Undeterred, Captain Rabaschnikow instructed the Water Police to post four men on the lake between 9 a.m. and 3.30 p.m. daily, effective immediately; British personnel discreetly removed them later that morning. Flt Lt Young, at the time OC of Havel lakeside, was told, 'to keep a close watch on their movements'. Unless they interfered in operations or started asking questions nothing could be done. This incident highlights a strange concept in post-war Berlin. Although the city was divided, movement between the four sectors was a daily routine for most Berliners. At this time there was no restriction policy in place in the British sector, so Soviet officers could visit and make 'recommendations'. However, not all interested parties were military.

Press agencies from around the world were located in the city and had reported the worsening situation throughout the preceding year. Many British newspapers had special correspondents stationed in Berlin, and these employed local staff for many of the tasks – including photography. On 10 July a German civilian, Gertrude Weise, was detained after being discovered photographing seaplanes from a barge on the lake. Water Police took the nineteen-year-old into custody and interrogated her as she carried no identity papers. It later transpired that Mr P.W.G. Burchett, a special correspondent for the *Daily Express*, employed Miss Weise. Officials took the young photographer to Mr Burchett's office at Hohenzollerndamm 81, part of the Kosmos Press Bureau, where her employment was duly confirmed. It was subsequently made clear to all press agencies that anyone wishing to take any further photographs of Allied installations should approach the appropriate authority in future. This was all the more important as the Soviet authorities, already practising a campaign of intimidation and kidnap, would not take so kindly to any infringements in their sector.

Questions

It took just two weeks before questions were being asked about the efficiency of the flying boat operation. Airlift HQ noted that in a thirteen-day period the average strength of Sunderlands had been ten but the average number of sorties was only eight. AC Waite requested, 'a substantial increase in the average effort if possible'. Further commenting that 'our customers at this end have the deplorable habit of eating on wet days and Sundays'. The inevitable choice was to resume Sunday flying, and from 18 July Sunderlands started operating seven days a week. This was not a moment too soon as it was now clear that the airlift needed to substantially increase imports if the city was to be supported throughout the winter. Flying hours suffered a number of restrictions. Obstacles just below the surface at the Elbe landing site restricted flights to daylight hours. Fuel was, in the early stages, ferried out to aircraft using a DUWK loaded with drums, it then had to be hand-pumped into the aircraft. This slow and laborious job added hours to the flying programme, greatly affecting turn-around times. Eventually a bowser capable of carrying 30,000 gallons of fuel was requisitioned and stationed at the base. The problem now was how to get the fuel from the bowser to the aircraft. Eventually, one of the section mechanics came up with an ingenious answer, the fuel pipe was attached to empty jerry cans that floated the pipe across the water. Later still, a mobile fuel point came into operation reducing the times even further. As the year drew on the amount of available flying time was reduced. Also the Air Ministry cut the total flying time available down to 480 hours per month, to facilitate servicing but ultimately impacting on the daily tonnage.

Aquila Airways' Short Hythe G-AGIA. Aquila operated three flying boats during the lift. This one carried 632.3 tons in 118 flights.

Aquila Airways

Aquila Airways was to play a major part in the flying boat contribution to Operation Plainfare. Originally registered as Aikman Airways Limited, Aquila was the brainchild of Barry T. Aikman, a former wing commander with Coastal Command. Before the war, flying boats had been the primary form of world travel. They exploited one simple fact – most of the world, especially on the Empire run, had no airfield infrastructure. Naturally the flying boat became the transport of choice. After the war the situation changed dramatically as thousands of airfields had been constructed worldwide. In direct consequence, BOAC ran down flying-boat operations in the immediate post-war years, concentrating on land-based aircraft. In May 1948 Aquila purchased two ex-BOAC Short Hythes, civilian derivatives of the highly successful Sunderland. By 21 July, at the request of the Air Ministry, two Hythes were operating alongside their military counterparts and a third was to fly for just six sorties as maintenance cover.

The majority of supplies arrived at Finkenwerder by barge or to the railhead nearby. Barge goods were unloaded by German Labour in aircraft payloads, just short of 5 tons, and then loaded into barcassas (small diesel craft). Once the craft reached the Sunderland, the consignment was loaded by British troops. Goods reaching the base by rail were off-loaded into DUWKs and then conveyed straight from the railhead to the waiting aircraft. At Havel supplies were unloaded to small boats and then transferred to barges or the shore for distribution. By 14 September the performance was 108 sorties carrying 487 gross long

Children were one of the more precious cargoes back-lifted to the British Zone. Here a boat-load make their way to the waiting aircraft.

tons of food, mostly meat, noodles and yeast averaged over a fourteen-day period. This sounded impressive; however, as always, statistics can be misleading. It turned out that the two Hythes of Aquila Airways had flown a whopping 40 per cent of the sorties, as they were not restricted in hours. But what the Sunderland lacked in tonnage hauled, it made up for in variety and novelty.

Cargo

A whole range of foodstuffs needed to be flown into the city if the population was to be kept going. On top of this, Western experts estimated that the city would need around 38 tons of salt per day, primarily for health reasons. In 1949 the Royal Air Force published an account of the airlift which read that 'now salt is one of the most troublesome of all things to carry in an aircraft', a typical military understatement. Aircraft are manufactured using specific types of alloys, and any hint of salt sets up a corrosive problem that very quickly scraps the aircraft if not dealt with promptly. This is where the Sunderland came into its own. Designed to operate at sea, the aircraft was virtually impervious to saltwater action. During production of the aircraft Shorts Brothers anodised the materials used for the fuselage, cutting down the amount of damage salt would cause. Control runs and cables were also roof-mounted wherever possible to take them out of harm's way. Berlin signalled that it was ready to accept salt from the 30 August, with an initial 1,000 tons to be transported, suggesting the whole consignment could be handled by the flying boat detachment. Flight Lieutenant Bailey of 230 Squadron flew over 18,000lb of salt into the city between 8 November and 12 December in just seventeen sorties. However, Flt Lt Bailey returned from Berlin with a far more precious cargo than salt.

On five of the return trips to Hamburg Bailey carried 179 children, accompanied by Red Cross helpers, to the West. The war had left many children in Berlin orphaned and many more suffering from tuberculosis or the effects of malnutrition. Sunderlands were to fly over 1,200 children (the airlift in total evacuated over 15,000) to Hamburg during the first four months of the blockade, for treatment or to be placed with families in the West. Unsurprisingly they came with their own problems. Airsickness was a major issue, especially since the Sunderland operated at a lower flight level which often made the two-hour trip very bumpy. And when one child was sick it naturally set the others off, making for some horrendous messes on occasion. Also, excited children invariably require the lavatory, usually at the most inopportune moment and a flight in a Sunderland often induced just such a situation. A small, rudimentary toilet was fitted in the Sunderland for the crew's comfort due to the long operational hours the aircraft was designed for. On more than one occasion aircrew reported trim problems with the aircraft becoming perilously nose or tail heavy. The handling problem, it turned out, was caused by children queuing for the toilet and thus moving the centre of gravity.

Other, less troublesome, cargoes were exported as backloads; however, these too presented their own unique handling problems. Ian Witter of 201 Squadron later described some of these in the squadron's history. The manufacture of goods in the city was encouraged wherever possible, primarily to keep the Berliners occupied but also to demonstrate a 'business as usual' attitude. Light bulb globes were manufactured in the city and then flown to a Siemens factory in Hamburg where the bayonet fittings were attached. Being light, the Sunderland could be packed to the roof with cardboard boxes of the globes; the problem was that to move round the aircraft crews needed to climb across the boxes. Inevitably breakage rates were rather high, prompting numerous complaints from the manufacturer!

Along with foodstuffs, children and light bulbs, the aircraft carried a wide spectrum of items including rolls of newsprint weighing 1,000lb each, sanitary towels and even bullion in 100lb boxes. Authority to fly in this special cargo was given by Airlift HQ in Berlin, commencing on Monday 19 July 1948. 208 boxes were involved in the consignment, and it would appear that whilst there was official sanction for the loads, nobody told the detachment at Lake Havel. Three days later airlift HQ requested that prior warning be given in future so that appropriate levels of labour, transportation and guards could be arranged. To date it has not been possible to ascertain why so much bullion was required by the city.

However, some loads were clearly more essential than others as a signal on 21 July demonstrates:

My dear Air Commodore,

You were asking Flt Lt Young the other day why he was not able to let the Americans know the firm ETA of the cigarette Sunderland.

The reason for this is that he receives no information from R.A.S.O. at Finkewade as to the loading of the aircraft. His responsibility is to unload what is given to him. In cases where special information is required I suggest you tell F.A.S.O. to tell the Wing Commander Flying at Hamburg when the ETA of the load is required. The Wing Commander will then notify the unit as to the nature of the load and who is to be told about it.

Yours sincerely,
Brian Yarde

Other requests hinted at deeper operational aspects and demonstrated that an intelligence war was underway. On 28 August a top-secret signal from HQ Intelligence Division BAOR 15 requested authority for operational moves as required by the division. The moves in question were to consist of, 'individuals, documents and operations stores'. Only two or three individuals a week would require transport, along with small packages with a total monthly weight of 2–3cwt. The operational stores would comprise 'radio sets, microfilms and possibly cigarettes and gin'. The signal emphasised that none of this equipment was for the use of individuals or messes but was required purely for operational purposes allotted by the foreign office.

As the detachment continued, renewed efforts were called for, eventually leading to an increase in October to fourteen sorties per day. Coastal Command was instructed to provide replacement aircraft for those requiring major inspections rather than leaving the post unfilled. Further aircraft requiring minor inspections would now remain in Germany and the servicing teams would work in the field. One casualty of this renewed activity was the backloading of cargo. From 5 October the HQ British Troops in Berlin signalled FASO that 'Backloading will be confined to the last wave of flying boats only'. Even that was not guaranteed. No backload was to hold up the aircraft 'so long that its take-off is delayed beyond 1545 hrs'.

Base

Assembling equipment for use at Lake Havel had been difficult and, in some cases, called for a high level of inventiveness. One unique problem with operating flying boats is how to load and unload while still on the water. The blockade was so unexpected that very few suitable short vessels were available. One organisation that was only too ready to help was the United Services Yacht Club, who gave up their entire fleet of motorboats. After two months' worth of use the boats 'got knocked about a great deal, as you can well imagine'. Air Commodore Waite now considered it only proper that the boats be repaired. Engine and hull repairs were no problem; however, sourcing other materials was another matter. In a demonstration of how scarce some items were, Berlin Airlift HQ had to specifically request 7kg of white enamel, 5kg of white undercoat and 10kg of 'good boat varnish'. Boats were, however, the least of the detachments problems. Whilst operations at Gatow, Tempelhof and later Tegel were near enough self-contained, the same could not be said of Lake Havel.

The Sunderland detachment utilised the United Services entire fleet of motor boats.
Understandably they 'got knocked about a great deal'.

A number of operational problems beset the detachment from the outset, not least
flying boat moorings on the Havel. To be effective the Sunderland needed to slip its
moorings as soon as the engines were started, otherwise twisting of the securing chains
destroyed their reliability. Those at the lake had been hastily brought into service and were
designed for ships, not flying boats. To inspect the mooring it had to be removed clear of
the water and lifting gear, along with manpower, was in very short supply. Eventually ten
sets, specifically for flying boats, were flown out from RAF Calshot, accompanied by Mr
Butters and Mr Connelly of the Moorings Branch of the Air Ministry.

To run flights effectively, a number of sites and facilities around the lake had also been
temporarily requisitioned. One such site was the boat harbour owned by Gerhus & E.
Westphal Bros, Klare Lanke, on the American side of the lake. A pier and surrounding
land was requisitioned for ten days from 4 July. Tents were erected and motor launches
intensively used the pier as the operation got under way. Three weeks later the lakeside
command moved across to the Gatow Royal Air Force Club in the British sector; however,
one tent was retained and the pier still used by airlift personnel and German River Police.
Unfortunately, over the following months no one settled the ground rent with Herr
Westphal and to add insult to injury the pier had, by now, sustained considerable damage.
The German Water Police at Spandau were duly informed. The problem was that the
requisition certificate only covered the initial ten-day period and that had been duly
honoured. The Public Safety Branch of the Military Government therefore suggested

at the end of October that a new certificate be issued, backdated to 14 July. Airlift HQ agreed that as 'the firm has been denied the use of the pier during the profitable months of the summer', some form of compensation was clearly due. AC Waite suggested any new requisition should run through the winter, even though it was clear that flying boat operations would cease in mid-December.

Furthermore, Military Government HQ was to be encouraged to release materials for repairs to the pier. By 9 November the issue had reached the Chief of Staff of Allied Kommandatura who suggested that, in the interests of good relations, the issue be settled immediately. However, even intervention from the top failed to solve the problem. Westphal, by now resigned to the fact he might not receive compensation, took the initiative. Repair work was carried out and bills were sent to Airlift HQ in the city who promptly redirected them to the British Forces Finance Branch. In typical accountant fashion Finance Branch was not impressed. Clearly no one had authorised the work to go ahead; 'half of Berlin could be rebuilt at our expense if we do not keep a tight rein on things' was the curt reply, however, it was stated that the bill 'would be settled within the next week', but just this once. That was on 30 November 1948. Clearly someone, as yet invisible to the record, thought otherwise. The unpaid bill out-lived the Sunderland operations, but Westphal continued the fight to the end. Under constant bombardment by letter and telephone, British Troops HQ in Berlin finally cracked, suggesting that, 'It would be appreciated if you would please check with the German Authorities and ensure that the bills are paid as soon as possible so that airlift HQ are not continually pestered by the contractor.' Whether Herr Westphal ever received settlement is not recorded.

Troublemakers

The art of creative writing has never been wasted on the Soviet press and the airlift was fair game. In the 14 November edition of *National-Zeitung*, the mouthpiece of the National-Demokratischen Partei Deutschlands (NDPD) and a Soviet-licensed newspaper, a story appeared highlighting the dangers of operating on Lake Havel. Apparently a Sunderland taking off from the Wannsee 'dashed into the route of a BVG-steamer'. Luckily, an 'awful traffic catastrophe was avoided' due to the 'meritorious presence of mind of the captain' of the steamer. The flying boat reportedly passed within a metre of the steamer, constituting 'The most serious incident' to date. The story advised readers that it would not be long before there was a disaster, especially since fog often prevailed and 'the English warning boats of the RAF have been withdrawn'.

Major General Herbert, GOC British Troops Berlin, was not impressed. Writing to Airlift HQ, Herbert pointed out that whilst the story was 'no doubt untrue… A collision between a flying boat and a passenger steamer would do us a lot of harm.' The GOC had spent time sailing from the RAF Yacht Club at the start of Sunderland flights and had 'not been impressed with the safety arrangements'. It was suggested that all craft should now be excluded from the landing areas, 'there was some excuse in the early days' but things should have been 'tightened up considerably' by now. Airlift HQ contacted OC Gatow suggesting an area be cleared of surface craft permanently, 'I have never seen a flying boat pilot take such a stupid risk and I doubt very much if the newspaper report, which is Soviet-licensed, is true; but, as the General says, we just cannot afford accidents of this nature'. Mischievous though the reports were, they had highlighted a situation of growing concern – weather conditions on the lake.

Rundown

By the end of November thoughts at BAFO were turning towards a rundown of the flying boat detachment. Conditions at Finkenwerder and Lake Havel were becoming increasingly difficult as fog and ice bit into the flying programme. Also the detachment had been on duty since 5 July, and whilst many aircraft had returned to RAF Calshot for servicing in that time, personnel had not and 'crews are well overdue for relief'. Also, work to complete the airfield at Celle was, by now, well in hand and full-scale operations by USAF C-54 Skymasters were expected by mid-December. In view of this BAFO suggested to the Air Ministry that 'RAF flying boats are withdrawn on 15th December or when Celle is fully operational'.

So, on 14 December the last Sunderland left the Havel en route for Finkenwerder without ceremony or send-off. A singular flight landed on the seventeenth to collect equipment, but it was not a freighter, and with its departure ended one of the more propaganda winning aspects of Operation Plainfare. By that last day flying boats had delivered 5,080.6 tons in 1,159 sorties and backloaded 1,269 children and 199 adult escorts along with 149 tons of goods manufactured in Berlin. All, most importantly, without incident.

Whether the flying boats were to return in the spring was the subject of much debate. BAFO suggested in mid-December that it may be better waiting until Celle was in full operation, as only then could an assessment be made into air traffic congestion. Tegel, in the French sector, would also allow for more tonnage to be flown in from land bases, again reducing the need for flying boats. The wooden police hut erected on the banks of the Havel to house wireless sets and a telephone would also remain for the time being, but without equipment. It was suggested that the long-suffering Herr Westphal should be made responsible for maintenance; his comments are not recorded.

By the beginning of February it was clear that the Sunderlands were not going to return to Operation Plainfare. Whilst their contribution in a visual sense had been immeasurable, practical use of the aircraft could not now be justified. 'Their potential lift is very small and the operation would unduly complicate the already difficult traffic problem in northern corridors', noted HQ BAFO in a telegram to the Air Ministry. The Ministry in turn added, 'Even if the difficulties could be overcome, the amount of effort required in provision of base organisation and maintenance is out of all proportion to their value.' Furthermore, 'It has now been agreed by all concerned that flying boats will not be required this Spring.' That was that, pleasure craft returned to the Lake, but elsewhere Plainfare was only just getting into its stride.

Seven

Atomic Bombers
and Mud Holes

The Berlin Blockade did much to change the political map of Europe. However, it also re-affirmed old ties, namely between the United Kingdom's and America's ground and aircrews. Britain found itself home to over 8,000 US servicemen, as first the B-29 bomber fleets and then C-54 maintenance programs were moved in to England. Both moves were to have a profound effect, not least the fact that USAF forces are still based in the UK today, a direct legacy of the Berlin Airlift.

Throughout the latter half of the Second World War, Britain had become a major detachment for the United States Army Air Corps (USAAF) working with RAF Bomber Command on the Combined Bomber Offensive. Officially this arrangement was catered for under the Visiting Forces Act (1942). After D-Day forward airbases were established in liberated Europe and as the front moved steadily eastward over the following year the majority of squadrons moved with it. By 1946 practically all bases had reverted to the Royal Air Force and were in many cases closed, although the Visiting Forces Act (1942) remained.

The first hint of a reversal in the reduction policy came in the summer of 1946. Whilst visiting airfields on the point of closure, Marshal of the Royal Air Force, Lord Tedder, and General Carl Spaatz, USAAF, discussed apparent Soviet belligerence on the continent. Tedder, at Spaatz's request, agreed to upgrade five airfields, Marham, Lakenheath, Scampton, Bassingbourne and Mildenhall, making them capable of supporting long-range heavy bombers, namely the B-29. Throughout 1947 the airfields received substantial alteration to their runways in both length and strength; interestingly not many in the Government were told the reasons for the work.

By 14 July 1948 it was clear that the Soviets had no intention of backing down over the city. Moscow cited Western interests as the main cause of Germany's division, especially with currency reforms. It noted that Berlin was the centre of the Soviet zone and any quadripartite control of the city was on the same footing as the administration of Germany as a whole. Clearly, in Soviet eyes, this had been breached and therefore any agreement over Berlin was null and void. This was the final straw for Bevin. It was now clear that the Soviets needed a show of strength not diplomacy and luckily Bevin, whilst waiting for the Soviet reply, had set those wheels in motion.

The stationing of the 'Atomic Bombers' in Britain from July 1948 set a precedent for the nuclear bases that were soon established and remain to the present day.

The British Foreign Secretary requested a show of strength, as that was clearly the language the Soviets understood. Of course Bevin knew that the only way Europe would be truly safe from the tide of communism would be with American military might firmly committed in Europe. And so on 16 July 1948 the National Security Council met in Washington to discuss Bevin's request. The debate that took place reveals the dire situation the United States Government considered itself in over Berlin, and indeed Germany. George C. Marshall, Secretary of State, was of the opinion that 'one advantage of sending the planes was that it would be a further indication of our firmness'. Also it would 'offset any tendency towards weakness and appeasement' on the part of the British, and more importantly the French. It was also clear that if the US were to remain in Berlin then the American people would need to get used to the idea. Sending in the B-29s was one sure way of 'conditioning' the population. Robert Lovett, Under Secretary of State, thought that a measured approach was far less provocative than 'if we pour troops into Germany'; after all Britain was 'a friendly country' and the B-29s would be there 'at the request of the Government'. However, the deployment of B-29s went well beyond the show of strength

Bevin had requested. It would eventually help cement an American presence in Europe well beyond the crisis. Indeed, Cornelius V. Whitney, Assistant Secretary of Air, rather astutely noted that 'it would grease the wheels for this kind of operation with the British by giving them experience in handling our planes'. The conversation between Spaatz and Tedder two years earlier now became reality. The NSC decided to order the detachment of two B-29 groups on the afternoon of 16 July.

The following day aircraft from the 28th and 307th Bomb Groups were in transit to their new bases. The first thirty aircraft of the 28th landed at RAF Scampton on 17 July. Scampton had been refurbished as part of the Spaatz-Tedder agreement and now had a new runway capable of taking the massive B-29. Aircraft of the 307th Bomb Group took up residence at Marham, and a few weeks later Lakenheath. Lakenheath had, towards the end of the Second World War, when the site was identified as a potential B-29 base, been designated a Very Heavy Bomber airfield. The upgrade cost over £2 million and two years to complete, by which time the war was over. Lakenheath was subsequently placed into 'care and maintenance'. By late July 1948 the base was reactivated and aircraft of the 2nd Bomb Group arrived. By the end of August ninety B-29s were in Britain on thirty-day temporary duty; however, this was steadily increased to sixty then ninety days.

One of those who crewed the B-29s was Joe Gyulavics, Master Sergeant with 28th Bomb Wing from Rapid City. He was in the first wave of B-29s to reach the United Kingdom and remembered his first tour at RAF Scampton:

> No one made provisions for our arrival, and the Royal Air Force was a bit overwhelmed by such a large group of personnel and aircraft. As a senior NCO I got to sleep in the NCO club, which had a little room upstairs. They put four of us in one room in double-decker bunks. We ate in a common mess. The British fare was not great by our standards, just stewed tomatoes for breakfast and meat pie for dinner.

The aircraft were quickly referred to in the press as the 'Atomic Bombers', but nothing could have been further from the truth. It transpired years later that the United States did indeed possess nuclear weapons, two to be precise, and both were still in storage in America. The B-29s on the original detachments were not nuclear capable. It was not until mid-1949 that 'Silverplates', the codename for modified B-29 aircraft, were stationed in Europe. It is therefore difficult to gauge what effect the use of such a deterrent had on Soviet attitudes. The B-29 was a capable and potent weapons platform as the Soviets knew only too well; they had, after all, copied the design from aircraft that had landed there during the war. However, use of the aircraft did demonstrate the resolve of Washington to stay in Berlin and support the European nations as part of the Truman Doctrine.

Burtonwood

When it became clear that the USAF intended to base B-29 aircraft in the United Kingdom a support depot was required. The former Central Repair Depot at

P-38 Lightnings being scrapped. Burtonwood was the scene of much destruction immediately after the war.

Burtonwood, Cheshire, was the obvious choice. RAF Burtonwood was opened in 1940 as No.37 Maintenance Unit and Repair Depot. The site received new aircraft from manufacture and prepared them for service. On 15 July 1942 the site became the home of Base Air Depot No.1 USAAF, carrying out the majority of servicing and repair on American-built aircraft and engines. Situated on England's west coast, close to major ports, it could readily accept supplies from the United States. In just two years Burtonwood grew into a site of gigantic proportions, employing upwards of 30,000 American and British staff by late 1944. By 8 May 1945 the site had prepared an incredible 15,575 aircraft and 30,286 radial engines for all theatres of war. After the war the airfield, like so many others in the UK, declined in importance. A small number of USAAF personnel remained to supervise the removal of equipment, primarily to the Erding depot near Munich in the American zone. Burtonwood controlled thirty-four other bases and airfields at its height, and was the last US base in Britain to close when handed back on 9 June 1946. At Erding the Centre Supply and Maintenance for US Air Forces in Europe was formed, the position of the site being considered far more central to military operations in Europe after the Second World War. Incredibly, over 200,000 tons of equipment and aircraft spares were in storage at Erding by 1947. From June 1946 37 MU re-occupied RAF Burtonwood, storing hundreds of Mosquitoes, Harvards and Lancasters. No.276 Maintenance Unit (MU) also took up residence, utilising some of the vast workshop facilities, primarily to scrap surplus aircraft. Along with 37 MU the Master Provision Office was also based at the airfield; its primary task to act as a central supply depot for all parts related to American aircraft in service with the RAF.

Tinker Hall site at RAF Burtonwood. The hangars to the top right are where the production line maintenance of C-54s was undertaken. The black sheds in the foreground are the USAF servicemen's accommodation.

A few weeks before the arrival of the B-29s, nearly 1,500 technical staff of the USAF moved to Burtonwood to prepare the facilities for bomber support. Low hours' C-54 maintenance work at this time continued to be undertaken at Erding and Wiesbaden, closer to the fledgling airlift routes. The problem was that most of this was being undertaken outside and as yet another European winter approached it became clear that covered facilities were essential. Deep 200-hour servicing of C-54s had been exclusively carried out at Oberfallenhofen, Bavaria, since 5 August 1948, however, Tunner, by now in overall command of the airlift, knew this could only be a temporary measure and the system would become totally overstretched by November. Burtonwood was duly identified as the ideal site for 200-hour inspections. It had both the space and facilities; all that was needed was the know-how and materials to make it work. In mid-September Major General Fred Borum and a small team of maintenance specialists were transferred from Tinkers Field Airbase, Oklahoma, to Cheshire. He had successfully pioneered a production line-type overhaul system for the air force in the United States, shaving days off the maintenance down time. Eventually a kilometre-long 'assembly line' was designed that could cope with eight C-54s arriving a day.

Personnel were drafted in from bases around the world and engineers were transferred from the airlift command to Burtonwood. The reduction in engineers in Germany seemed a sound enough decision, but was to leave the airlift servicing capability dangerously undermanned and short of serviceable C-54s. After an encouraging start servicings dropped to under two per day. Concerned, Tunner visited the base in late 1948 to investigate the lack of progress, by which time he was facing a deficit of thirty-five aircraft per week due to the slow turn-round. He found a site that in his own words was, 'dingy, dirty and depressing looking'. The majority of buildings had seen little maintenance since 1945 and were in desperate need of repair. Wooden huts and temporary buildings were cold and damp due to broken windows and leaky roofs. The equipment needed for aircraft servicing had become damaged due to the elements and the morale of the men stationed there was very low indeed. But this was not just the 'official' view.

In September 1948 Burtonwood, and for that matter England, was far from the mind of twenty-year-old Sergeant Allyne Conner from Worcester, Massachusetts. He was enjoying two weeks' leave at the time and was to be demobbed the following February. That was until he was telegrammed to report back to his unit, the 59th Air Depot Wing, and a few days later he arrived at RAF Burtonwood. Conner was in charge of a vehicle maintenance shop on Site 5, looking after transport on the base. The conditions he found 'were tough'. In fact the site was very quickly renamed the 'Mud Hole' and even spawned its own newspaper, the *Mud Hole Gazette*! The masthead of the first edition on 10 January 1949 proclaimed:

> The statistical boys can put it in pictures of box-cars, or tons, or trips to the moon, but never the less, it still takes hard work to insure continued delivery of the goods. You know whether or not you're putting out! It takes us all to turn out the necessary 200 hours inspections. They keep 'vittles' going.

But what about keeping the men going? Conner's accommodation was less than ideal. The hut he was billeted in had the standard-issue potbelly stove and two light bulbs. The ends of the tin building were rotten timber that let in wind and the rain and it felt like everyone was eating powdered egg every day. 'October through December was the worst time,' he later reflected. The only respite from the conditions was to 'get in' with local families, and being young men that is exactly what many did. Sgt Conner spent many stand-down days in and around Manchester and became quite proficient in the British sport of darts. At the time some areas of the city were still bomb-damaged, 'showing wall paper all the way up the sides of some apartment blocks'. Fish and chips made a welcome break from the monotony of powdered egg, but on rare days a real treat was in store. Occasionally, very occasionally, roast beef was on the menu – 'only problem was it was sliced so thin you could see through it!'

Just after Christmas the Bob Hope Show arrived at Burtonwood. Sgt Connor and his colleagues waited five hours for the spectacle to begin, 'but it was well worth it'. The show was held in one of the hangars, with a couple of aircraft surrounded by access staging as viewing platforms. Hope, despite the wait, played to a packed house. Photographs taken by International News Photos and wired around the world clearly demonstrated that the austerity of conditions at Burtonwood were not being exaggerated. Hope and a troupe of American screen stars were there to 'ease the mounting discontent of American airforce

From left to right: Colonel Walter Ott, Base Commander; Elmer Davis, Chief of War Information; Irvin
Berlin, composer; Bob Hope, entertainer. They are pictured here arriving at Burtonwood on
29 December 1948.

The Christmas Caravan. Hope's show in one of the hangars on site. Standing room only for the GIs.
(International News Photo)

officers and men who found themselves far from home over the holidays, with no war to occupy their minds'.

And whilst Hope was 'occupying their minds' the top brass accompanying him inspected the site. Stuart Symington, Secretary of the Air Force, was particularly concerned over the conditions and asked that anyone who had a suggestion should submit a 'gripe note'. He was inundated. Within a few weeks repairs had started. He told an *Express* staff reporter:

> It is an exaggeration to say that this is the worst United States camp in Europe, I have already asked for certain things to be done. We came in here awfully fast. It is Stalin who decides these things, you know.

Tunner later noted, 'Burtonwood was shaken from top to bottom'. By the end of January the situation had improved slightly. The walkways between huts, once just mud trails, had been replaced with concrete and the huts at least made waterproof. However, that was just the beginning. Symington demanded better personal conditions, eight men to a billet, each with their own light. The concrete floors in the huts were to be covered by lino, of which an incredible 56,000 sq.ft had been ordered from local suppliers. The US Secretary also promised 2,000 more stoves, enough to increase the number in each hut to a minimum of two, the problem being that it was already the depths of winter and supply in the near future was unlikely. Among the men, cunning heating plans were in the pipeline.

Just after Christmas, Airman Second Class Guy Kenney, a twenty-year-old aircraft Electrician from Stinnett, Texas, was posted to Burtonwood. By then many of the huts had been replaced with brick, and more importantly the rations had been switched from British to American! But some things took a little time. Kenney was billeted in Site 5, which by then housed the majority of maintenance specialists. In the depths of a true English winter, keeping the huts warm became a major problem. Each hut contained a charcoal heater that invariably went out whilst the men were at work and took two to three hours to warm the rooms up. Necessity is so often the mother of invention, and it did not take long before Kenney and his colleagues came up with an ingenious solution. One of the men 'discovered a 25lb spool of electrical resistance wire'. Seizing their opportunity, Kenney and his friends, 'wound coils and made a homemade electric heater, which worked great and solved the problem of a cold hut'. The problem was, good ideas never stay secret for long and within a week 'the entire squadron had converted to electric heat'. Unfortunately, 'as the last heater was plugged in the power failed'. It transpired that the local transformer was so overloaded it set fire to the pole it was mounted on, 'The next day the site was back to charcoal heaters'. However, not all homemade heaters were so reliant on the local electricity supply. Sgt Connor and his men came up with an equally ingenious, but far more reliable, method. One of the primary tasks of any vehicle maintenance depot is the oil change and with a base the size of Burtonwood there were plenty carried out each week. Fifty-five-gallon drums full of waste oil steadily accumulated at the oil store, and slowly a plan hatched. Many homes in America were heated by oil and it was not long before the men had built their own oil-fired heater running on the waste material.

Airman Second Class, Guy Kenney at Blackpool. Airmen took the opportunity to travel whilst stationed at Burtonwood. (With thanks to Guy Kenney)

The influx of American personnel caused problems for immigration staff, customs officials and local authorities, especially when requests were made for families to join the men. But the pressure was not just on the married men. With so many single Americans at the base it was inevitable that some would attract the attention of the local girls. And not just for a change of scenery as Sgt Connor and his boys had done. Towards the end of the airlift one young lady met with the base chaplain, complaining that she had become pregnant due to a liaison with an American serviceman. Unfortunately she could only remember his first name, Joe or Bill, but felt sure she would recognise him. The Camp Commander had all the Joes and Bills report to the parade square where the young lady was invited to conduct an identity parade. Luckily the perpetrator was not identified; however, Kenney recalled later, 'Believe me there were several hundred very anxious men in that line-up, all sure she would select someone. She didn't!'

With an American presence as large as Burtonwood this was unlikely to be an isolated case. In May 1949 the *Picture Post* dispatched the Member of Parliament for Preston, Edward Shackleton, to Warrington 'to make the first independent social survey of the situation'. The subsequent article discovered that stories of drunken debauchery were, for the most part, hyped stories from the British press. It transpired that three US soldiers had been set upon by a number of local 'rowdies' and the ensuing scuffle had to be broken up by the police. Later that same evening the servicemen headed for the station where one was attacked by a drunk who 'knocked him about very badly'. On convicting the drunk at the police court the local Justice of the Peace 'commented that the Americans only had themselves to blame'. Things deteriorated from then on in. Of course, soldiers with lots of pay and nothing to spend it on invariably ended up in the pub:

> Drunkenness always seems more offensive when the drunk is a foreigner, and some nights, especially after payday, there may be a number of drunk Americans in Warrington. Perhaps the fault lies with the comparative smoothness of Scotch whisky, for people who are unaccustomed to it do not always appreciate its kick.

And when they were not in the pub the troops were on the lookout for girls:

> The American courting technique is different from the European. Because it is different, it is apt to appear shocking, especially in places with the strong social customs of an English town like Warrington.

And the article went on:

> Some were unwilling to let their daughters out in the evening, and it was even suggested that for a girl to be seen walking with an American soldier was tantamount to admitting that she was a 'floozie'.

In fact the situation was nothing like the sensational stories that had appeared in the national press. Local police had indeed raided the base on a few occasions and did arrest a number of women, charging them in the County Court with the technical offence 'of being in possession of American bedding', but these were isolated cases designed to discourage others. American Military Police did patrol the town, often accompanied by British Police and one officer was permanently based at the local police station, in case trouble started in the pubs or dancehalls, however, things rarely did. Occasionally airmen making their way back from Manchester missed the last train and, luckily the railway police were often on hand and allowed them to use the second class compartments in carriages shunted into sidings, even giving them a wake-up call half an hour before the train to Warrington, Allyne Conner later recalled.

Fixers

The inspection regime was co-ordinated by staff at Wiesbaden, who notified Burtonwood of the aircraft's departure to the United Kingdom. A list of the faults the aircraft had been carrying was forwarded, allowing maintenance crews a 'head-start' on acquiring spares. Naturally, no flight was wasted and on trips to England mail, equipment and occasionally people were 'back-loaded'. The moment the aircraft touched down a waiting crew stripped-out all navigation and radio equipment, taking it to specialist bays for servicing and rectification. The aircraft was then washed. This was an arduous task, especially if the aircraft had been on a coal or flour run. Externally a thick layer of grime, cemented together by old engine and hydraulic oil had to be removed if there was to be any chance of inspecting the airframe and engines. A chemical solution was first applied and then washed-off under pressure. Inside was a different story. Any application of a liquid to the grime would have caked the (already black) morass into immovable blocks and washed it deeper into the inaccessible recesses of the airframe. In an attempt to combat this, teams of German workers religiously swept out the freight bays whilst the aircraft was operational and subsequently an industrial strength vacuum cleaner was employed. Interestingly, aircraft on the airlift continued to carry the legacy of dirty cargo around for their entire working lives, often leaving discreet piles of coal dust on hangar floors for decades to come.

After cleaning, the aircraft was given a pre-inspection engine run. This allowed engine performance and other associated systems to be assessed. Also, leaks showed up a lot better on a clean aircraft. It was now that the benefit of Borum's production line bore fruit. Rather than have a maintenance team descend on the aircraft fixing whatever snags they found, the aircraft was moved through a series of specialist stations. The production lines utilised all available hanger space and each building contained three maintenance stations. C-54s moved into the hangar at one end and moved through the three stations, leaving after a final inspection and panel close-up; finally the aircraft was given a pre-departure engine run, allowing all systems to be checked under operational conditions and finally all 'loose equipment' was refitted. The aircraft was then released back into service, the test flight being conducted on the way back to Germany. Competition was encouraged and by March the improvement in conditions and tools was starting to produce results. Airman Kenney recalled that his team 'completed a major inspection, including a double engine change, in an incredible 6½ hours'. 'The flight crews often complained that we finished too soon,' he added, 'since the only time off they had was while they were at Burtonwood.'

Thin end of the wedge

Burtonwood was, however, the visible end of a large and complex supply chain. If aircraft were to remain serviceable a constant flow of spares to the servicing line was needed. Logistically this rapidly turned into a nightmare. The airlift had come at such a bad time that many thought Stalin had actually planned it that way. The USAF was effectively on wind down as part of the Yalta agreement and so priorities in Europe were aimed at reducing manpower and equipment as quickly as possible. When the C-54 became the 'standard' American airframe of the airlift it became clear that a workable supply chain could, quite literally, make or break the US effort.

Eventually USAF internal politics gave way to common sense, allowing Tunner to run Operation Vittles as a full-blown detachment rather than a sideshow. A constant flow of spares and equipment were required, both in the field and for the scheduled servicing being carried out at Burtonwood. Rhein-Main was designated the central receipt depot

Competitions were set between maintenance crews in an attempt to increase production. Eventually it was possible to turn a round a C-54 on 200-hour inspection in just seven hours.

for German-based repairs, whilst the vast servicing facility at Erding covered the storage of parts common to the entire USAF fleet. A priority demand system ensured a quick turn-round for requested items, as Vittles parts were pushed to the front of the queue. Aircraft on Ground (AOG) spares were given top priority and were pulled from anywhere in the world. To ensure the quickest possible turn-round, all items were flown to Europe via a single airfield, Western Field, Massachusetts, whenever feasible. Here a two-stream system operated, one direct to Frankfurt for field maintenance, the other, 200-hour inspection spares, into Burtonwood. Sgt Connor at Burtonwood recalled many Lockheed Electra flights into the British base. This was as far as American civilian operators got on Operation Vittles.

Some idea of the amount of hours individual American aircraft were clocking up on the airlift can be gauged in an article in the *Task Force Times* from 26 February 1949. The headline proudly proclaimed 'Celle C-54 flies 1,000 hours in less than five months on lift'. The aircraft, originally based in Japan and operated by the 39th Troop Carrying Squadron, had been one of the first C-54 force planes to be stationed at the British base. Aircraft achieving 1,000 flying hours were returned to the United States for deep strip inspection, and often comprehensive repair. In the case of the C-54 this was carried out by the civilian contractor Texas Engineering and Manufacturing Company (TEMCO), taking around four weeks. In fact, with engine repair shops and stations around the United States involved in Operation Vittles over 40,000 servicemen and civilians were involved in support tasks for the fleet.

Eight

'Civvies'

The Berlin Airlift consumed a number of things: aviation fuel, tyres, spark plugs, aircraft fatigue life and more importantly both the RAF's and USAF's spare personnel capacity. It was not long before both had run out of trained aircrew, engineers and ground staff. For the USAF the answer was to set up the Replacement Training Unit at Great Falls Airforce Base in Montana. The Air Ministry, on the other hand, decided to contract in a diverse collection of civilian operators. This chapter will deal with the build-up of the civil operators and concentrates on the dry freight carriers. The next will cover the 'wet lift'.

Post-war blues

Civil airline services and routes were part of the programme of nationalisation orchestrated by the post-war Labour Government. Three airline corporations would, effectively, carve up the world, each owned by the Government. Commonwealth and transatlantic routes were operated by British Overseas Airline Corporation (BOAC), European routes came under British European Airways (BEA) whilst British South American Airways (BSAA) were to open up new routes to South America and the Caribbean. All licensing regulations covering civil operators had been rescinded during the war and so there were no restrictions to anyone who wanted to form a charter firm. Many former aircrew were eager to start their own businesses, and with the vast amounts of surplus aircraft available many did. Guy Halford-MacLeod noted recently that 'by the end of 1946 there were eighty-five firms engaged in air charter work'. The Government did not completely stitch up the emerging air transport market and accordingly small firms were allowed to conduct charter flying as long as it was not a scheduled service.

One thing that the small independent firms were increasingly getting involved with was the transportation of freight. This was graphically demonstrated with the large-scale importation of fruit and vegetables from Italy, Spain and southern France. With Europe's rail and road network in such a bad state of disrepair the traditional markets had dried up. As such, goods that would have been sent to Germany and the northern continent before the war now found themselves en route by air to the United Kingdom. Other loads

Bond Air Services' Halton G-AIWN. The aircraft delivered 2,189.4 tons of freight in 292 sorties.

included livestock, especially race horses, and large pieces of machinery. By 1948 over eighty charter airlines were operating nearly 500 aircraft, accounting for nearly 40 per cent of the total national air business. One area that was exploited right up to and beyond the Berlin Airlift was the transportation of milk from Northern Ireland to Liverpool and the Midlands. This was far more cost-effective than bringing it over by ferry and helped keep that nation supplied during the milk shortage of the late 1940s.

Some Operation Plainfare airlines had had previous experience moving large numbers of people around when, on 15 August 1947, India, as the British had ruled it, ceased to be. The Government required a number of officials immediately evacuated and air was the easiest method available. What it did do was give the big nationalised firms, in this case BOAC, the opportunity to work with charter airlines. Scottish Airlines, Silver City, Westminster Airways, all would go on to become Plainfare veterans.

Throughout early July 1948 the Royal Air Force, somewhat in the shadow of the USAF, struggled on, but manning levels and equipment were becoming major headaches. Then, on 27 July, a Flight Refuelling Lancastrian flew into Gatow from its home base in Dorset signalling the start of the civil lift. By 1 August a small armada had been assembled comprising a hotch-potch of charter operators. And so, on 5 August, the first charter freighter, operated by Bond Air Services and piloted by Captain Treen, flew into Gatow. Bond Air Services was typical of the charter firms of the time. It also introduced one of British aviation's more colourful characters to the scene – Freddie Laker.

Throughout the war Laker had worked as a ferry pilot, flying finished bombers from the factory to operational station. After the conflict he became one of British European Airways' first employees; however, this was a short-lived association and Laker soon moved into aircraft maintenance. When the Government was searching the country for

Bond Air Services' Halton G–AHDU. Seen here in BOAC colours, the aircraft was purchased by Freddie Laker and went on to deliver 2,505.1 tons in 363 sorties.

serviceable aircraft in June 1948 they called upon Laker. Interviewed in 1995, he explained his 'recruitment' and association with Bond Air Services:

> The British government discovered that of course the only aeroplanes they really had that could carry cargo were in fact owned by the air corporations, BOAC and BEA. And they couldn't take the aeroplanes off the commercial routes, so they had to employ almost anything they could lay their hands on. And there weren't many people in England that had any aeroplanes. But I was very lucky at the time in as much that I actually owned twelve converted Halifax bombers, and the government came along and said, 'oh, can we do something with these aeroplanes?' And I said, 'of course.' But remember, we all thought that the Berlin airlift was only going to last two or three weeks, or there would have been a war. No one expected it to go on for a year or more. So having got to the point of having some aeroplanes, I had to find a vehicle, so to speak, a business vehicle to use them. And I came across a company called Bond Air Services, which had an up and going operation but had virtually run out of money and had some substantial debts. So I did a deal with the owners whereby I would supply the aeroplanes and they would supply the company and sort of the end of the deal was rather like Christmas, you know, where you save up all year and hand the prezzies out at Christmas, and the deal was of course that we would share in the profits and whatever. And I sold six of the Halifax – or these Haltons, which was the civil name of the Halifax bomber, I sold six of them and kept six that we put on the airlift. And of course I had literally hundreds of tons of spare parts. So I started maintaining the aeroplanes and flying on these aeroplanes and we used Bond Air Services as a vehicle.

Joining Bond Air Services in the early days were the two Hythes, civilianised Short Sunderland sea planes described in chapter six, Dakotas from Westminster Airways, Kearsley Airways, Ciro's Aviation, Trent Valley Aviation, Air Contractors and Air Transport. Scottish Airlines supplied three Dakotas and one Liberator. In overall charge of the operation was Edwin Whitfield, British European Manager in Germany, who in turn had liaison officers spread across the airfields now being used in the British zone. When Whitfield arrived in Germany he found chaos. Many of the smaller outfits were being run on a shoe-string. The majority had no administration or, on occasion, maintenance staff, and all were convinced that they would be back home in a week or so.

To make matters worse the civil crews were fiercely independent. In a period of nationalisation and Government interference in the air routes of Britain, the airlift allowed, for the time being at least, a level of freedom. Unfortunately this had not been the Foreign Office's plan. They had requested that Whitfield organise the civil lift the day before operations began. Now two points became evident. No one had told any of the operators that they were in effect working for British European Airways. Effectively Whitfield was in control and the RAF was struggling to deal with this influx of 'undisciplined' crews who would only fly when they chose to. By the end of August things had settled down somewhat as it was now clear the airlift could be a long-term contract, with all the benefits that that would bring to the independent operator.

Air Transport Charter (CI) had one Dakota committed to the airlift. Pilot Sam Pover was in one of two crews the firm had flying from August to December. Their Dakota, G-AJVZ, had been purchased from the Ministry and refurbished at Prestwick and then flew passengers and freight from the Channel Islands before joining Operation Plainfare. As with service personnel, the accommodation was a little hit or miss:

I was billeted in the RAF Mess at Lübeck, this was wonderful, good service and the food was good too, this didn't last, when we moved up to Hamburg (Fuhlsbüttel) the accommodation was not good. We were crowded into old barrack blocks, which appeared to be temporary. We complained bitterly and were eventually moved to a hotel in town.

Eventually operations began to get organised and co-ordination between aircraft types and bases along with use of the air corridors led to a steady increase in tonnage. Captain Pover's description of a flight into Gatow became the norm for a while:

Dakotas left Lübeck at three minute intervals, you had to be on the dot. Our flight height was at 1,000 feet, making for a leisurely trip, we were so low that we were almost on nodding terms with the village postie! Other aircraft slotted into our wave at the Dannenberg beacon but were above our flight level. As we passed over the French Zone I could see great activity, thousands of men and lots of equipment constructing the new airfield. We would then fly east over Spandau and the Olympic Stadium before turning right over the Havel and down into Gatow.

Gatow was the scene of frantic activity, I was very conscious that as we landed the previous aircraft was still on the runway and one was coming in behind us. We were carrying flour at the time, I much preferred this to some of the other loads, one operator complained that he was carrying too many 'Stinkers' – kippers for the British messes. The turn-a-round took thirty minutes, just enough time to grab a coffee at the Malcolm van before joining the aircraft queue to depart. When taking off east to west we flew straight into the Soviet sector airspace as the perimeter fence was also the border. We exited via the central corridor back to Lübeck. Once the aircraft was reloaded and turned round again we were off. The flights lasted around an hour each way.

Initially, the civilian Dakotas were certified to carry 6,000lb, almost 1,500lb less than their service counterparts. The Air Registration Board eventually increased their potential to that of aircraft operated by the RAF. However, it was becoming clear that the aircraft was not good value for money when compared with its four-engine counterparts. Subsequently, as contracts ran out during November, they were not renewed:

> Now that the DC-3s have been withdrawn from Germany, the serious shortage of British charter aircraft has been eased to some extent. Operators report that although the aircraft were worked hard they were better off for spares whilst flying supplies to Berlin than before. This was because DC-3 spares were put at a high priority for aircraft in Germany, with a result that replacements of parts was considerably easier.[1]

Spares had frequently been difficult to source before the airlift and often meant civilian DC-3s carried lots of snags. Operators were coming back off the airlift with, in the main, fully serviceable aircraft. Unfortunately, moving back into the charter business meant loads were often radically different from day-to-day. Air Contractors Ltd, who, through their time on the airlift, had carried 1,376 tons in 386 sorties to Berlin, now got back to the challenges of touting for business:

> Air Contractors, Ltd, which had three DC-3s in Germany, began freighting cattle again this week. On November 15, British Livestock Export, Ltd,. which is working closely with Air Contractors, sent 19 pedigree pigs to Italy, 15 to Florence and four to Milan. Two days later a DC-3 left the UK for Nairobi with a bill of lading which would have done justice to a menagerie. On board were 18 pedigree calves, eight dogs, two goats, six pigs, two crates of poultry with six pullets and a cock in each crate, a canary and a chinchilla weighing 22 oz. worth £150.[2]

Diversity

By November the contract firms on Plainfare had risen to a staggering twenty outfits; some firms had just one or two aircraft, others were well-established operations. With this diverse collection of companies came a similar array of aircraft. Silver City Airways contributed two Bristol Wayfarers in September 1948 and later added two Bristol Freighters. Both types were derivatives of the Bristol 170, originally designed for vehicle transportation into jungle strips. Now the rugged aircraft was employed as an 'awkward'

[1] *The Aeroplane*, 19 November 1948.
[2] *The Aeroplane*, 19 November 1948.

Silver City Airways' Bristol Wayfarer G-AHJC. Employed to carry bulkier loads, the Wayfarer suffered from a lack of front-opening doors. This aircraft carried 141 tons in thirty-eight flights. (Bristol Aeroplane Company)

load transport. Silver City Airways had operated from Blackbushe, Surrey, since its formation in 1946 and had been developing a cross-Channel car-ferry service with the Freighter. Airwork Ltd also flew two Freighters for a limited period. Airwork was originally formed in 1928, and as such was seen as the senior charter company by many. During the airlift period Airwork operated a staggering 256 aircraft for organisations as varied as the Admiralty through to Sudan Airways. Unfortunately, the Bristol Freighters' and Wayfarers' input was to be short-lived. On 16 November freighters operated by Bond Air Services and Eagle Aviation were displaced from Wunstorf, finding a new home at Fuhlsbüttel. This was so that three Skyways Avro Yorks could be stationed with their military counterparts.

The first tragedy

December 8 was a moonless night at Gatow and crews were slowly making their way out to the aircraft for the return flight. Among them was the crew of an Airflight Tudor Tanker. The pilot, Clement Wilbur Utting, senior pilot, was a little way ahead of his crew. Suddenly, from nowhere a truck appeared, mowing down Utting as it sped past. It disappeared into the night, not even hinting at stopping. Utting later died of his injuries in the General Hospital in Spandau. His death was the first civilian fatality directly attributed to the lift and a major blow to Airflight.

Exhaustive investigations tried in vain to track down the culprit. With so many vehicles driving around RAF Gatow at any one time it was impossible to locate the truck, never mind the driver. Eventually conspiracy theories surfaced. Utting and Airflight's owner Don Bennett were the only two pilots cleared for night-time Tudor operations. That evening it was supposed to have been Bennett flying, but Utting had swapped with his boss. So it should have been Bennett walking to the aircraft that fateful morning. Theories covered two angles. Firstly, the driver was a German who had lost everything in the bombing raids Bennett had marked out as leader of the Pathfinder Force. Secondly, the driver was a Soviet agent, running over Bennett, who was clearly a high-profile character, was to have shaken the civilians' resolve. What it did mean was that Don Bennett flew two or three flights every night for nearly two months after the accident. Conspiracy or accident, Utting's death had made the civilian lift more determined than ever.

Rebecca

One major problem with operating a myriad of civil aircraft was the differing standards of navigational aids the aircraft carried. Top of the list was 'Rebecca'. The system had been developed during the Second World War as a way of supplying resistance units on the continent without any need for the rather obvious ground lamps. Military aircraft flying on Operation Plainfare were already fitted with the system. The problem was that the majority of the civil charter firms' planes were not. Suddenly a crisis loomed, a crisis made worse when 46 Group HQ issued a directive ordering that aircraft not fitted with Rebecca could only fly on visual flight reference (VFR). The Ministry had reduced the potential of the civilian effort in a single stroke. Throughout the run-up to the Christmas of 1948, London was warned that the lack of such a basic navigational aid would have serious consequences for the lift. As the Foreign Office saw the civil lift as a stop-gap affair it considered the fitting of units to aircraft already past their operational life expectancy a waste of money. Eventually they relented and the RAF was tasked with supplying the units. Naturally that is where the problems started.

The first issue was the serviceability of the equipment supplied. The RAF spent over a month trying to locate sets and when they did they were invariably unserviceable. The Haltons operated by Lancashire Aircraft Corporation (LAC) were in need of the Rebecca units and by January 1949 twelve sets had been located. Unfortunately they were not much use. Demonstrating the problems the civil lift faced, J.W. Hendry of LAC wrote to complain about the units with which they had been supplied. The majority had valves missing or broken, some units that were sealed in their packaging were found to be no more than empty shells and several had been stood unprotected and thus become dirty and corroded. All in all LAC technicians were able to cannibalise three and, using their own precious few spares, produce nine serviceable units. Airtech Ltd, the firm acting as intermediary between the RAF and the airlift, offered no answer as the units 'were released to you in the conditions as received. In fact, in many cases, as noted by yourself these were in sealed containers.' Luckily, Avro fitted their aircraft with the navigational aid as standard and managed to prop up the sortie total using Yorks and Tudors whilst the Haltons were grounded in bad weather.

An Airwork Bristol Freighter G-AICS. Seen here in later BEA colours, this aircraft only completed sixteen flights before the type was withdrawn.

By January British European Airways had decided to try and reduce the number of slower, less efficient aircraft on charter. First in the firing line were naturally the extremely slow Bristol Freighters. It was considered that the Handley Page Hastings with its wide doors, would now be able to cope with 'the awkward loads for which the Bristol Freighter was particularly suited', noted the Ministry of Civil Aviation. But other issues were conspiring against the aircraft. Firstly the Freighter had what was considered a 'moderate speed', 166mph (267km/h) in cruise-mode, this made them difficult to fit into any flight waves. Incidentally, the same reason made sure the Sunderlands did not appear back on the Havel See once spring arrived. Furthermore, the aircraft were not fitted with Rebecca, causing further headaches for ground control staff.

The Foreign Office's German section did not see it that way. The Bristol aircraft had made a valuable contribution to the lift. True they were not the most efficient of beasts, but Freighters had been brought into the civil lift to bring 'out of Berlin heavy pieces of machinery which it is said cannot be handled by other types of aircraft, at any rate at present. This might have originated in sales talk, but it does not come from the operators' pointed out Frederick Smith of the German Supply Department in a telegram on 26 January. Smith's department had called on the voluminous Freighters' capability more than once over the winter. Unfortunately, this was not the view of either the AOC 46 Group nor BEA Rep. Whitfield and the type were both withdrawn from service during the second week of February. Any loads that the Hastings could not carry were now to be loaded onto the Fairchild C-82 Packet. The expiry of the Bristol aircraft contract saw the end of Silver City Airways' and Airwork's involvement with the airlift.

January saw Scottish Airlines increase their fleet to five aircraft. The firm was founded in 1935 at Prestwick as part of Scottish Aviation. During the war the airfield had been an important ferry flight site due to its northerly location. The firm had become specialists in

Scottish Airlines' Liberator G-AHZP. This Liberator was used as servicing cover for fifteen flights delivering 110 tons to the city.

civil conversion after the war, Air Transport Charter's Dakota had been one of the aircraft modified at the site. Initially, Scottish Airlines flew two Dakotas as freighters; however, this was soon complemented by a single Liberator and then in January the operation placed a further two Liberators, a freighter and a tanker, on the contract. This had been accepted at a time when other firms were losing their contracts but, as the Ministry pointed out, the Liberators came at a very cheap price.

Staffing

One of the main reasons for contracting civilian charter firms in the first place was to relieve the pressure on Royal Air Force air and ground crews. However, by mid-January these firms were beginning to experience similar problems; this time bureaucracy was causing the headache. The situation was that civilian engineers and pilots were required to hold licences and type ratings in order to operate legally. Whilst firms such as Flight Refuelling Ltd had the training facilities, they did not have sufficient personnel to be able to rotate crews between Germany and the classroom. Wing Commander H.C. Johnson of Flight Refuelling Ltd commented in a meeting with the Air Ministry in early 1949 that:

> Owing to certain pilots having left the firm to various reasons (resignation, dismissal or death in an accident) and the decision to comply with the Foreign Office's requests to buy further aircraft, it was not at present possible to ground any of the pilots in command so that they might study for the A.R.B. technical examinations for their type ratings. Dispensation would therefore be desired, beyond the end of January, for the existing pilots and for seven more

men whom it was desired to use as pilots in command as soon as they have been passed as competent after flying along the corridor a few times as second pilot.[3]

And it was not just aircrew that were in short supply:

Accommodation facilities at Wunstorf and Bad Nendorf do not enable any further personnel of Flight Refuelling to be based at either of these places. Maintenance facilities and hangar space at Wunstorf are only just sufficient now to cater for the maintenance requirements of RAF and civilian chartered aircraft. An increase such as would be involved with transference of Flight Refuelling base maintenance facilities to Wunstorf could not be undertaken at the airfield, or at any other Plainfare airfield for similar reasons.[4]

When trained staff were recruited, bureaucracy often got in the way, as British South American Airways (BSAA) discovered when they tried to dispatch four engineers. The personnel officer, P.M. Polhill, with BSAA, wrote to the charter superintendent of British European Airways complaining of the situation:

The situation that arose last Friday night, illustrates the difficulties in this respect. The four engineers in question were rushed up from London airport Friday morning. Application for the entry permit was made at our west end office with the covering letter in triplicate to you. In the early afternoon they proceeded to your department and thence to Mrs Ryall at the Foreign Office. Although these applications were marked 'urgent' the men were told to leave them there and call again on Saturday morning at 11 o'clock. This would have meant that they could not have been ready for takeoff before midday on Saturday – a total period of 24 hours in obtaining permission to leave the Germany.

Rather optimistically Polhill requested that if BSAA found themselves in a similar situation that their staff could be rushed out 'without all this paperwork'. Once in Germany the stress of almost continuous operation, coupled with the dark, cold winter and poor accommodation, soon began to take its toll. Many turned to drink. Richard Collier later noted that to ensure flight refuelling could muster thirty-two sober pilots a day, the firm had nearly 150 on their books from which to choose. On one occasion, civil pilots out in Hamburg decided it would be fun to weld all the tramtrack points together, succeeding in sending trams way off route and securing themselves a rapid dismissal. The removal of staff at such short notice often meant they arrived back in Britain carrying all their paperwork. And with a shortage of personnel across the charter firms, it was not long before the individuals involved in such escapades found themselves back in Germany working through different firms.

---

[3] Wing Commander H.C. Johnson of Flight Refuelling Ltd, meeting with the Air Ministry on 14 January 1949.
[4] Report by Fredrick Smith of the German Supply Department to Flight Refuelling Ltd.

British South American Airways' Avro Tudor G-AGRH. Tudors were a major bone of contention between the Government and Airflight Ltd throughout the airlift. This one flew in 1,134 tons of freight in 114 flights.

Controversy

Nothing excites the press more than stories about Government spending, and it was inevitable that the airlift would eventually attract such attention. The ad hoc way the civil fleet had been assembled dictated that every firm had a different contract, each with its own unique rate per hour. This eventually caused friction, and some sought to use the press to air past grievances. On 6 February 1949 the *Sunday Express* ran a story that caused much consternation throughout Whitehall. Entitled 'The Big Money Being Made In The Berlin Airlift', the substantial piece written by Group-Captain H.S.L Dundas, DSO., DFC, the *Daily Express* Air Correspondent, chronicled expenditure of the civil lift. Whilst the article listed several companies, it was Don Bennett's Airflight Ltd that received the most attention, and not in a negative light, more the injured party. It turned out that when Bennett stood for Parliament in a recent by-election he had been strongly supported by both the *Daily Express* and *Evening Standard*. Clearly the piece was, at least partially, inspired by a conversation between Dundas and Bennett as it constantly demonstrated Airflights' struggle with the nationalised BSAA, Bennett's former employer.

It is worth exploring some of the allegations here as they serve to demonstrate two things. Firstly, the amount of work the Government was prepared to see go to the private sector when all policy direction led toward nationalisation of the industry. Secondly, the eccentric 'war hero' persona that Don Bennett clearly enjoyed in the eyes of the British population. 'One cannot assess Bennett's operating costs exactly', notes Dundas in the article; this is indeed true as there was no administrative staff, bar his wife, in the company, and it was not only the *Express* that had no idea. The Foreign Office had endeavoured to obtain an analysis of costs for months, noting that 'He says he does not know what the operation is, in fact, costing.' The newspaper article also suggested a conspiracy may be in force, preventing Bennett operating at the level he wanted. 'Bennett had hoped to add another five Tudors to his fleet. The sale was arranged, but before he could take delivery they were switched to government-controlled BSAAC who had previously turned them down.' The article went on, 'the corporation's name was substituted for Bennett's on the Certificates of Airworthiness, and they are now being used on the airlift'. This was not strictly true. BSAA's name was indeed on the Certificate of Airworthiness and rightly so. All five aircraft had been delivered to the airfield at Langley for flight trials during 1948 and given BSAA fleet names. However, they did not go into service until the beginning of 1949 and then it was as tankers on the airlift. Bennett was clearly in a position to have known this when he was employed by the company, and presumably now saw the opportunity to cause trouble.

Other airlines are mentioned (including Skyways) that Dundas identified as 'Believed to be the most successful money spinners in civil aviation'. They had negotiated a better deal than Bennett, presumably by holding out in the early days, not having a point to prove. Skyways pulled in a £3,000 per week initial payment with a sliding scale from loads paid as an extra. And, 'since York's are more economic to operate, Skyways profit is correspondingly higher than Bennett's'. As if that wasn't bad enough Aquila Airways also received a dig; 'In three and a half months this £20,000 company made enough profit to buy nine more Hythes from BOAC.' Fredrick Smith of the German Supply Department of the Foreign Office investigated the claim and found that Aquila had indeed bought aircraft. The Ministry of Civil Aviation suggested the price for each came to around £1,000. Aquila's gross revenue whilst on the airlift came to £64,066. He went on, 'The flying boats certainly rendered very good service'. This was hardly a revelation as, early in January, Aquila had been offering the Foreign Office use of up to six flying boats suggesting they could be used for the wet lift, utilising oil tankers and barges to load and unload.

The correspondent did achieve one thing, for later historians at least, he forced a review of revenue and rates that allows an insight as to the actual costs of such a venture. The gross revenue figure up to the end of January 1949 was estimated by BEA to be around £410,000; the *Express* put it at £483,000, 'but when the accounts are all cleared up there may not be very much difference between them', noted Fredrick Smith. Civil operators were aiming at a profit of around 10 per cent above overheads, depreciation of aircraft and flying costs, but this was being worked out on short-term contracts and Operation Plainfare had far outlived predictions by January. This meant that profits had risen for most to between 14 and 15 per cent.

Looking at specific aircraft types, Lancashire Aircraft Corporation, who was not specifically named but clearly appeared in the report, was discussed as an operator of 'Halifax tanker aircraft'. Each contract period spanned twenty-eight days, during which period the aircraft earned £85 per flying hour for the first ninety-six hours, thereafter the rate dropping to £45 per flying hour. The reason for the premium rate was to cover the cost of hire purchase and depreciation; it has to be remembered that LAC and other civil operators bought aircraft specifically for the airlift, and on a short contract this was a particularly risky financial move. However, the Government was in a strong position to renegotiate contracts, especially since the premium rate had paid for the aircraft outright in most cases. Smith noted that 'our agents are at present engaged in negotiations with the operators for a substantial reduction in the rates for extensions of the contracts'. The initial negotiations for the winter period had anticipated a substantially-reduced flying programme due to the 'typical' Central European weather. As it turned out the winter was not as bad as was first expected and, whilst this had made civil operators expensive, the benefits for the city far outweighed any cost. 'There is little doubt that the improved flying rate has offered sufficient inducement to fly to enable us to maintain a flow of supplies into Berlin which might not have been possible otherwise.' And this was the point, as far as London was concerned they were getting value for money. The alternative was to strip more transport aircraft from around the world, leaving the remnants of the Empire in a worse supply position than, in some cases, they already were.

Miserable March

On 14 March British European Airways, on behalf of the Government congratulated the performance of the civil operators the previous week:

> On Thursday the 10th March 232 tons of dry goods and 522 tons of fuel totalling 754 tons were delivered into Berlin, and on Friday the 11th March this record was again broken by the carriage of 274 tons of dry goods and 503 tons of fuel totalling 777 tons.

Events the following day were to quickly tarnish the sense of achievement that rattled through the civilian charter firms.

Crash, crash, crash!

15 March 1949 was pretty much a normal airlift day at Wunstorf, trucks were ferrying aircrew out onto the line, whilst hordes of German workers under RASO supervision were loading the day's tonnage. Christopher Gavon-Robison, senior pilot with Skyways Ltd, was catching up with events in the briefing room as crews arrived for the first of two sorties that evening. As he left he bumped into Peter Golding, another Skyways pilot. In true British fashion they discussed the weather before Golding said his 'cheery' goodbyes and headed off to collect his crew, First Pilot Henry Newman and Radio Officer Peter Edwards. By 4 p.m. they were en route to Gatow with a cargo of coal. After an uneventful flight and return the crew of Avro York G-AHFI readied themselves for the final flight that evening and by 9 p.m. they were back in the landing 'tunnel' approaching Gatow.

Airman Second Class Richard Jerkins, employed on marshalling duties at Gatow that night, witnessed what happened next:

> Aircraft were coming in regularly at about five-minute intervals. About 2100 or 2130 hrs one
> York had just landed and I was waiting for another, when I saw an aircraft approaching with

Skyways' Avro York G-AHFI. Skyways was the only civil operator to fly Yorks in the airlift. This one had delivered 1,364 tons before 15 March 1949.

the landing lights on. The landing lights came on soon after we saw the aircraft. At, what I estimate to be 200 feet, it suddenly rolled over and disappeared. I cannot give any reason for the aircraft rolling over. It was impossible for me to see or hear if the aircraft had engine failure. I could not tell what type of aircraft it was I reported the incident to the Marshalling Officer at once.

Flight Lieutenant Alan Guibal-Bradford, Medical Officer at RAF Gatow, received the crash call at about 9.15 p.m. that evening. He was following the station ambulance, accompanied by a fire tender, and reached the wreckage shortly afterwards. He later described the crash scene to the board of enquiry:

The aircraft was largely disintegrated and dispersed over some 25 yards. I found three bodies. I identified these three bodies as those now lying in the mortuary at Spandau Hospital. One body was lying relatively free. This person was dead and suffered multiple injuries. I examined him at once to see if he were alive or dead. I searched the wreckage and found two more bodies in the forward portion. Both had suffered a severe multiple injuries. There was no sign of life in either of three bodies.

A search of the wreckage was initiated but it was quickly found that, thankfully, only coal had been aboard. Captain Golding's body was discovered intertwined between the instrument combing and rudder pedals; the wreckage required some dismantling to recover his body. By 10.20 p.m. John Harrison, personal assistant to the BEA Civil Airlift manager Colin Whitfield, had visited the site. After confirming the aircraft was an Avro York of Skyways Ltd, he dispatched an accident signal to the Air Ministry and Foreign Office, whilst Whitfield telephoned Skyways operations office in Surrey to report the loss.

A wire photograph of the wreckage of G-AHFI showing the site being picked clean of cargo under British Army supervision. (ACME Newspictures)

Around 1.30 the following morning Captain Greensteel, Skyways' manager at Wunstorf, visited the site with a company engineer to confirm the registration and identification of the aircraft.

Others had also seen the aircraft plough in that day. W.C. 'Dub' Southers, a flight engineer with the 41st Troop Carrier Squadron based at Celle, had arrived at Gatow earlier in the day:

> On the 15th of March in Berlin we were one of the last planes in the block, and the British planes were landing as our plane was being unloaded. This was one time I was glad that we were not flying liquid fuels. A British York landed, one of the landing gears collapsed, the airplane with the gasoline went up in huge ball of fire, with the loss of all three crew members. That is an instance I will never forget. This was the only time that I was in Berlin more than 20 to 30 minutes on the entire airlift.

Clearly, from this account the aviation fuel contained in the York's tanks burned as the aircraft disintegrated. However, the fire must have quickly extinguished itself as Flt Lt. Guibal-Bradford, MO, recorded later, 'There was no evidence of incineration', on any of the crew. 'In my opinion death would have been instantaneous,' he concluded.

The British Government hired G-AHFI on 16 November 1948 along with two other aircraft from the company. Each aircraft was to attract £3,330 per seven-day period of operations; a further £50 was paid per hour flown. Skyways insured the aircraft through the British Aviation Insurance Company (BAIC) for £60,000 at a premium of £5,130 per annum. The airlift was considered a high-risk activity and insurers were not interested in taking on the liability. Eventually the Government covered operational flights with an indemnity. The aircraft remained the responsibility of the owner whilst on the ground;

however, between 'chocks away' and 'engines off' the liability against loss fell to the British Government. Interestingly, this loss included 'detention of the aircraft by a foreign power'; clearly, if the aircraft landed in the Soviet zone there was considered little chance of recovery. When BAIC inspected the wreckage at Gatow a few days later, they declared that the impact had rendered the aircraft a total loss.

Settlement was slow. With so many Government departments involved in Operation Plainfare it was inevitable that something would get lost. 'Receipt of the coroner's report in respect of crew of York aircraft G-AHFI was considerably delayed due to absence of covering note indicating for which Department of Foreign Office (German Section) it was intended.' This did not deter Group Captain Wilcock, a director of Skyways and Member of Parliament who 'has approached several ministers about the delay in paying out the claim – and is causing a certain amount of disturbance in Whitehall', wrote Sylvia Masel of the FO(GS) in a letter to the Treasury. On 5 May full payment against loss of the aircraft was authorised, although payments regarding the crew were being dealt with separately. 'We shall be interested to learn it in due course the method of disposal of the salvage and the amount realised therefrom,' added the Treasury. So were others as it turned out.

The BAIC report covering the damage G-AHEI had suffered concluded that the aircraft had been reduced to low-value scrap. Aircraft specification aluminium, due to the scrapping of large military fleets after the Second World War, held no real premium and was subsequently difficult to sell-on. There was also no way of transporting the wreckage from Berlin and with this in mind a local German scrap merchant removed the aircraft for 600 Deutschmarks. This was credited into the Hamburg account of British European Airways. The problem was that the insurance company was not authorised to actually dispose of the aircraft. Furthermore it was not Government policy to deal in German currency. Accordingly, the FO(GS) placed a demand for £44 13s 6d, the sterling equivalent, on BEA. Even with this settled, the question of pay-out to the families of the crew dragged on.

British European Airways, caught in the middle by now, wrote to the Foreign Office stating:

> I have today had an urgent request from the solicitors dealing with the estate of radio officer P.J. Edwards deceased, that the compensation due as the result of his death should be paid immediately in view of the fact that hardship is being caused to his mother, Mrs Edwards. It appears that this lady was entirely supported by her son and is now left without funds and has in fact, had to seek employment in order to obtain some income. As she is a lady of some 55 years of age and has not previously had to work this is causing some distress.

The major delay centred on who had actually insured the aircrew. Unfortunately, whilst the Government agreed to indemnify the periods not covered by Skyways insurance, it did not cover the death of the crew. Eventually, seven months after the accident the Foreign Office decided, under mounting political pressure, to pay out to the next of kin; however, if Skyways Ltd benefited from any subsequent insurance policy then 'it must be paid to His Majesties [sic] Government'. Such was the legacy of the Berlin Airlift to families in both Germany and Britain.

Eagle Aviation's Halton G-AIAP. This aircraft delivered 2,727.8 tons in 390 sorties.

Eagle Aviation's Halton G-ALEF. Note that this aircraft has the freight pannier removed. G-ALEF carried 1,481.4 tons to Berlin.

In April the civil effort really got into its stride. Issues surrounding both qualified aircrew and the level of competent ground crew had been solved and new servicing regimes were allowing for more available serviceable aircraft. To help the situation along, the weather was much improved, allowing the average daily sortie level to be raised to nearly seventy-four per day. One Halton of Eagle Aviation operated for the entire month, turning in three sorties per day, without any major level of un-serviceability. Eagle Aviation had been formed in April 1948, initially flying fruit between Italy and northern Europe. The company initially flew out of Aldermaston with Halifax and Halton aircraft. Unfortunately the month did not end on a high. On the night of the 30th, a Halton freighter, one of three World Air Freight operating, came down in the Soviet zone. The aircraft was returning from Tegel. Captain W. Lewis, Navigational Officer E. Carroll, Engineer J. Anderson and Radio Officer K. Wood died. These were to be the last fatalities of the civil lift during the blockade: twenty-one men had lost their lives in air crashes and ground incidents in the name of freedom. This was not the end of the civil effort; like its military colleague it would continue for some time yet.

Nine

The Wet Lift

One area in which the British, or more accurately British civil operators, excelled was the movement of liquid fuel. At the time of the blockade neither the Royal Air Force nor the United States Air Force had the capability to transport liquid fuel of any kind in bulk. Both relied on road transport or pipelines, that was until the blockade shut down all chance of supplying the city by those methods. Initially fuel was flown in onboard the Dakotas, but this was in no way ideal. 55-gallon drums were difficult to load and even more difficult to secure once loaded. The answer came in the form of the civilian operators that had sprung up since the war. Some, such as Flight Refuelling Ltd, specialised in such work and had been working with the Air Ministry since before the war. Others, like Airflight Ltd, saw the opportunity to make some quick money and had their one or two passenger or freighter aircraft converted to the task. This chapter will look at the 'wet lift' and some of the operators who made this a successful part of the supply of Berlin.

Requirement

In the immediate post-war years, Berlin's ability to generate its own electrical power was seriously curtailed. As the Red Army settled into the role of conqueror it systematically stripped the city of machinery and equipment under the auspices of German reparations. This had, in July 1945, included the large power station located in the Spandau region of the city. Power, albeit intermittently, was from then on supplied by the Klinkenburg station in the east of the city. Eight smaller generating stations spread across Western Berlin and supplemented the power output in high demand situations. The main supply came to an abrupt end when the blockade severed power, forcing the three Western sectors to rely on the smaller, inefficient stations. Of course the Soviets cited a chronic fuel shortage which had 'prevented resumption of electricity'. Generators were quickly flown in for essential services such as the telephone network and hospitals, but the private consumer was restricted to four hours a day. Industry suffered too, with many companies closing as the 80 per cent reduction in their supply bit deep. As the number of generators flown in increased, so naturally did the demand for diesel to power them. Furthermore, some

Liquids were originally flown into Berlin in drums; however, with the contracting of British Civil firms the task fell to the experts.

smaller stations were converted to liquid fuel in an attempt to relieve pressure on the coal lift. This reliance on wet fuel called for specialist transport and it was to come in the form of British civil operators, the subsequent 'wet lift' was to become an integral part of the airlift. Nearly fifty percent of the city's power was generated using fuel directly flown in by the British, continuing until the new power station for the Western sectors came on line in December 1949.

Civil companies

The transportation of fuel by air brought a myriad of personalities and companies into the limelight. Some, such as Flight Refuelling Ltd, were well established by 1948 whilst others, like Airflight Ltd and Lancashire Aircraft Corporation, were formed out of the necessity to fly in the post-war air cargo world.

Flight Refuelling Ltd

Flight refuelling was the brainchild of Sir Alan Cobham, one of Britain's foremost aviators through the 1920s and '30s. After initially serving in the Army Veterinary Corps from 1914, Cobham transferred to the Royal Flying Corps in early 1918, eventually becoming

Flight Refuelling Ltd was the world leader in bulk liquid carrying at the start of the blockade. Avro Lancastrian G-AKDS, seen here in its Trans-Canadian Airlines colours, delivered 2,784 tons of fuel.

Flight Refuelling Ltd also relied on original types converted for the task. Avro Lancaster G-AHVN delivered 1,586 tons during the blockade.

an instructor. On demobilisation in February the following year, Cobham joined the Berkshire Aviation Co., conducting pleasure flights from many sites around the United Kingdom. From here he went on to fly for the newly formed de Havilland as an air photographer-pilot, and was influential in the design of the classic DH Moth. Pioneering long-distance flights to India and South Africa followed along with a publicity stunt in 1926 involving delivering a letter to the Houses of Parliament via Australia. All this earned Cobham widespread fame and a knighthood. Throughout his long-distance exploits it became clear that if an aircraft could be refuelled in-flight then the time it took from one airfield to another could be dramatically reduced, especially on the Atlantic run.

By late 1934 this dream became a reality as Cobham formed Flight Refuelling Ltd (FR); however, the concept of air-to-air refuelling took ten years to be accepted by the Air Ministry. For the task FR initially used Government surplus Lancasters stripped of all their wartime equipment and machine-gun turrets. Trials were carried out throughout 1946–47 with minimal government funding, and whilst the concept was proven orders were not forthcoming. Undeterred by this Cobham purchased four more Lancasters from the Ministry's stockpile at RAF Kemble for £1,000 each and surplus engines at £100 a time. This was stock was bolstered by the delivery of Lancastrians recently sold by Trans-Canadian Airlines in late 1947. Little did Cobham know that he was positioning his company at the forefront of fuel transportation.

Aircraft and crews from Flight Refuelling Ltd were the first of the civilian companies to be involved in the airlift. On 27 July 1948, an FR Lancastrian took off from Tarrant Rushton, Dorset, en route for Berlin. At least twelve aircraft were utilised during Operation Plainfare, delivering 27,114.6 tons over 4,438 sorties. As with other operators, the airlift signalled a growth period for Flight Refuelling Ltd, and at its peak over 650 staff were employed across sites in Britain and Germany. Initially operations were conducted from Bückeburg alongside other civilian organisations; however, this site was severely limited by the lack of fuel storage facilities, and by the beginning of August FR had relocated to Wunstorf in the British zone.

Tragedy struck the Flight Refuelling detachment when, on 22 November 1948, Lancastrian G-AHJW was lost during a return flight to Tarrant Rushton. This accident had the dubious honour of becoming the first Operation Plainfare civilian aircraft to crash causing fatalities and was, as Colin Cruddas noted later, the only fatal crash the company experienced. The aircraft departed Wunstorf for the company's base in Dorset in the afternoon and progressed without incident until well over England. A second crew and three FR captains, all returning for leave, accompanied the flight crew on board. The Lancastrian was due to be serviced, having completed just over 130 flying hours while delivering 221 tons of fuel into Berlin. At some point the aircraft changed course, probably onto the wrong navigation beacon, taking it over Andover and in the direction of RAF Netheravon on Salisbury Plain. Just beyond Andover the Lancastrian entered some haze and struck a hillside in Conholt Park, killing all but one member of the crew.

The Avro Lancastrian was a development of the famous Lancaster bomber. Intended as a transatlantic airliner, the aircraft saw varied service in the immediate post-war period. By 1947 the aircraft had been superseded by types built specifically for the air charter market and the Lancastrian became the mainstay of many small 'one-man-bands'. After slight modification the FR aircraft were commissioned by the Foreign Office to fly fuel, both petrol and diesel, into RAF Gatow. Initially this was solely the responsibility of FR, but before long it became clear that more tanker provision was needed and other charter firms joined the fuel run.

Airflight Ltd

Airflight Ltd was born out of necessity as a vehicle to prove a point, or rather prove an aircraft. Air Vice-Marshal D.C.T. Bennett had staked his reputation on the Avro Tudor, Britain's first pressurised airliner, but the aircraft was shunned after an unexplained loss north-east of Bermuda on the night of 29–30 January 1948. Bennett had flown the proving flight and stood by the aircraft's airworthiness but, with the loss of thirty-one people, the Government-owned British South American Airline (BSAA) dismissed him. A crushing blow to such an ego.

Donald Clifford Tyndall Bennett was born in Australia in 1910. By 1930 he had joined the Royal Australian Air Force and a year later was on secondment to the Royal Air Force, initially serving on flying boats at Calshot. Bennett left the service in 1935, retaining a reserved commission, and joined Imperial Airways. Whilst there Bennett broke the world's long-distance seaplane record using a Shorts-Mayo composite aircraft working on the 'piggy back' system. Basically, a large powerful aircraft carried a smaller one up to the cruising height and part way to the destination. On separation the smaller aircraft carried on whilst the launcher returned to the originating base, thus giving the smaller aircraft added range. By 1941 Bennett was back in the Royal Air Force. As a wing commander he commanded 10 Squadron equipped with Halifaxs and went on to attack the *Tirpitz* whilst she was moored in a Norwegian fiord. During the raid his aircraft was shot down and he spent many months evading the enemy, eventually making it back to England. In July 1942 Sir Arthur Harris appointed Bennett commander of the new Pathfinder Force, designed to spearhead large bomber formations, marking out targets for the waves to home in on. Eventually there were nineteen squadrons of pathfinders, mainly equipped with the highly successful mosquito aircraft. After the war Bennett went on to join British South American Airways where he was appointed managing director. On 28 May 1947 he joined forces with Sir Alan Cobham to demonstrate that it was possible to fly the South Atlantic non-stop using aerial refuelling techniques. The flight from Heathrow to Bermuda in a BSAA Lancastrian took twenty hours and the plane was refuelled in-flight by aircraft from Flight Refuelling Ltd, stationed at Santa Maria, Azores.

After the loss of the aircraft in 1948 near Bermuda, and his subsequent dismissal over the affair, Bennett was determined to rescue his reputation. Undeterred, he insisted the Tudor was a good aircraft and set up a new company, Airflight Ltd, based at Blackbushe, to prove the point; buying two government surplus Tudors with his payoff. The first, a Tudor II, flew from Wunstorf to Gatow on 3 September. Initially Airflight carried low-density supplies such as baby rusks, biscuits and butter, the load being built up to a maximum using sacks of flour stacked over the centre section of the aircraft. Meanwhile a Tudor V, originally destined for Bennett's former employer BSAA, was fitted with five 500-gallon fuel tanks at Blackbushe airport; eventually both Airflight aircraft were on the fuel run.

Airflight Avro Tudor undergoing routine maintenance in the field.

Lancashire Aircraft Corporation

Lancashire Aircraft Corporation (LAC) was more typical of the privately owned airlines that sprang up after the Second World War. Formed in 1946, it comprised a mixture of civil and military personnel and equipment, flying unusual cargoes such as football supporters to destinations in the north-west of Britain. The company offices were based at Bovingdon, Hertfordshire, and from there Air Vice-Marshal Frazer oversaw the running of the operation.

Chief pilot, Captain Wallace Lashbrook, had led a distinguished career throughout the war earning the DFC, AFC and DFM. This included escaping through France into Spain and finally on to Gibraltar after being shot down in 1943. On return to Britain, Lashbrook was assigned to the Empire Flying School as a flight commander before he finally retired from the military in November 1946. He went on to work for Scottish Aviation before joining Lancashire Aircraft Corporation in 1947. Others included the Polish Battle of Britain veteran, Jan Malinski, who had escaped the Nazis via the Balkans and France before finally arriving in Britain. From 1941 Malinski flew with 307 Squadron operating night-fighter Beaufighters, and later Mosquitoes. He joined Lancashire Aircraft Corporation in 1947 and flew throughout Operation Plainfare. Others on the airlift had initially started their civilian careers with LAC, this included Barry Aikman of Aquila Airways, now a major airlift participant. Aikman had been instrumental in the corporation's post-war activities, especially the conversion of war surplus Halifax bombers into profitable post-war freight carriers. Although he was Lancashire Aircraft Corporation's general manager and held a director's post, Aikman decided to form his own airline business and left in mid-1947. His legacy did, however, live on, as aircraft on the conversion programme were

Lancashire Aircraft Corporation Halton G–AJZY. This tanker flew 1,282 tons of fuel into the city.

the initial airframes used on the airlift. Lancashire Aircraft Corporation initially supplied three Halton freighters on contract from 16 October 1948. This was quickly added to by the arrival of a single Halton tanker two weeks later. By the end of the airlift LAC was flying just liquid fuels into the city with a fleet of twelve aircraft.

Lancashire Aircraft Corporation suffered a number of losses whilst involved in Operation Plainfare, including a tragically avoidable ground incident. John Dury, Flight Mechanic with 297 Squadron, Hastings, Schleswigland, was on the line that day:

> My own worst experience was one evening in Jan. 49, when hearing a commotion near our dispersal, we rushed across to witness a terrible scene after one of our Hastings had taxied into the rear of a truck on the perimeter track, driven by a careless German, the propellers killing 4 and injuring 2 others I believe.

A Fordson truck taking ground engineers out to the aircraft line had driven into the path of a taxiing Hastings. The propellers made short work of the scant protection afforded by the truck panels. Within seconds three of the engineers, Theodore Supernatt, Patrick Griffin and Edward O'Neil, along with the German driver, Richard K.O. Neumann, were dead.

Build-up

The 'wet lift' had humble beginnings, but it quickly grew into a major part of the operation and one that brought with it a number of unusual problems. Flight Refuelling

Ltd, the first civil contractor on the airlift, commenced operations on 27 July from Bückeburg in the British zone, but poor fuel storage facilities hampered operations and the Foreign Office soon moved the 'wet lift' to Wunstorf. By mid-September they had been joined by Airflight and British South American Airways Tudors, and by December Wunstorf was home to all civilian tanker detachments except the Haltons of Lancashire Aircraft Corporation. They were stationed at Schleswigland.

Initially the Haltons had been based at Wunstorf, but they were relocated to Schleswigland on 24 November to share the base almost exclusively with Royal Air Force Hastings. The facilities at the airfield were far superior to those experienced by other 'wet lift' operators. Schleswigland had a good rail network supplying both coal and fuel oil to designated parts of the site. Rail wagons decanted their loads into underground tanks, which were then used to load the Haltons. The system had been built for the Luftwaffe and now proved invaluable for the airlift. With slight modification it was possible to reload the Haltons four tanks with 1,300 gallons of fuel in less than fifteen minutes. The system contained an automatic meter that cut the flow when the desired load had been reached. This cut down the amount of aircraft out of service due to overfilling, something the Lancastrians operating from the Wunstorf suffered on more than one occasion.

At Wunstorf loading involved a far more convoluted process. Fuel was delivered to the airfield by rail and deposited into 'cistern wagons' at the railhead. The correct aircraft load was then drawn into bowsers that took the fuel across the airfield to the waiting aircraft. A Tudor with a typical load of 2,100 gallons took forty minutes to completely fill, but if there was a problem then the aircraft very often missed the flight slot. This situation prevailed until mid-April 1949 when purpose-built facilities increased the speed of a fuel uplift to 100 gallons per minute, halving the loading time.

By mid-December 1948 the worsening fuel situation had reached critical levels. The problem was that there was just not enough fuel being brought in and by Christmas Berlin was almost totally reliant on the airlift with little in reserve. The expected daily target of 220 tons was optimistic to say the least; throughout December the average was more like 150 tons per day. And surprisingly a lack of tankers was only part of the problem. Many aircraft had been recalled to the United Kingdom for modification from freighter to tanker and part of that work included fitting the navigational aid Rebecca. The problem was that there was a shortage of Rebecca units, so rather than proceed with the conversions, companies such as Airtech Ltd allowed the work to pile up.

Christmas breakthrough

Throughout January, British European Airways representative Whitfield oversaw the construction of a credible tanker force. What had started out as Flight Refuelling Ltd rapidly expanded as the Lancastrians were mixed with aircraft from other operators to create a fleet of over forty aircraft. Contracts from the Foreign Office, along with the push for more flights per day, dictated that serious money was now being earned. Ironically, Avro at Manchester was now being pressurised to produce Tudor tankers for British South American Airways, even though Don Bennett's Airflight appeared to be the only

Avro Tudor G-AKCA, operated by the Government-owned British South American Airways, flew an incredible 4,480 tons of fuel into Berlin on 529 sorties.

true champion of the aircraft. During a publicity tour around the airlift, Avro company representatives made the following observation, one of them summing up the general feeling at the time:

It was inevitable, standing there in the heart of Germany surrounded by Manchester-built aircraft, that we should feel a glow of pride and satisfaction. Here was the aircraft which had been turned down before they had been given a chance to prove their capabilities in service.

Subsequently, Avro pulled out all the stops and produced two further Tudors two weeks ahead of schedule. The Foreign Office was 'considerably relieved by this information'.

By 25 January it was becoming clear that the tanker fleet was almost at full strength. Two further Liberators had initially been requested but would not become available until 19 February and the Foreign Office wondered whether 'it would be necessary to explore the possibility of other tanker aircraft being made available earlier'. But the point was that there had been a substantial improvement already in the daily oil and petrol lift. Aircraft were now being loaded more efficiently and many now carried the Rebecca navigational aid allowing for tighter timing in and out of the city. So much so that the Foreign Office quite happily commented, 'it rather looks as if there will be sufficient carrying capacity available in Germany to carry a tonnage substantially in excess of your stated current daily requirements, and to provide for building up of stocks'. So the Liberators were put on hold, especially since a further civilian operator meant yet another unique contract, but not for long. By the end of the month the required total lift had increased again, and it was now 'confirmed that the Liberators are required... Objections you refer to must give

Scottish Airlines' Liberator G-AHZR. This aircraft delivered 1,182 tons of fuel into Berlin.

way to the immediate necessity of increasing the fuel lift to Berlin.' By 11 February the Foreign Office were exploring an increase to the daily lift of petrol, diesel and kerosene to 520 metric tons a day. Survey teams were already scouring the United Kingdom for suitable aircraft, while companies such as Avro saw the opportunity to off-load further redundant types, including Tudors.

Logistics

Handling facilities varied considerably throughout the early days of the lift, but by March 1949 the situation had radically improved. Gatow had been quickly identified as the primary liquid-receiving airfield within the city. It had none of the hazards encountered at Tempelhof and, more importantly, if a crash did happen it was unlikely to be in a built-up area. The main problem was that housing surrounded Tempelhof, and an aircraft coming down short of the runway laden with fuel would be a major disaster, especially on the political front. Gatow benefited from underground tanks and a large area of hard-standing, all constructed as part of the 1947–48 upgrades to the airfield. These valuable assets now saw extensive use throughout the blockade. However, only the Lancasters and Lancastrians used the subterranean tanks initially. Others, such as Airflight and British South American Airways (BSAA), both operating Avro Tudors, decanted their loads directly into waiting fuel tankers. This process was time consuming and meant very little room for error. And errors there were. A report investigating tanker problems in April 1949 identified a lack of trained groundcrew at Gatow as a major reason for missed flights throughout the airlift. The BEA representative G. Foster had noted for the inquiry that he 'doubted whether there were sufficient de-fuelling teams available to enable a proper check that the aircraft

British South American Airways' Avro Tudor G-AKCD. Seen here in Dempster colours, this aircraft carried 3,288 tons into the city.

was completely empty'. 'De-fuelling crews,' he went on, 'had not time to do more than connect the discharge hoses to one aircraft before proceeding to the next one.' As a direct consequence the aircraft returned back to base still with tanks full. When reloaded for the next trip fuel poured out from the tanks drenching the aircraft internally, and forcing it to miss one or two sortie slots.

Airflight Tudors had a turn-round time of forty minutes at the Gatow airbase. Internal fuel tanks were situated over the centre of gravity in five 500-gallon tanks making, on the Tudor V, for lots of wasted space. The tanks were fitted in line with a single delivery pipe to a fuel stopcock near the rear passenger door. This arrangement was beneficial as the Tudor had a tail wheel undercarriage layout, meaning fuel would naturally drain to the rear of the aircraft, helping fully deplete the load. Even with this layout there were sometimes problems. To get the fuel into the waiting bowser it had to be suction-pumped by the vehicle. By February the bowsers were suffering serious fatigue, as was all equipment in Berlin. 46 Group HQ pointed out that, 'It has always been recognised that the pumping equipment was liable to failure as it was not designed for the task.'

Clearly then, the transportation of liquid fuel posed many problems; however, one stood out above all others: the volatile nature of the vapours, especially petrol. Diesel was unpleasant and could be smelt for days on clothes. Philip Kidson, Avro's publicity manager, nicely summed up the experience of flying in an Airflight Tudor to Wunstorf: 'Conditions were just above the minimum laid down for Ground Controlled Approach (GCA) landings and the extremely bumpy conditions combined with the reek of diesel oil, made the journey anything but pleasant.' Petrol, however, was far more dangerous and, given half a chance, would cause explosions. This was especially the case with the Haltons operated by Lancashire Aircraft Corporation and Westminster Airways, where the aircraft had no cargo bay. Tanks were fitted in panniers slung in the bomb bay and in the spaces either

Halton G-AIAR. This aircraft operated on both the wet and dry lifts. British American Air Services delivered 1,805 tons of fuel before Eagle Aviation leased the aircraft as a freighter. It then carried 432 tons of freight.

side of the spar; this made venting the fuel vapours difficult. Often crews flew with the direct vision cockpit window open in an attempt to shift the fumes. To exacerbate matters further, as the aircraft taxied in it was a ticking time bomb; if defuelling procedures were not followed to the letter more than one aircraft could be lost, along with anything else around it. By 12 January the Ministry of Civil Aviation, now tired of the near-misses and mindful of the field day the Soviet press would have made, limited the carriage of petrol to those aircraft fitted with adequate venting systems.

The restrictions did not stop there. The Air Registration Board also decided, on safety grounds, that aircraft carrying petrol in pannier tanks were now considered dangerous. No further Certificates of Airworthiness would be issued for aircraft carrying such loads, regardless of requirement; the order effectively removed the majority of Lancashire Aircraft Corporation Haltons from the petrol lift. The decision was sound enough. An aircraft landing wheels-up would naturally end up skidding down the runway on the pannier tank; any sparks would ignite the petrol and up would go load, aircraft and aircrew. However, AVM Fraser of LAC had been converting Haltons for fuel carriage since the beginning of Operation Plainfare and was insistent that, with slight modification, the aircraft were safe. He suggested work to fit a vent system was cost-effective at £10 per tank, and he had also developed a large tank capacity for the aircraft. However, the Foreign Office thought otherwise; they instructed him to stop the modifications and had the Air Registration Board throw out his large tank plans.

Loads could be increased by other means, as British-American Air Services Ltd demonstrated. The firm, based at Aylesbury & Thame Airport, Haddenham, Buckinghamshire, increased the load capacity of their Haltons to 1,550 gallons of fuel without fitting additional tanks. This had been achieved 'by carrying out considerable modifications to the aircraft'. Basically, company engineers accompanied by a team from Airtech Ltd had systematically stripped everything out of the aircraft that was deemed unnecessary. This was a risky tactic as the Ministry of Civil Aviation (MCA) had already warned Skyways and Flight Refuelling Ltd of the consequences. 'The only way in which payload can be stepped up is by stripping the aircraft of some equipment thought to be unessential. This unfortunately, probably means some modification which would require the consent of the Air Registration Board.' To cope with any possible payload increase FR Ltd fitted 'a special type of undercarriage' to the Lancastrian and after the figures had been worked out the aircraft was found to be capable of much more than the operator had planned. The MCA decided that a temporary increase in the all-up landing weight to 59,000lb would be allowed, a concession extended to the Halton too, reviewed after six weeks. This was a bonus for the wet lift as it enabled the Halton to fly at maximum capacity, 1,800 gallons. In the event this arrangement was to remain under a 'special circumstances' Certificate of Airworthiness until the end of the contract.

PLUTO

One problem with RAF Gatow was the lack of a railway from the airfield to central Berlin and with the blockade in place there was very little chance of building one. So the easiest way to transfer fuel and other supplies from Gatow to the city was via Lake Havel. The trick was to find the most fuel-effective method of transport. The Air Ministry efficiently summarised the situation in 1949:

> If, for example, a load of 3,000 tons of freight had to be moved from Gatow to the various depots in Berlin, it could be hauled by petrol-driven vehicles, by oil burning vehicles, or by barge. The petrol vehicles would require, taking into account the return journey empty, about 15 tons of fuel to make this haul. Diesel vehicles could have done it with the consumption of some 5 tons of oil. But the whole load could be delivered in barges drawn by a single tug, which would burn, in 24 hours, only one ton of coal.

When the Soviets imposed the blockade they stranded around forty large barges on the lake. These had been 'stolen' by the Nazis from Belgian and Dutch companies and luckily had not yet been returned. The small fleet was capable of moving around 15,000 tons, including a large tanker capacity. The lake and a large number of tributaries lay within the UK-US sectors and were linked by a series of canals and waterways into the city. There was no way of avoiding the transportation of food and coal to the Havel by road, but fuel was a different matter altogether. Luckily, the British Army logistical teams were experts at moving fuel over large distances and came to the rescue with a proven system. It is surprising what an army carries 'just in case'. When the British took up residence in their sector they brought with them sections of PLUTO (Pipeline Under The Ocean). PLUTO had been developed to get fuel over the English Channel in support of the Normandy landings and subsequent liberation of France. The original idea was to utilise it in Berlin repairing water and sewage services; however, it was soon identified as essential for the airlift. Two 3km lengths were laid between December and March, one for petrol, the other diesel, terminating at the site of the United Services Sailing Club, under Allied control. A specially built pumping station then decanted the fuel onto six of the barges, where it was then delivered into fuel depots in Berlin.

Problems

Inevitably there were those in the Government who resented the involvement of civilian operators in what was essentially a military operation. The crunch came on 8 April, when the Foreign Office complained that, 'We are frequently informed that tanker aircraft do not get full payloads because POL [Petrol, Oil, Lubricant] is not delivered to them in full quantities by the time they must fly', in a signal to HQ 46 Group. They concluded that 'this has a serious effect on total lift into Berlin besides being expensive of aircraft'. It transpired that Skyways had been operating three Lancastrian tankers contracted to an agreed payload of just over 2,000 gallons per flight at loads less than guaranteed. Unfortunately, two out of the three had been carrying 600 gallons less than expected and as all three were hired for the same load capacity this 'makes the difference even more remarkable'.

An investigation was demanded in order to ascertain whether full loads were now being flown by Skyways, and 'if not why not'. Furthermore, the whole situation needed to be reviewed, as other tanker firms might also be 'short-loading'. Edwin Whitfield, British European Airways area manager for Germany, was tasked with designing a more representative and advanced plan. Meanwhile, a board of inquiry was convened at RAF Wunstorf on 12 April in an attempt to discover the truth behind the allegations. The board, chaired by Brigadier J.A. Dawson, Commander of the Army Air Transport Organisation (AATO), interviewed a number of staff, both civil and military, over the serious charges. Clearly, defrauding the Government through short-loading could not be allowed to continue as if one firm got away with it others would surely try. However, the board was surprised at the findings.

It transpired that between 1 January and 12 April 2,827 civilian tanker sorties had been flown from Wunstorf, whilst only fifty (or 1.8 per cent) of flights had been cancelled. The time allocated to refuel a tanker was forty minutes and this Major Joyce, OC 74 Company RASO, considered wholly adequate. In fact, 'the task could be completed within 30 minutes if nothing untoward happened'. G. Forster, the BEA representative at Wunstorf, added, 'that the acceptable time allowed was 40 minutes, and no complaint was justifiable unless this time is exceeded'. Any aspect of the operation that caused an aircraft to miss a time slot was fully investigated that day and the findings presented at the station commander's 'morning prayers' the following day. To demonstrate the point, Joyce produced the details of the investigations into the fifty missed sorties. Contrary to the procedures used in aircraft 'short-loading', they were not being completely de-fuelled at Gatow. Often the belly tank of the Lancastrian, containing 400 gallons, was still full on arrival back at Wunstorf. The loading crew would be unaware of this until an overflow occurred. The aircraft was subsequently grounded until the fuel, now causing a major fire hazard, could be removed. The problem was that there was no way of knowing what fuel load was left in the tanks; in the rush to provide tanker aircraft for Operation Plainfare no one had considered fitting content gauges. Also, there were not enough unloading crews at Gatow to cope with aircraft if they came in too close together. Often, whilst one aircraft was connected to the ground tank another was taxiing in. But what about short-loading? It transpired that the two aircraft named by the Foreign Office as cheating the Government were not actually capable of carrying the loads expected in the first place. Skyways had operated the two Lancastrians, G-AKMW & G-AKBT, at the reduced capacity until extra internal tanks had become available, after modification each had carried over 2,000 gallons per sortie.

One dangerous practice did come to light during the investigation. Companies were paid per sortie, making it critical that aircraft hit the designated slot. An example of the hazards caused by this kind of pressure was brought to the boards' attention. Twice Avro Tudors from Airflight and a Lancastrian operated by Flight Refuelling Ltd had started up whilst the RASO troops were still refuelling the tanks. Each time this had been within the allotted forty-minute loading time and the load crews had been forced to abandon the operation. As the aircraft taxied away there was no opportunity to amend the manifest to agree with the reduced load. Clearly, the aircraft had indeed 'short-loaded', but in each case the incident had been logged and reported to BEA for action.

So it transpired that any problem the Foreign Office had centred on just three incidents from over 2,000 sorties, and that all had been promptly reported to the relevant authorities by the RASO loading team. Far from being an epidemic the board of inquiry considered, 'that best utilisation is made of all civil tanker aircraft and that max. payloads are carried'. In the event, only one recommendation was made and is summed up in the closing paragraphs of the board's report, 'this is not the first time such charges have been made and as it appears BEA are unaware of grounds for these allegations, it would be appreciated if the Foreign Office could name the source of such rumours'. The culprit was never revealed.

Facts and figures

As is so often the case with endeavours such as these, the total wet lift effort changes from account to account; however, it is worth demonstrating the figures such as they are. The civil airlift formally closed on 16 August 1949, ninety-six days after the blockade was lifted. By that date forty-eight aircraft had flown a total of 13,208 sorties, spending over 37,156 hours in the air. In that time they delivered a staggering 92,345 tons of liquid fuel. This had comprised petrol, diesel and, to a lesser degree, kerosene. This had not come cheaply, there were seventeen casualties on the civil wet lift alone. All are named on the monument at Tempelhof.

Ten

The Blockade Busters

January was a month of mixed blessings for the airlift. Within the first few weeks three C-54s had crashed, one on its way to Burtonwood for servicing, killing six aircrew. However, this was also the month the United States Air Force began rotating staff on temporary duty. Technical innovations also came online, as the 'search radar system' installed on top of the Tempelhof terminal building was finally commissioned. This reduced most of the building clutter echo the GCA teams had suffered at the city base, it also complemented the CPS radar sets that had arrived a month earlier. Now British and American air traffic controllers were able to dictate flight times whilst aircraft were still 50 miles from the city, the airlift now had the edge over the weather.

The pace now increased considerably across the whole CALTF effort as the coordination of both bases and aircraft waves began to bear fruit. In the period 3–10 January a staggering 30,073 tons of supplies were delivered by air, 18,779 of which were coal. The Soviet authorities had no reply; short of an act of war it appeared that for once their old ally – winter – had let them down. Harassment seemed the only recourse and so the SMA announced at the Berlin Air Safety Centre its intention to carry out exercises in the air corridors. Interference had always been a possibility, but in the face of failure it now became an increasing probability.

American flight crews noted over seventy incidents of 'buzzing' and just under another hundred that should have been noted as such. This caused great unease, as the previous year just this kind of action had brought down the BEA Viking, killing all on board. But this was not the only scare tactic employed. The SMA built new ranges below the corridors and proceeded to use them for live firing exercises. In what must be classed as the most reckless of the activities undertaken, fighters would stand-off at around 6,000ft and wait for a transport aircraft wave. As soon as one started up the corridor they would shallow dive through the wave, firing into the targets below as they passed. And when this was not enough the ranges were used to practice anti-aircraft fire in front of a wave. And, as an added obstacle, the SMA announced on 26 January that parachute jumping was also to be carried out. However, the biggest fear of the airlift command was that barrage balloons might appear; luckily they never did.

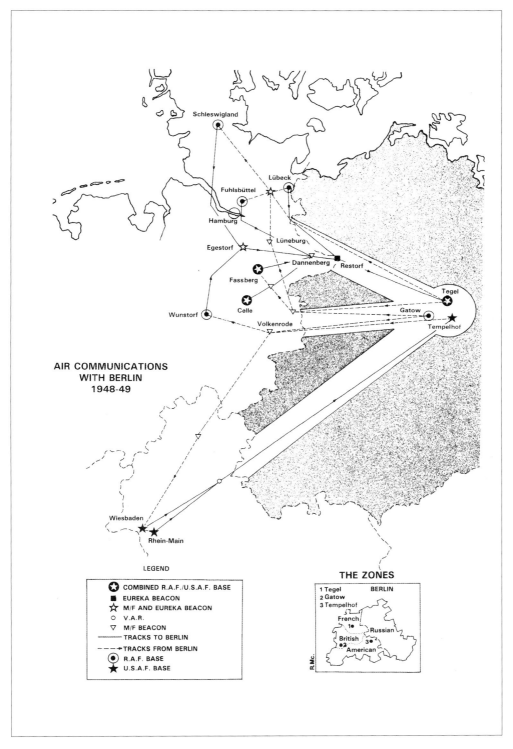

By January 1949 the network of beacons across Germany, coupled with accurate weather prediction and load matching, all but ensured victory. (Map after Dr Bob McManners in Jackson R. 1988)

The steady increase in flights to Berlin prompted Moscow to increase 'training flights' across the city. A line of C-54s and an Avro York stand ready for the off at Gatow.

C-54 down

Burtonwood Tower this is 45543, over.

The voice came over the radio, the weather conditions were atrocious. The Skymaster C-54, 14th Squadron Troop Carrying Squadron of the 61st Troop Carrier Group was en route from Rhein-Main for its 200 hour inspection. Pilot 1st Lt Richard Wurgel struggled with the aircraft from the outset. Carrying a load of engines due for refurbishment along with two passengers, Capt. W. Rathgeber and Pte R. Stone, the aircraft was slightly heavy, and now the weather over north-west Britain was making a routine flight anything but...

45543 this is Burtonwood Tower, What is your present position and what are your flying conditions?

Tower, I am approximately two miles South of the field and have just broken clear of the clouds at 2,200 feet. I will be completely VFR in a few seconds, over

Roger 45543, this is Burtonwood Tower. Liverpool Control advises they have no known traffic in Control Zone and you are cleared into the Control Zone, over

45543 to Burtonwood Tower, Roger I am now completely VFR at 1,700 feet
Burtonwood Tower, Roger. You are cleared to make a VFR approach. Advise tower before

you encounter instrument conditions. For your information the Burtonwood Range may be used for homing purposes only on 214 kcs, over

Roger, 214 kcs

That was the last contact with the aircraft. At around 4.45 p.m. on 7 January a number of eyewitnesses in the village of Garstang heard a roar of engines as the aircraft broke through the cloud. Within seconds it had struck the face of Stake House Fell, a few miles to the north-east of the village, and exploded. Co-pilot 1st Lt. Lowell Wheaton Jr, Engineer Sgt Bernard J. Watkins and Radio Operator Cpl Norbert H. Theis died, along with the two passengers and pilot and, according to later accounts, a dog that had been on board. What made this tragedy even more keenly felt was the circumstances that had caused it. It transpired that the signal of a local radio mast had affected the C-54's radio compass, making the crew think they were still south of the airfield. In reality they had passed quite a few miles beyond to the north by the time of the crash. Wreckage still litters the site nearly sixty years later. January, however, had yet more lives to claim. On the 14th another C-54 crashed near Rhein-Main, killing three crew, and four days later a further C-54 put down east of Fassberg, killing the pilot.

Frank Watt AC1 at RAF Fassberg Station Sick Quarters was involved in recovering the bodies:

We had a few crashes, mostly through tiredness, and I recall two bad ones. One Skymaster fully loaded with coal took off and engines cut and it dropped like a stone off the runaway and blew up. Next day all the SSQ staff were out picking up the human pieces and bagging them. I was nineteen years old and had never seen a dead body before. I picked up a large piece of rib cage still with the nipple on it hanging from a tree, for days after I was upset and sick. The other one was a returning plane which did not make the runaway and hit a fence, it blew up and all the crew were killed. A sad postscript to all this was that my boss the Dental Officer was called out to cut the gold rings from the pilots fingers using our dental gear. I often wonder what one mother thought of the Berlin Airlift when all she had of her son was a couple of broken gold rings, a sad end to a bad day.

Near misses were also becoming a regular occurrence as W.C. (Dub) Southers, Flight Engineer with 41st Troop Carrier Squadron explains:

In the early days of the airlift the C-54s were not equipped with radar IFF and the ground control approach system was in its early stages. There was no way the GCA operators could completely identify the target on the screen. Most of the landings at Celle were straight in approaches. On one of our attempts to land we were informed that we were on the glide path and were to continue our landing approach. When we were told we were over the end of the runway, we broke out of the fog, but there was no runway in sight and there were lights all around us and in front of us, nearly at the same height. Needless to say it was urgent to get some altitude as soon as possible. The pilot then returned to the regular traffic pattern for another approach and to a safe landing.

The Royal Air Force did not fair much better. Dakota KN491 crashed just inside the Russian zone near Lübeck, again in bad weather, this time killing one crew and five civilians, including one child. On this occasion the Dakota, piloted by E.J. Eddy, was on a return trip from Gatow. After delivering coal the aircraft had been quickly turned round, loaded with twenty-two passengers, a number of whom were children, and then took off at 5.00 p.m. for the return trip to Lübeck. As the aircraft entered the last leg of the flight it experienced severe turbulence. Even under GCA control the aircraft proved difficult to handle in the conditions, and eventually it struck several trees before going down in a forest. Fires quickly started and although some passengers and crew escaped, six did not. A further three who were pulled from the wreckage succumbed to their injuries a few days later.

Naturally, the Soviet authorities made great capital from the situation, especially since a child had been killed. A number of Soviet-sponsored newspapers carried the story of the crash on their front page. 'Airbridge = Deathbridge' and 'One Dakota Less – One Lesson more' were some of the more inflammatory headlines. Of course, as the aircraft had come down in the Soviet zone the survivors had been 'cared' for by the local Army unit. Interrogations ensued before, surprisingly in the case of the German passengers, they were allowed across the border.

Future plans

January also saw the Royal Air Force committing itself to a long term airbridge, possible lasting a further two or three years. The directive issued by the Headquarters of BAFO noted that Plainfare would continue; however, major modifications would be needed if it was to remain successful. Such was the conviction of the British to continue that plans were being formulated at the highest levels.

On 27 January 1949 Brian Robertson wrote to Ernest Bevin outlining the proposed requirements for supplying the city during the winter of 1949–50. Bevin had requested a forecast on the 18th and was duly furnished with quite a telling report. The information not only indicates the enormity of the operation, it also shows the depth of the problem.

Industrial output

Industrial output and the ability to export a proportion of it were considered essential to Berlin's future. If the city could produce then it could raise the standard of living and levels of self-esteem. This was clearly advantageous to the success of the airlift. If the population could be kept going it would resist any temptation to side with the East:

> The broad conclusion reached is that, in order to maintain the morale of the population of
> the Western Sectors through a second year of blockade, measures must be taken to provide
> for certain appreciable improvements in the conditions of daily lift and for a reasonably

high level of employment. In the latter respect a 36-hour week has been taken as reasonable in the circumstances, except for the building trade in which activity will necessarily be limited.[1]

This would not come cheap. Robertson proposed a daily average of 9,500 short tons from April to October, followed by 7,500 in the winter:

> To increase the lift to the figures referred to above may well necessitate the development of a new or reserve base in the British Zone and further development of the airfields in Berlin. It will also be necessary to make considerable improvements in the domestic accommodation at airfields in the British Zone in order to bring them up to the standard required for long term operations.[2]

A few days later, Command Sections (Plans) of the British Element, Control Commission for Germany (Berlin) issued its airlift requirements up to 31 March 1950. The Top Secret document assumed that the level of blockade would continue at the same level with no Soviet interference in the air corridors. It was predicted that the winter would be a 'moderately severe one', and that the power station at Berlin West was still non-operational. Further public transport around the city was also seen as essential to maintaining the morale of the population. In yet another example of the complexity of the Berlin Blockade, public transport was operated by both East and West:

> The population depends on the S-Bahn, U-Bahn and trams for movement in the Western Sectors. The latter two are worked on the current provided by the Western Sectors, whereas the former is run on current provided by the Russians. If the S-Bahn service was suspended, an alternative plan requiring an additional 60 tons of coal and 2 tons of diesel a day is ready.

Transport was not the only critical element to morale: potatoes, it would appear, came a close second. In fact the report suggested that 'the German is a big eater of potatoes'; unfortunately they were not thriving on the dehydrated variety. The point was that fresh potatoes weighed considerably more than dehydrated ones and as water was freely available in the city it made sense to fly in the powder. However, dehydrated potatoes were not entirely to the taste of such a discerning audience and, to make matters worse, it had not been possible to issue any fresh potatoes through the winter of 1948–49. As such it was, 'considered essential, therefore, by next winter to issue a proportion of fresh potatoes'. To give some sense of perspective to this seemingly easy request it was estimated that to feed the Western sectors with a third of its ration in fresh potatoes, around 45,000 tons would need to be flown in over five months.

---

[1] Robertson 27 January 1949 (BT 217/2270).
[2] Robertson 27 January 1949 (BT 217/2270).

Coal posed another problem. As the winter had been fairly mild the population had managed on just ½cwt per household up until January. A winter of standard severity would require around 4cwt as a safe measure. This could be topped up with wood as, 'A fair quantity of standing timber will still be available for felling without de-forestation reaching the danger level for soil-erosion.' However, the deposits of brown coal in the local area were not considered worth exploiting, as local timber would have to be used for pit-props, roofing and flooring if mining went ahead. There was an alternative to coal consumption – kerosene. The beauty of kerosene is that it has twice the heat efficiency of coal and so only half the amount is needed. Estimates put the required oil stoves at 500,000 and, whilst they could be flown in, it was thought that 'These can be made in Berlin – providing that the firms concerned have a guarantee that the kerosene will be available to cause a ready sale for the stoves.'

Other items discussed included the need to increase the daily tonnage of newsprint to 35 tons as technical literature was now required by the University. To complement the airlift of fresh food, further areas of the city would be brought into production and so 6,000 tons of fertilizer and 600 tons of seeds were needed. One additional Dakota for transporting civilians, especially German businessmen, would also be required and all this with just the capacity supplied by the existing airfields.

However, issues within the city itself were only one side of the story. The entire infrastructure of the British mission would need to be radically upgraded to keep the efficiency at established levels. At the time, many of the aircrew had had little time off and even fewer had been stood down for any length of time. In fact, Transport Command had all but abandoned training for any other world route, and the entire organisation was beginning to show signs of collapse. Furthermore, the groundcrew and support staff were also in need of serious re-organisation as young National Serviceman Neville Cox explains:

> I started my National Service early 1948 expecting to serve 18 months. After training I was posted to RAF Finningley flying school as an aircraft electrician. When the Berlin crisis happened we knew how the situation was developing from the news. Suddenly one afternoon the whole station was ordered to assemble on parade in 3 hangar at 3.30 p.m. We duly gathered and the station C.O. started to speak. "At 3.30 today the prime minister or the minister for war will make the following announcement in the House of Commons." My heart hit my boots, I thought 'we are at war with Russia'. He went on to say that links with Berlin had been blocked and it was decided to supply Berlin by air. The consequence was that all RAF demobilisation was stopped and national servicemen would serve for two years. I was not concerned it was so far away anyhow but there were airmen actually 'clearing' the station ready for demob in a day or two. They had to stay as well. I will never forget that day.

The problem was that some of these men and women would, very soon, have to be released and they could only be replaced by trained individuals. The accommodation would also require serious work if it was to be used intensively. Flight Mechanic John Dury with 297 Squadron (Hastings) described the accommodation at Schleswigland:

A refuelling crew working on Hastings at RAF Schleswigland in the winter of 1949. (With thanks to John Dury)

This was in a building on the edge of the airfield with large sleeping areas which were basic, crowded and with little privacy (originally used during the war by the Luftwaffe personnel), but toilet and washing facilities were quite adequate. The canteen was a short distance away.

Of course, working though the winter was not the most pleasant of experiences and at Schleswigland, just about as far north as you could go in Germany, the conditions could be dangerous. Flt Mech. Dury noted later:

Hastings Squadron 47 and 297 (ours) had a number of ground crews, each consisted of 5 people; an engineer in charge, a flight mechanic (engines), flight mech.(airframes),also two German helpers, usually ex-servicemen. The crew were responsible for ensuring that directly the aircraft had completed its flight from Berlin, it was refuelled, inspected and serviced, then loaded with 7 tons of coal. It was then ready for its next flight. Our crew experienced very few snags, except for bad weather grounding aircraft, and lost very few flying hours that were available. At times, snowfalls and extremely cold causing severe icing up of aircraft control surfaces that had to be de-iced before take-off. Ground crew were responsible for climbing onto wings with de-icing sprays. More than one mechanic was injured after falling twelve feet or so during this operation.

'Plumbers'

Naturally, when aircraft required deeper servicing than could be provided on the line, they returned to Britain. The myriad of different types being used complicated the issue and did not allow for centralised servicing. Subsequently aircraft were dispersed across a number of bases and contractor sites.

Transport Command's main DC-3 spares base had been located at RAF Honington, Suffolk, shortly after the USAAF had vacated the base in 1946. Known as the 'Plumber Flight', Honington owned six Dakotas that constantly tramped around Europe delivering spares. An estimated 400–500 tons were delivered in an attempt to keep the aircraft operational. On more than one occasion the depot at RAF Burtonwood, operated by the USAF, had to be raided. When it was clear that more aircraft were needed for Plainfare, those Dakotas in storage around the UK were regenerated for flight. In all, over seventy that had been stood out in all weathers underwent refurbishment with civil companies taking the lead. Scottish Aviation at Prestwick, who had been refurbishing aircraft for the civil market, now took on Government work. Airwork Ltd worked on components at their Eastleigh base near Southampton, the airfield at Sywell, Northamptonshire, was used for major servicing and Field Aircraft Services refurbished engines at their Croydon site and carried out aircraft maintenance at Tollerton near Nottingham.

Bill Ball, Fitter with 77 Squadron, remembers:

> It wasn't long before the Daks were being used well past their major servicing dates. When they were finally released they flew back to RAF Oakington. The dust created from carrying coal and flour got under the floorboards and as the majority of control cables were under there, caused some problems. Many pilots complained of sluggish controls.

Avro Yorks were serviced at RAF Abingdon and, on occasion, at RAF Lyneham. They too brought their own problems. The type had been developed from the Avro Lancaster as a stop-gap transport aircraft, and as such was nearing obsolescence. The sturdy nature of the airframe allowed the York to withstand the additional fatigue imposed during the airlift. However, many were grounded due to a lack of spares, especially windscreens. Conditions at Wunstorf often varied considerably. Ankle-deep mud would turn to concrete, which would then turn to fine dust. And when it started to rain aircrew naturally turned on the aircraft windscreen wipers. For the first few traverses it was like rubbing a sheet of sandpaper over the window. Very soon the entire supply of windscreens and wipers had been used up.

Len Guyatt, an Air Radar Fitter stationed at Wunstorf, remembers a problem to which the Avro York was prone:

> To refuel the aircraft, check the upper surface or aerials you had to climb onto the top of the aircraft. Behind the engineers position was a small ladder up to a hatch. You released the hatch to get outside. Problem was the hatch was fiddly to refit and on occasion it was not done properly. Now the Yorks left Wunstorf with 8 or 9 tons of coal plus a big fuel load. One day I remember an aircraft taking off and the hatch coming adrift as it did so. It promptly knocked

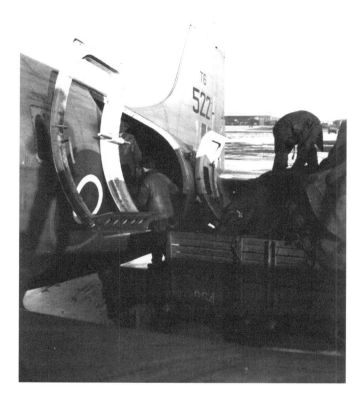

More coal is loaded onto TG522 Hastings. The crew were bitterly disappointed when they discovered the intended cargo for their brand new aircraft. (With thanks to John Dury)

off the central vertical stabiliser, I think it was only made of wood and fabric. Well the aircraft couldn't land with all that cargo on board so it circled the Steinhuder Meer, a lake nearby, whilst the crew flung all the coal sacks out so they could land. I wonder if any are still in the lake!

In 1948, 47 Squadron had moved to RAF Dishforth, North Yorkshire, and in the process became the first squadron to operate the Hastings. On 1 November the aircraft was on detachment to Berlin. By April 1949 the majority of servicing was being done at RAF Topcliffe, a few miles north of Dishforth. Naturally, both air and groundcrews were proud of their new aircraft, and were more than a little put out to discover they too would be hauling coal. As with other aircraft types, minor servicing was undertaken back at base.

Harlan Senior, National Service instrument fitter at Topcliffe from 1948, remembers the aircraft when they were first delivered:

I was at Topcliffe as NS Instrument Basher on repair and rectification when these beautiful brand spanking new aircraft arrived complete with civilian technicians carrying out modifications, and when the aircraft took off for the Berlin Airlift the civilians went too. I remember the smell of 'newness' and also the coating of coal dust on everything when aircraft returned for servicing, after carrying coal to Berlin, and after a short time we looked more like coal miners.

The Hastings aircraft was considered reliable from the outset, and the type rarely went unserviced. Spares were initially a problem as the aircraft was in production right through the airlift period; however, suppliers soon recognised the benefit of producing extra parts – courtesy of lucrative extra Government contracts. AC Senior describes the 'Fairy' (instrument) servicing team:

> The servicing team was limited to Instruments and the two of us, my partner was usually a WAAF, hard working and reliable, we had a Flight Sergeant or Sergeant to oversee our work and sort out the snags, again two first class NCOs. The Electricians again were usually two, Radar one, and Radio one. Topcliffe was very busy during my time there during the Airlift, and the Hastings always seemed a very reliable aircraft.

Working with a member of the WAAF brought with it some unexpected benefits:

> The young lady WAAF I worked with was engaged to a Sergeant Engine Fitter, and sometimes we needed high steps and other gear to get to the engines, and of course any requests for the loan of same from engine or airframe fitters were greeted with the usual, ahem!! 'polite refusal'. So when I could not get any help, I used to retire from view, and Muriel, my partner, would turn on her feminine charms to her fiancée for help, and out he would come from his hangar office to detail 'You and you put those steps in position for this LACW', so this was done and then I would appear and we get on with the job!

Gap

Despite all the uncomfortable aspects of spending January away from home in less than palatial surroundings, and in the depths of winter, the crews from both countries ensured the airlift did not falter. That month the highest monthly tonnage so far was set at an astronomical 171,960 tons. Clearly, the writing was now on the wall and Stalin decided to answer a set of questions the International News Service had submitted to him. Usually such requests never resurfaced or were answered with propagandist statements. This time it was slightly different as Stalin made no reference to currency reform, one of the instrumental issues surround the blockade; a rivet had just fallen out of the Iron Curtain and the question now was how to exploit the weakness. At the fledgling United Nations, Dr Philip Jessup, the US delegate, discussed Stalin's currency omission with Jacob Malik, the Soviet delegate. Had it been significant or even intentional?

Throughout February the pace continued. It was announced in the first week that Celle was to be considerably enlarged to almost double the capacity, then already over 1,000 tons per day, and Tegel was to receive a second runway. Western reports placed the Tegel runway upgrade as a move to increase flights into the city to an average 900 per day; however, there was an ulterior motive. It had been very quickly recognised that if Tegel continued to take the hammering it was under the whole thing would need to be rebuilt; a second runway was clearly needed. Gatow, meanwhile, was preparing for its third, and

On 18 February 1949, the airlift's millionth ton was loaded onto an RAF York at Wunstorf and flown to Gatow.

the construction of a third was underway at Tempelhof. It was during this month that the first million-ton milestone was passed.

The millionth

On Friday 18 February an Avro York took off from RAF Wunstorf en route to Gatow. On board were five crew: Squadron Leader Eric Best, pilot; Flying Officer Derek Jeffery, navigator; Signaller II John Fulker; Flight Lieutenant Kenneth Ryall, engineer and, acting as second pilot, Air Marshal Williams, Air Officer in Chief of the British Air Forces of Occupation. And this was not the only important item on board. Somewhere in among the rather confusing mixture of load 309, which that day included raisins, meat, potatoes, butter and hay, was the 1 millionth ton delivered into the city.

Landing at just after 4.00 p.m., involving a fog-bound flight, the aircraft taxied onto the hard standing where it was met by a small crowd of dignitaries. The city Magistrat had dispatched Herr Klingelhofer to meet the crew armed with a speech:

> The people of Berlin are aware that their whole life, their strength and the power of their resistance has depended on the airlift since the beginning of the blockade. For eight months it has prevented their starvation, enabled them to live, to work and to maintain the civilization of Berlin, which will be defended at all costs.

He then turned to Air Marshal Williams, announcing:

> I beg you sir, to pass our gratitude to all persons involved in the airlift and to those who love peace. We will never forget it.

Naturally, the airlift couldn't have it all its own way, and the winter weather soon made flying so difficult that operations were almost totally suspended for a few days. On 20 February just twenty-two flights made it through to the city, delivering 205.5 tons. Helpfully, the weather stations reported on the twenty-first that, 'yesterday was the foggiest day since November 1946. Berlin resembled a laundry room and traffic moved at a snail's pace.' Stating the obvious aside, weather reporting was now becoming increasingly accurate. By now the British forecasting network was being complemented by corridor flights of B-29 weather ships. This had a two-fold effect; more accurate − real time − prediction, and it didn't hurt to let the Soviets see the aircraft from the ground. However, reducing the flight totals now had an effect like placing more tension on a spring, as soon the tonnage record was to be smashed yet again:

Airlift Carries 7,639 Tons In The Fourth Straight Big Day

Proclaimed by the *Task Force Times*, the article went on to say that:

> HQ CALTF, Feb. 25 - striking at the Berlin blockade with the greatest continuous high tonnage streak in its history, the airlift delivered 7,639.7 tons in 879 flights for the 24-hour period ending at noon today. It was the fourth consecutive day of more than 7,300 tons production. Today's tonnage was second only to the 7,897 tons hauled in 905 flights Feb. 23rd, and marked the fourth day in a row that Operation Vittles has exceeded its air force today (Sept.18) peak of 6,988 tons. Other high points this week were 7,513.9 tons on George Washington's birthday and the 7,301.3 tons yesterday. Barring the weather which could force virtually a complete cessation for the remainder of the week a new seven daily record was assured.[3]

And assured it was as February, traditionally one of the worst months of the year, produced in the last week a record lift of 44,612 tons. Clearly the airlift had now won, it was just a matter of getting the Soviets to admit defeat.

The consistent increase in flights began to take its toll on the aircraft, and it was not long before a rethink on how first line maintenance and repairs were to be carried out.

---

[3] The *Task Force Times*, Saturday 26 February.

At Fassberg, the maintenance depots were reorganised so that as much fixing of snags as possible could be carried out undercover. This also allowed for major inspections if Burtonwood had problems. Operations at Celle were covered by much the same servicing. However, cutting corners during servicing was often a dangerous and expensive way of saving time; 'Dub' Southers described one such incident:

> One night while performing maintenance on my plane, the airplane in front of mine had completed their maintenance and decided to power check their engines. There were two men in the cockpit, each one proceeded to run a power check at the same time, instead of each one running up one engine, and then the other. Each decided to test both the engines on their side at the same time. It so happened that both men reached full power at the same time, the airplane jumped the chocks, and started towards the plane in front of them. The man in the pilot seat quickly turned the nose wheel to the left, the wing of their plane struck the tail of the plane in front of them. Heavy damage was sustained on both aircraft. Official ruling was that there was air in the brake lines. I don't think the brakes were set. As soon as this happened the two men had jumped out of the aircraft and started messing with the brakes on their machine.

On occasion servicing the aircraft was the easy part, finding it in the first place was the hard bit. Val Spaven, AC First Class, Flt Mech. with 77 Squadron Dakotas remembers the winters well:

> The dispersals of the DC-3s were not regimented and you had to drive around looking for the aircraft to be refuelled, at night this was hopeless with only a Woolworth's torch to find the right aircraft number. We worked long shifts on a 24 hour system which meant sometimes you had lunch at midnight. Two miles north from the runway was the Russian sector, we quickly forgot about this. Everything went well until we struck winter where temperatures dropped to below 0°, the Northern Lights were good to see but not the snow! The winter was a bad one but nothing stopped flying. We were issued with Russian fur hats, thick navy socks, Wellington boots and leather jackets.

Life further north was no better. John Dury worked the Hastings line at Schleswigland and remembers some of the hazards of the German winter:

> Refuelling Hastings aircraft necessitated ground crew climbing out onto the wings where the filler connections were situated, and this being on a sloping surface approx. 12 feet from the ground was extremely hazardous [wearing rubber boots] when the wings were coated in ice during the very cold weather conditions often experienced during the winter of 1948/9. More than one injury was caused by airmen falling.
>
> In fact one of the main causes of grounded aircraft was severe icing up of control surfaces, this again required ground crew walking over wings covered in ice and spilled fuel, spraying de-icing fluid over the elevators and ailerons etc. immediately before the aircraft could take-off enabling the transport of another 7 tons of coal to Berlin.

C-54s at Tempelhof in February 1949. By now the Soviets were opening dialogue in an attempt to save face. (Air Force Photo)

Mad March?

On 5 March the airlift received one of its most important visitors – Clement Attlee, the British Prime Minister. Attlee visited a number of airlift installations, meeting military and civil dignitaries including Professor Ernst Reuter and the British Military Governor Major-General Bourne. Attlee later described the airlift as 'one of the wonders of the world'. It had become so partly due to the competitive spirit that Tunner had initiated between squadrons and bases, especially within the USAF.

Stories of large tonnage efforts, crews flying round the clock and aircraft clocking up enormous hours in short periods graced the *Task Force Times*, the daily bulletin of the Combined Airlift Task Force. This single-sheet publication was very effective on a number of levels. It gave all participating units, and more importantly the Soviets, a running total through the 'Howgozit Board', whilst informing those on temporary duty of when they were likely to go home. It also became the quickest way of transmitting technical instructions and changes to flight crew orders. However, the *Task Force Times* was most effective when used to throw down the gauntlet, as exemplified by this extract:

British Prime Minister Clement Attlee described his visit to Gatow as, 'one of the wonders of the world'.

Fassberg Crew Reports 26-minute Turn-around

Fassberg, March 25 – A turn-around time of 26 minutes from touchdown to takeoff has been recorded here. An airlift plane, landing at 11:48, took off again fully loaded at 12:14, officials reported.

An impressive set of figures and one published just to spur on the groundcrews and loaders at Celle. It is also probable that this was no more than a generalisation designed to build rivalry between the two bases, as there is no mention of aircraft number, crew, or anyone attached with the record. With such competition it was inevitable that flight crews would be exposed to some dangerous situations. Flying C-54s 'Dub' Southers experienced many such incidents:

> The stacking of planes was not allowed in Berlin, but at times this will be necessary in extreme weather conditions at our home bases if aircraft did not land on the first approach. On one occasion we had flown all day and had not been out of the fog or clouds at any time during that day. Upon approaching Celle, we were directed to go to a specific altitude and circle. Planes were separated by 500 feet and as the ones below were able to land we could drop down 500 feet. As we were circling our plane and another plane broke the clouds at the same time and were heading directly towards each other, both pilot spotted each other immediately and were able to take extreme corrective action, thus avoiding a midair collision by a few feet.

Cartoonists kept up with events in the *Task Force Times*. This one is by Jake Schuffert, a regular American contributor.

On 15 March 46 Group HQ finally moved from Bückeberg to Luneberg. The staffing levels at Bückeberg had steadily increased since the previous December, and now the HQ team were consistently overloading the poor communications network. Luneberg offered more office space and a more central location, making communications with the airlift bases easier. The whole move was in advance of the amalgamation of 46 Group HQ with the British Air Forces of Occupation. Tragedy struck the British contingent again when, on the 22nd, Dakota KJ970 came down in the Russian zone, killing all three crew. It had been returning to Lübeck at night when, during the Blind Approach Beam System (BABS) approach, it flew into the ground. This, along with the Skyways York crash at Gatow and Lancashire Aircraft Corporation Halton at Schleswigland, made the week ending 22 March one of the worst months for the British.

Significantly, things were starting to move in Moscow. All had been quiet on the United Nations front: it had been a month since the discussion between Malik and Jessup as to Stalin's intentions, and then out of the blue came a sign. On 5 March Stalin replaced two top policy officials, Foreign Minister Vyacheslav Molotov, with Andrey Vishinsky and Minister of Foreign Trade Anastas Mikoyan, with Mikhail A. Menshikov.

Flight Lieutenant 'Frosty' Winterbottom kept the British end up with offerings such as these.

The replacement of Molotov was significant as it signaled a change in Soviet foreign policy. Ten days later Jessup received the news that Stalin had indeed omitted the currency issue, and by the 21st it was clear the Soviets were willing to lift the blockade in exchange for a meeting with the Council of Foreign Ministers. Stalin also wanted the counter-blockade to be lifted and the proposed formation of West Germany to be put on hold. A few hours before the meeting on the 21st, Washington decided it was time to inform the British and French Governments of what had been going on. Naturally London, and especially the Foreign Office, was upset by the situation, but not Bevin. Being a negotiator for the unions he saw an opportunity when it arose and this was just such an opportunity.

With agreement now possible and the weather showing signs of relenting, an air of complacency began to set in, especially when the month passed with yet another record total, this time 196,160.7 tons. What was to come would make this figure seem a drop in the ocean as the Allies planned the *coup de grâce* for the Soviet blockade.

The Easter parade

By April it was clear that the airlift had won. The air armada at this time numbered 154 British service and civilian aircraft, with 225 American C-54s and a further seventy-five undergoing maintenance at Burtonwood. The Combine Air Lift Task Force had done a superb job. On 7 April a Fassberg C-54 had completed the entire round trip in one hour fifty-seven minutes, and that included the fifteen-minute, thirty-second turn-round. But some in command were still not happy and were worried that complacency could set in,

Tunner devised the Easter parade to check complacency had not set in. 12,940 tons later the Soviets were ready to throw in the towel.

eventually affecting performance. Gen. Tunner decided that with Easter just a few days away, 'we'd have an Easter parade of aeroplanes, an Easter Sunday present for the people of Berlin!' after discussions with his team Tunner decided on a quota of around 10,000 tons – 50 per cent higher than had been achieved before. There was logic behind his thoughts. During the war the supply route over the Himalayas often ran 'one-day Derby'; the tonnage the day after naturally tailed off as everyone relaxed, but it always levelled out higher than previously. Eventually the idea was accepted by Washington and the push was on. Base commanders were told to keep a close eye on the serviceability of aircraft. Those that were carrying snags would need to be sorted before the big day. Meanwhile, coal stocks at the air heads ensured that the chosen cargo, coal, was ready in sufficient quantities to pull off the biggest daily tonnage flown in history. Just before noon on 15 April the predicted loads were chalked up at airbases across West Germany to many a raised eyebrow. By noon the following day, the Easter parade had delivered a staggering 12,940 tons on 1,398 flights. Colonel Bill Bunker, head of Army Transportation, summed up the situation for the press, eloquently stating that, 'You guys have hauled the equivalent of 600 cars of coal into Berlin today, have you ever seen a fifty-car coal train? Well, you've just equalled twelve of them!'

This superlative effort turned in some interesting statistics. A total of 3,946 landings and take-offs were made during the twenty-four-hour period. Over 80 per cent of all aircraft were committed and in some cases 100 per cent utilization was achieved. An aircraft was landing at Tegel, Tempelhof or Gatow every fifty-five seconds and during their time in the air crews made 39,640 radio contacts, averaging one every four seconds. The last C-54 to carry an Easter load from Rhein-Main had inscribed on its load in hurriedly applied red paint – 'RECORD TONNAGE 12,941 FLTS 1,383'. The Easter parade demonstrated the Allies' ability to operate high density air traffic; they had smashed their own limit and now appeared invincible. And after the process, as Tunner predicted, the average tonnage increased from 6,729 to 8,893 tons per day.

Such high density flying was only possible as long as there was no 'log jam' at the Berlin airfields, and so, in order to ensure that this didn't happen, aircraft were allowed to make the return trip carrying a certain amount of snags, snags that would have grounded the aircraft anywhere else. One of the most common problems with the C-54 was the constant use of the starter due to the short-hop flights. Inevitably these would 'drop out', meaning that the only way to start the engine would be to windmill the prop once in the air – effectively 'bump starting' it. The only problem with that was that a 'windmilling' prop caused lots of drag on the side it was positioned, violently yawing the nose port or starboard. Taking off on three engines also meant the aircraft needed a longer runway and would not climb as readily. And as if that wasn't enough the aircraft had to take off with the prop feathered (with the thinnest part to the direction of flight) until the airspeed was over a certain point, or this too would cause loads of drag. Two such incidents at RAF Gatow that almost ended in tragedy are described here by Flt Eng. Southers of the 41st Troop Carrier Squadron based at RAF Celle:

The pilot of the aircraft insisted that it was not necessary to feather the prop, as it would windmill way before we reached take-off speed. I informed him that it would not windmill before take-off and that it will be a tremendous drag, and to make matters worse it was an outboard engine. At that point I was overruled and told we were going to take-off without feathering the prop. The takeoff runway at Gatow was blacktop part of the way and the remainder was PSP. We started our takeoff roll and had reached a minimum takeoff speed and at that moment the plane reach the PSP part of the runway. The engine had not started to windmill and with the excessive drag the nosewheel slipped sharply to the right and the pilot pulled the plane off the ground. I pulled the gear immediately. The pilot then panicked and reached the throttles as he was going to cut the power and set the aircraft back down. At this point the co-pilot, an ex-bomber pilot, took over the controls and managed to avoid a crash. Once we had become airborne the outboard engine started to windmill and the pilot assumed command of the plane. He instructed me to bring in the engine and then proceeded to push the throttle fully open, I thought the increase of power was going to roll the aircraft. Again the co-pilot took control and manage to straighten it up. With all of the manoeuvres we had made on takeoff we were out of the corridor when everything was finally straightened out. On the way back to the British Zone we broke out of the fog over a Russian airfield with hundreds of Yak fighters. This was one of the times that we went over the specified airspeed in order to get out from over the Russian Zone as quickly as possible.

Just a few days later:

The next time we had a starter failure in Berlin there was a storm in progress. We were able to obtain takeoff speed with plenty of room on the runway but the aircraft would not gain altitude. We got about 20 feet from the ground and it stayed at that altitude until we were most of the way across a lake that was at the end of the runway. On the other side of the lake

Successes on the lift were broadcast to the population using mobile units developed by Radio in the American Sector (RIAS). This unit is broadcasting in the British sector.

was a Russian military base. As we approached the base with less than normal takeoff altitude it was a very critical time for us, not knowing if we're going to get enough altitude to clear the base. Watching the Russian soldiers scatter, thinking we were going to crash into them was funny -- after we had time to think about it.

On 21 April the airlift celebrated its 300th day of operation with 927 aircraft carrying over 6,390 tons into the city. Professor Reuter said of the day, 'This achievement has fulfilled all our wishes. It will certainly make a great impression on those responsible for the blockade of Western Berlin.' The further expansion of RAF Gatow also started as the first sods were cut for the paved third runway. It had also become clear that the improved weather conditions were now allowing a comparable weekly tonnage to be flown in as had been previously brought in by rail. By 25 April the endeavour had indeed made a 'great impression' as the Soviet news agency Tass was openly talking of ways to lift the blockade.

'The Greatest Triumph'

Clearly, the secret talks between Malik and Jessup were now out, and the US State Department confirmed talks had been going on behind the scenes at the United Nations. Soviet ministers now tried one last time to manipulate the proposed peace. They reiterated that a condition of lifting of the blockade was the stalling of the creation of a West German state from the three allied zones but this demand fell on deaf ears. The two met again on 29 April in optimistic spirit; unfortunately the whole process hit the buffers and suddenly appeared in danger of de-railing. By now the meetings involved all four representatives and so when Malik and Jessup met, Jessup would not agree to any movement without his three allied counterparts being present. Malik, on the other hand, was furnished with a full and final agreement and was eager to accomplish settlement. The Soviets proposed a meeting of the Council of Foreign Ministers (CFM) sometime between 10 and 14 June and that all restrictions should be removed in the week prior to that. Why so long, queried Jessup? No firm agreement was forthcoming and agreement suddenly looked further away than ever.

Jessup, under instruction, wrote a strong note to Malik outlining the Allies position. It was important that the Soviets accept the start date of the traffic restrictions into Berlin as being 1 March 1948, lifting of the restrictions must be on 12 May 1949 and the CFM must meet by the end of the month. Surprisingly, Malik replied the following day and, having conceded every point, invited all the main UN delegates to a meeting on 4 May. And that was it. Agreement was swift. The following day press releases were issued – the blockade would end on the 12th. Naturally, in the run up to the 12th things were less than organised, and the Western governments viewed the announcement with an air of caution. Clay and the USAF both underpinned the airbridge and vowed to continue for the foreseeable future. Berlin could not be caught in the lurch again. Clay remarked that the current level of flights would be maintained until the pre-blockade stock of coal, around 200,000 tons, had been accumulated. The USAF also indicated they would not reduce manning levels of squadron strengths until it was absolutely clear that the Soviets did not intend to re-impose the blockade. The RAF, declared Bevin to the house, would also maintain its current level of deployment. He also told them he was to fly to Gatow to personally thank as many Operation Plainfare personnel as was possible.

Almost unseen through all this was the arrival at Rhein-Main of the United States Air Forces' latest transport aircraft, the Boeing C-97. Capable of carrying a 26-ton payload, this massive aircraft visited Tempelhof on the day the UN delegation met. It transpired that the aircraft was only carrying 10 tons, primarily due to safety concerns; however, it was clear that the C-97 demonstrated a new commitment to supplying the city from the air.

At 12.01 a.m. on 12 May the lights came back on, in some Western sectors at least, and the crossing points into the Soviet zone were unblocked. As the barriers were lifted so were the border checks; Soviet troops simply waved through traffic. Clearly there was no real point trying to hinder passage. Just over an hour later a British Military Train had also entered the Soviet zone heading for Berlin. Would life now return to normal, wondered the city's population? Or would the Soviets try a new method of repression? Reassuringly, the drone of allied aircraft continued.

Eleven

'In the Tug-of-War for Berlin, these people are the knot on the rope itself.'

As the battle to beat the blockade gathered pace, so did the fight for the hearts and minds of the citizens of Berlin. The struggle was multi-faceted. If they were to be successful then the Allies would have to beat the effects of Soviet intimidation, depression, creeping hunger and cold, boredom and the black market. This chapter covers those aspects and introduces some of the experiences of those stationed in and around the city at the time.

Police

The Soviet Military Authority (SMA) had instigated the creation of a new police force by the middle of May 1945. In line with other city organisations it was heavily controlled by the SMA through its new chief, Colonel Paul Markgraf. Markgraf had been a prisoner of war in the Soviet Union and later undertook communist training. Throughout the years between the end of the war and the airlift Markgraf ensured that the police stayed firmly under communist control, often ignoring the requests of the Kommandatura and later the Magistrat. Whilst the police contained factions of both East and West it was still strongly influenced by Markgraf who was, by 1948, in control of the Soviet sector.

As movement in the pre-blockade city was almost totally unrestricted, the Eastern sector police intimidated and kidnapped as many opponents of the SED as they possibly could. This shook the faith of the Berlin population as it appeared that the Western Allies were turning a blind eye to the situation. However, strong representations were being made at the Kommandatura, though unfortunately the proceedings were closed to the public making the process invisible. Things came to a dramatic head when Markgraf's men aided a mob that attacked the City Assembly, held in the Soviet sector. Shortly afterwards 240 police members were sacked for being non-SED as Markgraf streamlined the force into a pure communist organisation. The Magistrat could do nothing – it was the job of the Kommandatura to sack him, if four-power agreement could be reached over the issue.

On 26 July the Magistrat made a stand. With the backing of Reuter and Schroeder, acting mayor Friedensburg dismissed Markgraf by letter, accusing him of failure to control

Up until 2 August 1948 the police were a mixture of anti- and pro-communist groups. Eventually, the city Magistrat expelled the communist elements. From then on two forces presided over Berlin. (Presse-Remus)

his staff, lack of discipline and anti-social, un-German conduct. Police vice-president Stumm would take over. However, as with so much in Berlin politics it did not quite work out that way. Colonel Markgraf refused to acknowledge his dismissal, instead staying at his post. Kotikov supported him wholeheartedly, demanding that the usurper Stumm should be the one who was dismissed. By 2 August Berlin had two police forces, one allied to democratic principles, the other the instrument of the SMA, each accusing the other of theft as officers loyal to Stumm carried files across to the West.

Whilst the dispute had split the police it had also led to a potentially explosive situation. The Magistrat, who had the majority of its departmental offices in the Eastern sector, now looked increasingly like they would be shut down by the SED and communist movements. The West had offered sites in the more secure American sector but the assembly argued that no one should dismantle the Magistrat for the Soviets and so they stayed put.

Counter-blockade

The blockade was not all one way. The Western Allies quickly imposed a counter-blockade, primarily using sanctions, in an attempt to force the Russians' hands. This loose set of directives was poorly matched to the situation, but it was the Soviets' own communist ideals that were to make it effective. Food production suffered enormously in the years after the war and this was now hindered further by the creation of state-run cooperatives. Any machinery or seed had to be drawn from centralised pools and was thus difficult, if not impossible, to obtain. As the Western zones and those countries that had accepted the Marshall Plan started to invest back into agriculture, so the Eastern Bloc countries were stripped of their produce. This was a direct result of supplying the Russian sector of Berlin with attractive, inflated rations.

Industry fared little better. The aggressive reparations policy adopted by the Soviets meant that by the time of the airbridge over 60 per cent of the Soviet zone's manufacturing sector had been taken to Russia. And of that which remained, tooling, facilities and raw materials were in extremely short supply. If the firms did manage to produce anything they often lost up to 90 per cent of it, as it too was taken in reparations. On top of this there were many economic migrants across the porous zone frontiers, and of those who did stay nearly 400,000 were out of work whilst another 250,000 at least were in prison camps. And so the Allies' blockade did not need to be 100 per cent effective to cause the SMA, and ultimately Moscow, some serious headaches.

Of course there were ways around the sanctions. The first point was that nobody actually knew if the zonal border was indeed a border and whether it could be used legally as a customs frontier. It was a long, ragged line across former German territory and as such cut lots of roads, rail-lines, canals and minor tracks. It was the tracks that made the counter-blockade almost impossible to control. The Soviets made smuggling a lucrative pastime and even, on occasion, paid in dollars. And so all manner of goods and raw material headed into the Russian zone from the West, often on the nod of a guard at the zonal crossing point. Some trade did not need to cross the border at all, just go round it. Satellite countries would legally buy raw materials and then ship them into the Russian zone, whilst finished goods were still reaching Holland, Belgium and the like through the Baltic ports. But this was just a drop in the ocean, and it was not long before factories were closing down due to lack of components or raw materials. But the counter-blockade was only for show, another demonstration of 'tit-for-tat'. British economists were convinced that any economical damage would only be short-term, and eventually the Soviets would find other markets and supplies. This they did, and by doing so they strengthened the Iron Curtain.

'Whoever gives up Berlin, gives up a world and himself too.'

By early September it had become clear that a united front was needed from the Magistrat for it to remain effective. The communists were arguing that no meetings were being held, and therefore the assembly was clearly ineffective. If representations were not quickly made to the military government then maybe the Allies might start agreeing and remove what little freedom they had. And so, on 6 September the Assembly met, the police in the Soviet sector ominously refusing to give protection. The day before a broadcast by Assembly officials had pleaded with the population at large to allow the meeting to go ahead unmolested – it was like a red rag to a bull.

The meeting was scheduled for 12.00 p.m. and a large crowd had been gathering all morning. They were mainly communist activists intent on being heard. A number of Western police officers in plain clothes had accompanied the delegates to city hall and were ready in case of trouble, and trouble they got. No sooner had the meeting come to order than the mob stormed the building, smashing windows and ripping the main doors off, meanwhile, the Soviet sector police followed events from across the street. Once in the building the mob displaced the assembly, forcing them to flee; by now the Soviet sector police had also entered the building looking for the plain clothes police. Nineteen were found taking refuge in the US liaison officer's office and were quickly arrested. Several international pressmen were also set about, having their cameras smashed, and one was even thrown down the stairs. By now the remaining Western police had barricaded themselves in the British and French representatives' offices, and, short of burning the building down were unlikely to be dislodged in the near future. A cordon was thrown around the building, reinforced with Soviet troops. Eventually the French brokered a deal to extricate the remaining police under military escort – General Kotikov gave his personal guarantee on the safety of the men. No sooner had the vehicles got underway than they were stopped by Soviet soldiers and the Western police were removed at gunpoint. General Ganeval, the French officer in charge of the convoy, could not believe Kotikov had gone back on his word, and said so in a letter to him. The Russian accused the Frenchman of clearly being drunk and relations took a nose dive; France would never look at the Soviets' viewpoint over Berlin as being remotely credible again.

On Thursday 9 September nearly 300,000 people gathered in front of the shell of the Reichstag to demonstrate over the behaviour of the Soviet sector police and the Soviet Military Authority. In the opening address Franz Neumann, chairman of the Berlin Social Democratic Party, declared:

> The Berlin population is willing to make every sacrifice to maintain freedom in Berlin. In the struggle for Berlins democratic and civil liberties we need the assistance of all other nations. Berlin appeals to the world.

By 7 p.m. the crowd was dispersing without incident. It looked like a peaceful demonstration had finally taken place. The British sector commandant, General Herbert, had wanted to ban the meeting but Robertson had said no and proposed that troops be stationed discreetly out of sight, just in case. Clay had also held reservations, but this had not stopped him sanctioning RIAS to spread the word. It now looked like their fears were unfounded. Unfortunately, the day was not to end peacefully. Many of the protesters were from the Soviet sector and were passing back through the Brandenburg Tor when they noticed a truck full of police. Naturally they started to jeer and tension continued to mount to a point where some police started to point guns in to the crowd.

Then, a party of Russian soldiers drove past on their way to the Soviet War Memorial in the British sector and attracted a downpour of stones and bricks. In a flash there was shooting – whilst the troops were taking cover the police had opened up – one youth falling, mortally wounded. The crowd took cover, but when another of their number was shot, several climbed the Tor and ripped down the red flag. It hit the street below and was immediately torched. More shooting ensued and by now further Soviet soldiers had reached the scene. Machine guns at the ready, they pointed them into the crowd; a massacre was now possible. Luckily, a small contingent of British Military Police managed to get themselves between the crowd and the Russians and convinced the troops to stand down. In the end one civilian was killed and twenty-two injured, mostly from stones; it could have been much worse. The following day Markgraf condemned the speeches and conduct of the meeting as anti-communist and threatened serious consequences. Across the world Truman had been following events – the question of the 'bomb' arose more than once over the next few days.

Schwarzmarkt

Of course, large open areas of the city were not only used for political meetings and wherever groups of people encountered one another the black market flourished. Everything had a value, especially immediately after the war, and now in blockaded Berlin the ability to trade became increasingly important. It also became lucrative for the servicemen stationed on the airlift, as Air Traffic Controller Richard Wilson, billeted at Tempelhof explained:

> We sold cigarettes, coffee, chocolate, soap and items of military clothing. I never engaged in any large-scale black marketing, but I had a friend who did. In preparation for stepping out in the evening he would make the rounds of every room on our floor checking if anyone had anything to sell. The big thing was cigarettes.

And the black market was not just confined to the city; the whole of Europe was still operating some form of it in 1948–49. Wolfgang Samuel was a refugee from the Soviet zone living in a displaced persons' camp near Fassberg in 1948. His recollections were published as *German Child*; they reveal the less glamorous side of the *Schwarzmarkt*:

> Although everybody at one time or another had to fall back on the black market to obtain something to keep a family functioning, it was not a frivolous choice. It was usually an act driven by the necessity to stay alive, to maintain the body if not the soul. The family that did not count a young woman among its members was at a disadvantage in the day-to-day struggle for survival. The black market, the conditions of scarcity it thrived on, and our years of living in the rotting Wehrmacht barracks had stripped our lives to their bare essentials. Sex was so pervasive in our environment that it had become currency for us, the destitute. Personal humiliation had become our daily norm, and most of us didn't even recognize it for what it was anymore. The dirt of our lives was not only under our fingernails and on our

The black market with its currency of cigarettes flourished, and was even supported by the Soviets. However, if you operated independently you could soon attract the attention of the Soviet army and police, as this couple found out. (Dr Wolfram Kahle)

unwashed bodies but had penetrated our souls. Barracks life, poverty, untold needs, and the usurious market that satisfied them ate away at our self-respect. With the currency reform, I had hope that the black market would at least change its nature.

John Dury, flight mechanic with 297 Squadron (Hastings) at Schleswigland remembers:

German people were very friendly and many would give anything in exchange for soap, cigarettes, chocolate etc,. inevitably there were quite a few servicemen seeking medical help after being involved with local girls.

Surprisingly the black market, to a certain extent, was actively encouraged by the Soviet Military Authority. They ensured that their version was outside the jurisdiction of Markgraf and his police, but still encouraged him to close down ' illegal' operations run by Germans. The Soviets used nationals from other countries to front their operations and disguised them as shops with names such as 'Texta', 'Ballorex' and later the enigmatically named 'Handelsorganisation'. Here the key function was to collect Western marks at knock down prices. This proved a far more cost effective way of gaining the currency as the exchange rate between West and East had rapidly settled at 5 to 1.

In a city where two currencies were legal it was not long before one outstripped the other. The rate settled officially at around 5 to 1, some deals were many times that amount.

Displacing the displaced

As previously mentioned, Germany contained around 7 million Displaced Persons (DPs) at the beginning of the blockade, and around 5,000 were still located in the Western sectors of the city in 1949. The Allies, primarily the British, had been flying out the old, sick and undernourished children for some time – in fact during September and March 15,426 children were moved; however, it was always the intention to remove DPs as well. The early repatriation of DPs in 1945 had been largely successful, returning over 80 per cent to their countries of origin. To assist in this process a Soviet Repatriation Mission had been set up in Frankfurt under the command of Colonel Lazarev of the Russian Military Mission to the US zone. Now, four years later, the Mission had grown somewhat with a small garrison of 'officials' in post. Naturally the Soviets kept quiet when the blockade started and for a while were overlooked. But by the end of January 1949 it became clear that the mission was doing nothing towards the repatriation of displaced persons and they were requested to leave.

General Clay formally requested the removal of the Russians on the grounds that they had completed their task. Naturally, Colonel A. Lazarev, who was based in Berlin, was in no rush to withdraw his men and pointed out that without the authority of Moscow they would be staying put. Colonel Sterling of the Frankfurt military post was subsequently tasked with removing the Russians. Sterling pointed out that the mission was, in fact,

'This is the first group of 5,000 D.P.s that were flown from Tempelhof to Frankfurt.' Eventually they would be rehoused in a transit camp. Note the jam jars used as drinking glasses. (US Army Signals Corps)

illegally operating and it was the US Government's intention to remove all occupants,. They would, naturally, receive a 'suitable escort' to the border. With that a cordon was thrown around the compound and all telephone, gas and electricity was cut. Being the end of February this was very effective, and after a few days the order was issued for the troops to withdraw to the Soviet zone. On the night of 3 March the electricity was restored, and in time-honoured tradition the Soviets were allowed to burn all sensitive papers and load as much as possible onto their trucks before being escorted to the border. Not surprisingly the SMA expelled the US mission from their zone on the same day – they left with more dignity.

Displaced Persons in the city began to be flown out to Frankfurt and Wunstorf, and from there they were placed into new camps until they could be re-housed. Unfortunately, as numbers increased so conditions became unbearable. In January 1949 Rudolf Kipp shot a thirty-seven-minute film *Report on the Refugee Situation in January 1949* for the Control Commission for Germany (British Element), documenting life in the camps. Kipp discovered that compounding the already cramped conditions was the influx of refugees fleeing across the border from the Soviet zone. The guards on the British side were unwilling to turn back the human traffic and readily allowed asylum seekers in, whilst the Soviets, mindful of the headache it was causing the West, initially allowed people through. That was until they realised that a great many engineers, doctors and other necessary professions were also making a break for the West. The refugee camps were a mixture

Soviet troops leave the Repatriation Mission in Frankfurt after just over a week without power or heating. It was February. (US Army Photograph)

of structures, including allied prisoner of war camps and military barracks. There were hundreds spread across Germany and Kipp concentrated on those at Schleswig-Holstein, Niedersachsen, Uelzen, Ehndorf and Nordrhein-Westfalen.

Once at the camp the refugee was registered, fed and de-loused. After they had been assigned accommodation the interview process began. Officially known as the 'Admission to the West' procedure, the applicants, as they had now become, were subjected to a series of interrogations. These included racial background, ethnicity, religion, profession, activity during the war, number of family members and, most importantly for those who had recently crossed the border, reasons for leaving. Naturally, any Germans not able to present de-Nazification papers stood little chance of remaining in the West, but generally the system was ad hoc and a lot of innocent people spent years under suspicion in the Eastern zone, and later East German state, after being returned across the border. Their plight did not go unnoticed.

Len Guyatt, AC1 Air Radar Fitter, RAF Wunstorf, recalled that:

On the few days off we got every so often we used to go to the local town. One day me and my mate hitch hiked to Hannover. No mean feat as there wasn't much traffic around. We eventually got a lift in a Red Cross truck. The driver told us it was their job to drive up and down the autobahn picking up DPs and taking them to camps. We gave away all our cigarettes that day.

Ehndorf Camp near Neumunster. These were the conditions most Displaced Persons experienced throughout the late 1940s. (From the film *Report on the Refugee Situation*, January 1949)

Main Living Quarters in Uelzen Camp. Overcrowding meant the threat of disease was always present. Some stayed in the camps for years. (From the film *Report on the Refugee Situation*, January 1949)

There were always vast convoys of trucks from Hannover heading for Wunstorf and as they passed through the gates an army of DPs would appear from the camp down the road. I specifically remember one chap on a unicycle of all things. They look poor. After they had unloaded the trucks into the various storage sheds on the base they made their way back to the camp.

Severance

After the events in front of the Reichstag it was clear that democratic assemblies would no longer feature in Eastern Berlin, if not the entire Eastern zone. For a while some ministers continued to go to the city hall, but their number dwindled and, eventually, they too gave up. On 3 December the SED elected a new Magistrat, replacing all those with ties to the old regime with communist sympathisers. Two days later the Western sectors conducted their own municipal elections, Ernst Reuter's SED was now firmly returned in a majority position. The Christian Democratic Party lost seats primarily since they had requested caution over currency reform in the interests of preserving the unity of the city. In the current climate of near anarchy this had been seen as a point of weakness, and what the populace needed was strong direction. Reuter ensured that both the CDU and Liberal parties retained an active share in the administration of the Western sectors, citing that all should be involved in the democratic governance of their side of Berlin. They now set about building an efficient and reliable administrative structure, excluding any influences from the East.

Winter

> This winter, for the first time since Napoleon's day, the weather could tip the balance of power in Europe. The lethal coldness of their capital could drive Berliners into the Russians' arms for fuel, for groceries – and for good.[1]

This was declared by an article in a December issue of the *Picture Post* in 1948. Winter, both sides realised, was make or break in the battle for control of the city. It was clear that there would be great hardship for the Western sectors, and the Soviets hoped that this alone would be enough to drive the population into their arms. Travel restrictions around the city were light, primarily because Soviet sector businesses needed to run just the same as those in the West, and at this time people were still travelling the length and breadth of the city to their offices. There was also an underlying reason for 'free' travel. Any Western citizen could free themselves of the hardships of the blockade diet simply by registering for rations in the Soviet sector. Luckily, very few did. Also, as people travelled into the Russian sector they brought with them, occasionally, Western marks and they were encouraged

---

[1] The *Picture Post*, December 1948.

to spend them on the black market. In order to encourage this spending cigarettes were made available at major meeting places, well above the price that the Soviet mark spender could afford, but still competitive in relation to Western sector prices.

The true victors over winter were the CALTF planners and the British logistical load specialists in the army. They worked out that many loads had not only a calorific value, but also a major impact on morale. One classic process was the production of bread. Would it be more effective to bake the loaves and then fly them into the city than to fly in the ingredients? Once it had been worked out that bread can be upwards of 40 per cent water it was decided to bake loaves in the city. This increased the workforce and morale as the population at least received fresh bread, even if the majority of other foods tended to require hydration. The humble potato was a classic example of this. Berliners ate potato as part of their staple diet and so it was important, for morale if nothing else, to continue that tradition. The problem was that potatoes are around 80 per cent water so, again, in terms of payload they were not very effective cargos. Subsequently, the planners saved the airlift around seventy flights a day by flying in dehydrated potato. CALTF were delighted; the same could not be said for the population.

The majority of milk was also imported in powder form, although children received bottled milk as part of their ration. The number of children in the city was being steadily reduced through flights conducted by the Royal Air Force: it was far safer to have them fostered in the Bizone than exposed to a level of nutrition that would adversely affect their health in later life. Victory was, however, given a helping hand. The typical winter every forecaster predicted never materialised. True, there were severe frosts and ice did cause some problems, but it was a mild winter. There were more days lost to fog than ice, and these were conditions that could be combated by GCA and instrument-landing assistance. Neither did fog have anywhere near the same effect on fuel stocks as a winter with temperatures consistently down to -20° would have done. And then it appeared that the airlift had received a divine seal of approval when almost 7,000 tons of coal were discovered in a stock yard and a further 4,800 were located a few days later.

Tobacco was a hit or miss affair. Large stocks were already available in the city at the beginning of the blockade, and to ensure fairness the ration was maintained at that level. However, cigarettes became one of the primary currencies of the blockade and so quickly became a much sought-after commodity. It was not unknown for the American authorities to release Government stock in an attempt to devalue its runaway success, and occasionally home-grown German cigars were flown into the city. The police did come across large quantities and often confiscated them in the process, but these were destined to return onto the market as they were often given away to workers at Gatow. On 26 February the *Taskforce Times* proudly explained, '30,000 black-market cigarettes were distributed to German airlift workers at Gatow in recognition of their contribution to the success of Operation Vittles', going on to say that 'The cigarettes were confiscated by British authorities.' Presumably many of those were destined to appear back on the market that evening.

Sweet tooth

One commodity that had not been in ready supply for years was chocolate. It became one of the major 'currencies' alongside cigarettes on the black market, and was available if you could scrounge it from a GI. Occasionally chocolate was flown in, if only to give a slight boost to the younger population. On 14 January *Der Tag* reported that 100 tons of raw cocoa had been processed in factories in the Western zones into more than 2 million 50-gram chocolate bars. Unfortunately, the distribution of this and subsequent cost to the Berlin 'consumer' was far beyond the reaches of those it was destined for – children.

'Little Vittles'

Gail Halvorsen, like countless hundreds of other airlift pilots, took a tour of the devastated city whilst at Tempelhof. He noticed lots of children living in amongst the ruins, and later at the airfield fence had the opportunity to speak to some of them. The one thing he noticed was that, unlike children in other parts of Germany, they did not immediately ask for gum. Once Halvorsen mentioned it, though, it was a different story and 'Little Vittles' was launched.

Dieter Hesse was an eight-year-old boy in the city and remembers the 'Candy Bomber' missions:

> What I remember so vividly is the excitement stirred up by all the kids in my neighbourhood, Nehringstrasse in the British, I think, sector of Berlin. All the kids in 'our gang' would go en masse, maybe fifteen or twenty of us, and head for Tempelhof Flugplatz to watch the planes come in at house-top (those four-storey blockhouses in the working class neighbourhoods) level and then descend to touch ground beyond the fence. It simply was fun to watch planes land every 60 seconds, or so.
>
> One marvellous day when I was not present, an American pilot opened his cockpit side window and threw out some tiny parachutes with a heavier weight to make them drop slowly down to the ground. Of course, the saga of Gail Halversen began and he became known as the Candy Bomber because the weight was candy. When the word filtered through the city that the Americans were bombing Berlin again, but this time with candy, there were hundreds and hundreds of kids at the end of the runways always looking for that one plane with the generous American pilot who threw out candy. We were still very hungry with little food so anything was welcome. What we didn't know was that Halversen was reprimanded because the Berlin newspapers actually used the 'Berlin is being bombed again' line in good fun, but Halverson's superior officer chewed him out for stirring up a potential news mess! Quickly that superior, I guess the CO of the unit, brought Halverson's tormentor to heel recognizing that this was not a 'mess', but a genius stroke in public relations. Virtually all planes from then on threw out the little parachutes. That may have been an exaggeration, but lots of planes participated. And I was one of those kids who caught the candy. Oh, the fist fights over that candy! That was one of those unexpected results from doing a kindness. There

were so many kids not every one always got one parachute. So the 'strong took from the weak.' You'd think we'd learned something from the great war we had all just survived! But we were kids and precious candy was at stake. Moral lessons would surface in later years.

Operation Little Vittles became a major undertaking and soon candy bars were being imported from the United States in an attempt to supply the city. Halvorsen rapidly became known as *der Schokoladenflieger* – the chocolate flyer – attracting hundreds of letters of thanks and requests for further drops, often with co-ordinates. Drops from the air were one thing, but with large amounts of candy being donated by firms in Europe and the US it soon became easier to deliver it by jeep. Captain Eugene Williams started deliveries to schools whilst Halvorsen conducted PR visits to children in hospitals around the city. Other ways of raising morale and, more importantly, cash for 'care packages' were explored. That January an unusual book was published by the wives of servicemen, predominantly American, in the blockaded city – *The Operation Vittles Cook Book*.

One of the entries was headed with a story that gives some idea of the power of the domestic electricity supply, or rather lack of it:

> The battle between electricity cut-offs and the unfinished roast has often taken a roast from an oven in one sector to the oven of another where the electricity was still on. We think a lamb roast established the record when it went in and out to a total of 22 hours baking and travelling time.

Interestingly, the note does not elaborate on the edibility of the roast once finally cooked! It does help us understand the situation though. The majority of the current generated was earmarked for industrial or transportation use. The situation dictated that the domestic supply was invariably not available at peak demand times, i.e. late evening or early morning. Announcements were made in the press as to which areas were to receive two hours' supply and when. This eventually drove entire households: the family would rise at 3 a.m. to do the washing, ironing, cleaning and cooking, often with the radio tuned in, and then return to bed for a few hours when the lights went out two hours later. Some flats cooked on gas, and this too could be rather intermittent. Naturally there were one or two explosions when the supply was re-established.

Travel was a different matter, but with careful planning the voltage could be put to very good use. One major headache was that some subway trains had to stop in the Soviet sector and the passengers had to change there for other Western sector destinations. Naturally the SMA and Markgraf's police took advantage of this and regularly harassed the passengers, searching them and confiscating what they were carrying. By March this had become intolerable and *Der Tag* announced:

> Beginning on Monday, the subway line B between Uhlandstrasse and Warschauer Bruecke will again operate continuously from 0006 to 1800 hrs., since the required current in the amount of 4,000 kilowatts has been allocated. This will enable people to ride on the subway from the British to the U.S. sector without changing in the Soviet sector.

Travel around the city was kept as normal as possible. However, by 1949 some trolleys were in desperate need of repair. Note the clippy's home-made shoes, another privation.

Throughout all this hardship the Berlin population had grown hard, weary and cynical of the situation. The population was predominantly female, estimated to be at least 20 to 1, the majority of whom were, or had been, employed in some form of heavy manual labour at one time or another. To many the blockade became a way of life. The Soviets did punctuate this existence with the odd tantalising act of 'compassion', although it would often cause much anguish. Richard Wilson, based at Tempelhof, remembers just such an occasion:

> I was in a train station when a train arrived from the east. The train was full of German prisoners of war who the Russians had just released. The scene in the station was the most emotionally wrenching thing I've ever seen. Hysterical women – wives and mothers, I suppose – were screaming, asking the men if they knew this name or that name. I saw two women and one older man faint when they found a loved one. The men disembarking from the train were gaunt and hollow-eyed; most of them appeared to be totally confused. Some were amputees, and I saw at least one blind man being led along.

Basic Law

During the period of the Soviet blockade of the city, moves had continued for the formation of a West German constitution. This would, as all concerned were aware, split the country if the concept went ahead. Discussions by a 'Parliamentary Council' had been underway since September 1948 in the town of Bonn, investigating the concept of a 'Basic Law'. This was not designed to be a constitution, just a framework that could be utilised until Germany was reunited. As it transpired it would be the basic principle behind the Bonn administration for over forty years. Driven by the West, the 'Basic Law' was to be a decentralised system devolving control to the Länder at a provincial level. As the blockade lost its grip through early May the population realised it was a very hollow victory. It had cost the country its unity.

One immediate benefit of surface access to the city was the reintroduction of proper potatoes. No longer restricted to the dehydrated variety, the population now thought normality might return. That first day lemons and fresh vegetables arrived, as did fish and several train loads of coal. This load was matched by that carried on the C–54s: the blockade had finished but the airlift would continue. The following few days were days for wise words. Ernst Reuter was in belligerent mood: 'Since midnight the "technical traffic restrictions" have been lifted. The blockade is over! The attempt to force us to our knees has failed, frustrated by our steadfastness and firmness.' He echoed the sentiments of millions when he added, 'We will say farewell to dehydrated potatoes without regret.' General Clay addressed the City Council the following day and called both pilots and Berliners heroes. Then the names of those who had died during the airlift were read to the assembled chamber. The square outside Tempelhof was renamed *Platz der Luftbrücke* (Airlift Square) and the council vowed to erect a 'simple monument' to those who had lost their lives supplying the city.

Life on the Lift

Naturally many service personnel were detached to Germany due to the airlift and quite a large number found themselves in Berlin itself. The following accounts cover some of their views and experiences.

Young men away from home inevitably gravitate towards the bar, as do the local women, so it is no surprise that many airlift veterans recall events surrounding girls and alcohol. Richard Wilson, Tempelhof Air Traffic Controller, USAF, recalls that:

> I spent most of my free time drinking and chasing women. I was sixteen years old when I arrived in Berlin, having lied about my age to join the army. You could get away with that in those days. This was 1948 and the battle of Berlin had been fought only three years previously. During the battle many, many of the male Berliners had been killed or captured by the Russians. This left a population almost entirely made up of women. I remember hearing that the ratio of women to men in Berlin at the time was 28 to 1. I have no way of knowing if that figure is accurate, but I must say that it can't be far off the mark. So that's where my energies went.

John Bevin, 80 Squadron (F) Detachment remembers:

> We would wander where the mood took us, and since we couldn't afford to visit the city every day we would go down to the lakeside mainly because there was a hospital there with lots of nurses to chat to.

But even this had its hazards:

> There was an organisation that did all our guard duties, made up of displaced persons of dubious nationalities. They wore a uniform, British Army battledress dyed green and were called the GSO. They were a right scruffy lot and would not hesitate to clobber you if they caught you breaking into camp, yes we often broke out of camp and therefore had to break back in, 2359 was no use to us!

Frank Watt, AC1 at RAF Fassberg Station Sick Quarters remembers some potent concoctions:

> We did not have a great number of sick, minor things only, quite a few bad doses of clap which was a chargeable offence! Another nasty was the local wood alcohol hooch, some of the more unscrupulous locals had seen a chance to make a buck and sold it to the yanks as vodka scotch and schnapps, lovely labels but deadly, caused blindness and sent the boys crazy, they reckoned it was originally made for rocket fuel for the V2s.

However, not everyone got the opportunity to go out 'socialising'. Personnel with RAF Dakotas appear to have drawn the short straw – long shifts and not much time off. However, they did go sightseeing, as John Beauchamp, rigger with 99 Squadron RAF Wunstorf explains:

I did visit Gatow but it was a heap, as was Berlin, they were still digging a lot of the streets out. The kids were so thin I remember. We were too tired to think about going out, on the go all day every day.

Bill Ball, Fitter with 77 Squadron RAF Lübeck had a similar experience:

We didn't see much time off, we worked around the clock night and day shifts. I did go for a trip to Lübeck, it had seen a bit of a battering.

Val Spaven, Engine Fitter, 77 Squadron RAF Fassberg, remembers:

We worked long shifts on a 24 hour system which meant sometimes you had lunch at midnight, after so many shifts you had 24 hours off. This gave us the chance to visit the nearest town Celle. Celle was not bombed and the three storey buildings with the sharp roofs were picturesque. There was a church army canteen by the river which after exploring Celle was a welcome sight.

Bella, ACW1 Bad Elsen RAF Signals, tells us that:

I so wanted to go on one of the trips [flights], but we were not allowed, my friend and I attempted to go, but were found out and taken off the plane, what a shame we couldn't have gone and seen the other end of our operations. The men were allowed to fraternise, and one of our men arranged a wedding to his German girlfriend, we were all allowed to attend. The reception was held on her fathers farm, he did a barn up, and the seating arrangements was on empty coffins, with blankets over them… after a while we had the opportunity to try them out!!!! On our time off we would go into Lubeck, and sit in the cafes with the oompah bands playing, and enjoy ourselves with other members of our camp. At other times, we sat around on camp in the N.A.A.F.I, talking and drinking cups of tea etc, until our money ran out.

Despite the hardships endured by servicemen there were some perks, as Bella, ACW1, explains:

For leave we were allowed to go to Bad Hartsburg in the mountains and stayed at a lovely hotel, at the very high cost of ONE SHILLING PER DAY! We also used a Hotel on the coast it was called THE STRAND, and we were charged again, ONE SHILLING PER DAY (forces prices I think) But were not allowed to stay in the same hotel as the men. Times have changed drastically I think!!!!

And what about those down times between aircraft flights?
Len Guyatt, AC1, air radar fitter, RAF Wunstorf:

There was often nothing to do at Wunstorf between waves, and very quickly a card school developed in our Nissan hut. We were paid in BAFS at the time. I remember opening the door one day and the middle of the table was covered in the biggest pyramid of 3d & 6d notes you could imagine.

How did the Western service personnel view the Germans? With the war still prominent in people's minds they had to try and understand how Hitler had stayed in power for so long. Richard Wilson, Tempelhof Air Traffic Controller, USAF, recalls some frank exchanges:

I do remember an odd conversation I had with a young German guy in a bar. He was about my age, meaning he would have been about 13 at the end of the war. He declared that Hitler 'was the best thing that ever happened to Germany.' Here we were, in a pub at the bottom of a bombed-out building, surrounded by miles of rubble, and he's telling me that 'Hitler was good for Germany.' I still don't understand what he meant.

John Collier, RAF Regiment Gatow, gives a viewpoint similar to those of many at the time:

When I discovered I was posted to Germany I wasn't too impressed. My older brother had been killed in the war and I thought 'there's no love lost here' but when I saw what conditions those people were living in. They had nothing in the towns, absolutely nothing.

Sam Pover, Pilot with Air Transport Charter (CI), Lübeck and Hamburg:

The fact that Britain had a flour ration on the go through 1948 made a big impression on the German population, especially since it had not been experienced during the war. However, it has to be remembered this was a political not a mercy mission.

Interestingly, by the time of the airlift Hitler and the Nazis had become a bit of a joke to the occupying troops.
Frank Watt AC1 at RAF Fassberg Station Sick Quarters:

They say every picture tells a story, that one of me on the tail of the plane, if you notice I am wearing the German helmet back to front, this was intentional much to the annoyance of our German staff, we were lampooning the swastika and, at that time, that didn't go down too well. There was still a lot of sympathy for Adolf and the village of Fassberg was an old party haunt of the Field Marshal.

But not all Germans were set in their ways, as John Dury, Flight Mechanic, 297 Squadron RAF Schleswigland, found out:

Hastings squadrons 47 and 297 (ours) had a number of ground crew – including two German helpers, usually ex-servicemen. – Our German crew friends often invited us to their club (Kinderheim?) for drinks , table tennis etc.. Heinz Peter an ex-serviceman, one of the two Germans in the crew, a great guy, always smiling, hard working and eager to help with

'Der Huckle Blister, Luftwaffe.' AC Watt enjoys the spoils of war. (With thanks to Frank Watt)

anything. He was a member of the Hitler Youth movement before the war. I have recently been in touch with him, 57 years after the end of the airlift.

Sometimes contact could not be avoided. When eleven WAAFs were posted out to the communications centre at Bad Elsen in Lübeck there was no service accommodation for them. Subsequently they were billeted with local families.

Bella, ACW1, Bad Elsen RAF Signals:

My friend Marjorie and I were billeted with a very nice German family near the camp, we had sauerkraut and black bread with our meals, and we thought the feather duvets, were really lovely and warm for the German winter we arrived in. The frau washed our things for us, and ironed and pressed our uniforms, we kept in touch with her after we were given a billet at the camp, just for us girls!!!

So clearly attitudes had changed towards the Germans; however, fear of the Russians was still very strong.

John Bevin, 80 Squadron (F) Detachment:

I first went to Germany in June 48 and was very surprised at how friendly the vast majority of the people were, even among the ruins of Hamburg, I would go as far as saying they were jolly pleased to have us there, when I was posted from Lübeck I had to tell my current girl friend we were leaving, (meaning just my unit) she just went to pieces because she thought I meant the whole air force. They really feared the Russians, with some justification.

But not every encounter was stressful, as Bella, ACW1, Bad Elsen RAF Signals, recalls:

We did meet some Russians one night on the way home, as we were on the border, they stopped us and of course no one could converse, but they shared a drink with the men, it was quite an experience for us.

John Bevin, 80 Squadron (F) Detachment:

In those days though, Germany was overrun with something like eight million displaced people from Eastern Europe, Latvians, Lithuanians, Ukrainians, Austrians, all of them fleeing from the red hordes. One day my mate and I got a little off the beaten track near the Russian Zone, we called into this bar for a beer and all conversation stopped, You could sense the hostility, eventually one man plucked up enough courage to ask who we were, They had never seen our air force uniforms before and thought we were the hated Russians. I will wager that even today in Germany the same feeling prevails.

The Christmas caravan

When Bob Hope visited the airlift stations, General Tunner ensured as many personnel as possible got to see the show. For those who did it made a great impression.

Frank Watt, AC1 at RAF Fassberg Station Sick Quarters:

The highlight of the year was Christmas, we had a German choir who came and done the rounds of the wards singing carols, to hear silent night sung in German with snow falling outside is quite something. We also had the Bob Hope Christmas caravan, we all queued outside the stadium snow on the ground and bloody, bloody, cold. Hope comes along in a jeep with a gang of MPS and says let these guys in the theatre their my future fans! We all rushed in and got the best seats. He had his wife Dolores and Irving Berlin and a heap of dancing girls the Rockettes, he visited the SSQ and joked with the sick boys. He held

Arguments over where the sector line actually was became a bone of contention. The Soviets are accusing US servicemen of overstepping the line. (ACME Pictures)

the show two hours had us all in tears some of his jokes very risqué but the lads lapped it up. Afterwards we waited and got his autograph before he was shot off to the officers mess – quite a guy.

Not all had the same experience. Len Guyatt, AC1 air radar fitter, RAF Wunstorf:

At Christmas a York was loaded to the gunnels with booze for Berlin. It was the only time I saw an armed guard on a loaded aircraft. I remember I missed the Bob Hope show as I was on shift. All American shows were free of charge, all the Brit ones you had to pay for – typical!

Even the most innocent of days out, like taking a boat on the lake, could have its downside if you strayed too far, as Richard Wilson of the USAF ATC discovered in May 1949:

During a day off work, a friend, whose last name was Georges, and I rented a small motor boat from a recreational area on Lake Wannsee, which is a large lake in Berlin. We motored along the shoreline, taking in the beautiful sights (during the Nazi era, Lake Wannsee was where many powerful people had their homes). We decided to proceed up one of the many small canals that emptied into the lake. As we motored along one of these canals I marvelled at the beautiful houses and canal-side pubs, all of which were closed. Not a soul to be seen. Eventually, we came to a sign jutting out of the water:

IT IS FORBIDDEN FOR BRITISH, FRENCH OR AMERICAN PERSONNEL TO PROCEED BEYOND THIS POINT!

In our ignorance (and some might say our stupidity) we assumed that the sign was there for safety reasons, because the water was becoming more shallow and the canal was narrowing. At any rate, we continued and shortly emerged from the canal into a large open area. I was manning the outboard motor, so I was sitting in the rear. As we left the canal, I looked to the left where another canal entered the lake. I noticed a couple of small bombed-out bridges in the canal. I thought this was odd; in West Berlin most of the rubble around waterways had been cleaned up. Anyway, I was enjoying my reverie when Georges clapped me on the shoulder and pointed in the other direction.

What he was pointing at was a soldier who was standing on the bank aiming an automatic weapon at us. The soldier motioned for us to come. Needless to say, I killed the motor and we started paddling to the bank (come to think of it, we could have just as easily motored). My friend asked me who I thought the soldier was. I replied that maybe he was French – wishful thinking, obviously.

He motioned for us to come up where he was, which we did post-haste. He was standing next to a dirt road. He ordered us to sit down which we also did with alacrity. Then he went a few yards away to where a portable telephone was hung on a tree trunk. As he spoke on the phone, we passed time with observations like, 'Siberia, here we come.'

He began talking to someone, and I heard the word 'Amerikanski' or something like that. It was the only word I recognized. Perhaps an hour passed with us sitting in the grass before some more soldiers came walking up the road. Their sergeant was very friendly; he showed us some family pictures which he carried in his pocket. Then he took our wallets and examined their contents.

After some more time passed, a vehicle containing two officers came driving up the road. One of the officers was an older man of very senior rank, as we later learned, but the other was a young guy who spoke perfect, unaccented English. He sounded like he had lived in the U.S. for all his life.

The two officers questioned us at length about our jobs at Tempelhof, what were we doing with that boat in the Soviet Zone (which was outside of Berlin), and did we want to return to our unit. We assured him that we did indeed want to return. We each told lies about our jobs. My friend worked with secret material in the teletype room. Georges told them he was a cook. I told them I was a typist. They seemed to accept our fabrications.

They took us in their vehicle to an area where I saw some American Constabulary soldiers. We were giddy with relief -- we weren't going to Siberia after all. We were made to sit down in a small room. After sitting for a short while an American army captain came in and told us to come with him.

The captain drove us to Tempelhof, and it was a long ride of maybe 1½ hours. During the entire time he screamed invective at us, saying things like, 'I'm going to see that the two of you are court-martialled. You will wish the Russians had kept you. How could you be so god-damned dumb?' (A reasonable question, considering the circumstances)

At any rate, we survived his tirades and arrived back at Tempelhof. The captain ordered us to report to the OSI (Office of Special Investigations) the following morning.

We reported as ordered, with some trepidation, and we were questioned about our experience. They were only looking for intelligence information. We identified the senior Russian officer from a picture, but they were most interested in the English-speaking officer, of whom they had no photo.

We were released and never heard any more of the incident. It's a memory I treasure. Our initial fears about Siberia were probably justified, because many British and American soldiers had disappeared in Berlin. There were always rumours that the missing people had been seen by somebody in the gulags.

By May the main blockade was over and it was time to celebrate. Frank Watt, AC1 at RAF Fassberg Station Sick Quarters:

… soon the Ruskies got a bit fed up with the lift and had had enough so they called a halt. Fassberg and Celle decided to have one hell of a Piss-up called the Blockade Busters Blowout started in the morning in the big hangar, barrels of beer, lager, schnapps and food for the multitudes, my first introduction into bar-b-que and yank burgers.

Twelve

'Two Camps'

Misjudgement

On 13 May thousands gathered outside the Schoenberg Town Hall. The Soviets had lifted the blockade, but Berlin could quickly be sealed-off again. Many Berliners feared this would be the case and that Moscow would wait until after the Council of Foreign Ministers' meeting before re-imposing restrictions. The week ending 18 May saw 5,456 tons flown into the city; stockpiling was now the order of the day. That week 3,000 gallons of petrol were released for public consumption and private cars now started to reappear. This fortuitously coincided with the Western sector rail workers strike over the amount of Deutschmarks they received in their pay.

That was not the only sign of tension. Whilst the blockade had been officially lifted, it seemed no one had told the SMA. Officials there considered this a lull in which supplies could be built-up, ready for the blockade to be re-imposed ready for winter. The story filtered out into the media and confidence was once more shaken. In an attempt to worry the population, the SMA decreed that all trains transiting the Russian zone would have to be pulled by Soviet engines and crews. Further to this, they arbitrarily altered timetables and delayed military trains, again citing 'technical difficulties'. It looked very much like a return to the blockade was on the cards. Road traffic on the Helmstedt autobahn was also disrupted due to changing paperwork rules. The only course of action left open to the Allies was to continue with the airlift.

The Council of Foreign Ministers met in France on 23 May. The meeting went on for nearly a month, due in part to the lengthy speeches of the Soviet representative, Andrei Vishinsky. Vishinsky proposed that a four-power agreement be constructed allowing the Soviets a level of control in the Ruhr. Also, a new Berlin Magistrat encompassing all the city sectors should be formed, in the interests of the new found 'understanding' between East and West. The problem for Moscow was that the West now 'understood' all too well how the Soviets operated. A new city Magistrat on Soviet lines involved the reformation of the Kommandatura and reinstatement of its powers and, naturally, its veto process. If accepted, stalemate would quickly return to city politics until, that is, the Soviets could influence the appointment of sympathising trade unionists, police, council members and

Free land travel did not last long. This sixty-strong convoy of GMCs was escorted through the Soviet Zone by the 759th Military Police Battalion. (US Army Photograph)

other civil service positions. Donald Acheson, the US representative at the talks, noted that the only thing the Kommandatura 'would not be in control of was dying'. Clearly, any move like that would be a major step in the wrong direction and Vishinsky was given a flat no to the suggestions. Bevin had struggled from the outset of the talks; he obviously found the other three ministers, with their legal training, very hard work; their attitude seemed to be 'why use one word where a thousand would do?' Bevin was relieved when he could finally leave for the Labour Party's annual conference at Blackpool. On his return, he discovered little progress had been made. Even though discussions dropped onto menial topics in an attempt to get things moving, Moscow managed to frustrate the process. A final communiqué was issued on 20 June. It said practically nothing.

The Lift continues

As if to prove a point, the monthly tonnage for May was a staggering 250,818 tons delivered in 27,718 flights with a total of 76,000 hours in the air. This was the clearest demonstration yet that the Allies could service every need of the city by air cargo. Even though the Soviets were now allowing freight trains in they were still intermittent, and whenever mail was discovered the train was turned back. Items by road fared little better, and so mail continued to be brought in and out of the city by air. Work was also continuing on the new power station for the Western sectors. A number of 11m-long supports were needed during construction, and these too were delivered by air, utilising the C-82 Packet. This was another clear message to the Soviets that practically anything could be brought into the city using aircraft alone.

Handley Page Hastings' TG510 of 47 Squadron, little worse for wear after a wheels-up landing at RAF Schleswigland on 19 May 1949. The aircraft was repaired.

From May, a large number of National Servicemen were being released from duties and this caused major problems. With no immediate reduction in the flying programme, the British Government realised that some parts of Operation Plainfare were now close to collapse. Manpower shortages were having a detrimental effect on operations staff, especially Air Traffic Control. Shift patterns were changed in an attempt to compensate for postings back to Britain, but all recognised that this was not ideal. The following paragraphs demonstrate that desperate search for manpower. On 10 March Flight-Lieutenant W.K. Ongley, Operations Controller, Gatow, came up with a suggestion:

> It is understood that difficulty is being experienced by Higher Authority in replacing Junior Officers employed as Deputy Controllers, who, after six months have requested to return to productive flying or other employment which would enable them to improve their service knowledge. May it be suggested that there are a number of pilots in the glider pilot Regiment who are fully trained pilots and who would be only too keen to be associated with Operation Plainfare.

Glider pilots were already employed on the airlift, nine at Wunstorf and eight at Schleswigland as co-pilots, and a further eight as air movements assistants at Gatow. It was proposed that the air movements assistants be replaced by RAF personnel, but further glider pilots could be despatched to act as co-pilots. This would 'enable a new detachment of glider pilots to take advantage of the valuable training opportunities offered on the airlift. And assist in maintaining the morale of the regiment which, under present circumstances, has too few chances of doing interesting work.'

Headquarters 46 group at Luneburg requested that:

… if Operation Plainfare is to continue for any period, it is suggested that a proposal be put to Officer Commanding, Headquarters the Glider Pilot Regiment for six glider pilots (officers) to be attached for at the least two-monthly periods to this group for duty in the operations room at Gatow. This would alleviate our manpower problem to no small extent.

Unfortunately, events had conspired against them. In a demonstration of just how far-reaching the effects of the airlift had been on flying training, the Glider Pilot Regiment replied, 'replacements are not available owing to the dislocation of the glider flying training programme by Operation Plainfare'. By 1 August 1949 the original glider pilots were still detached to Gatow, Wunstorf and Schleswigland; all were now under the direct command of Captain P.G. Scott. They were employed as operations staff, air movements assistants and second pilots on Yorks. All had returned to the United Kingdom by the end of August.

June saw no let-up in the air effort, and by the end of the month another 250,000 tons had been flown in. By now the Soviets were smarting. Clearly, their blockade of Berlin had achieved absolutely nothing, their vision for Europe was now in ruins. So the SMA reverted back to a blockade mentality. Trucks carrying manufactured goods on the autobahn were stopped and searched; any paperwork carrying the stamp of the Magistrat's Traffic Office meant the load was turned round and sent back to the city. The reason? – signatures and not stamps were required. A few days after that the Soviets began refusing entry to their zone and closed the Gleinicke Bridge because it was being used by East Berliners to travel to the Western sectors. Some British politicians questioned whether the blockade had been re-imposed.

Luckily the rail dispute was settled by the end of June allowing some semblance of order to come to transport around the city. However, road traffic continued to come under increasing military scrutiny causing traffic jams miles long. This eventually prompted the US Army to declare their intention to send a weekly convoy of sixty trucks under military guard. Not quite Clays Armed Convoy, this had by then been discounted as being too dangerous, as Robertson had predicted a year before, but a statement of intent none the less. Surprisingly the Soviets 'welcomed' the proposal.

Planners at Airlift HQ had for some time been considering when, and indeed if, the effort could be reduced in any way. The rail strike had increased the pressure on supplies held in the city, but by the end of June over sixty-five days' worth of food was stockpiled around the city. Accordingly, the airlift was to be reduced in scale from July. The lift went out with a bang as 253,090 tons were flown that month, the highest tonnage ever. Flights from Rhein-Main were suspended in late July, and as August approached more bases were earmarked for closure or reversion to their pre-lift tasks.

The lift was not totally abandoned as Berlin was still within the Soviet zone and could quite easily be threatened again. And so the National Security Council and Cabinet in London agreed to maintain a basic level transport capability in Germany, including the upkeep of some infrastructure. Nobody intended to be 'caught with their pants down again'. Throughout August the fleet numbers dwindled. Aircraft on the civil lift began to leave as contracts ran out, and the C-54s began returned to bases around the world. One by one the squadrons pulled out. Dakotas, now well past their best, began to return

On 30 September the last Operation Vittles sortie landed at Tempelhof. The pilot was Captain Harry D. Immel. (US Air Force)

to Britain, some being disposed of immediately. The Yorks returned to Abingdon and Lyneham whilst the Hastings, looking decidedly older than their airframe hours suggested, flew back to Topcliffe. On 1 September the Combined Air Lift Task Force (CALTF) was disbanded and operational control reverted back to national status.

The finals

On 16 August 1949 the first in a long line of final missions landed at Tegel. The Halton (G-AIAP), owned by Eagle Aviation, delivered 14,400lb of flour signalling the end of the civil operation. On 26 August a Avro York of 59 Squadron landed at Gatow for the last time and by 6 September the final Plainfare Hastings flight took place. The RAF Dakotas were last in attendance on the 23rd and eight days later a C-54 delivered its load to Tempelhof. Those aircraft that remained were now on standard cargo flights: Operation Plainfare was at an end.

'The Big Lift'

A number of films were made during the blockade along with newsreels for public consumption. Many were filmed by the various organisations attached to the services, including the US Army Signals Corps, who incidentally produced a massive archive of photographs, and the Crown Film Unit. However, with such a good story it wasn't long before Hollywood was on the scene.

The Big Lift, a Twentieth Century Fox film directed by George Seaton was released in July 1950. The film crew had been in the city filming from July 1949, and had managed to capture the look of Berlin before it returned to normality. Hollywood actors Montgomery Clift and Paul Douglas played the leads but Seaton used original aircrew members including Captains Dante V. Morel, John Mason and Gail Plush, wherever possible. A number even became minor celebrities afterwards. Unfortunately, it did not receive good reviews; ' *"Big Lift"* more like a *"Big Letdown"'*, reported the *New York Times*.

The Berlin blockade in a European context

NATO

If the blockade of Berlin achieved anything it was a demonstration to the West the intent of the 'red menace'. Stalin, who had been known to the free world as 'Uncle Joe' during the war, was suddenly cast from a similar mould to Hitler. Movement towards an alliance had become inevitable in the face of Soviet pressure, and with the formation of the North Atlantic Treaty Organisation (NATO) Moscow now found itself faced with an even stronger, more resolute Western Europe.

The first steps towards this iconic Cold War institution came in the wake of the Marshall Plan. On 17 March 1948, the Benelux nations signed an alliance with Britain and France forming the Western European Union (WEU). This 'self help' organisation, known as the 'Brussels Treaty', drove public opinion in the United States. It was clear that Marshall aid would not halt communist expansion on its own, and the Europeans would need help from the US if any alliance was to hold firm. Events in Germany and further afield underpinned this thinking, eventually forcing those isolationists in Congress to reconsider their opposition. As the blockade began to bite, funding was sought for the organisation; however, many considered the WEU to be too small for European defence and its application was rejected. Work on recruiting further nations received a boost when the Soviets started to pressurise Norway into ceding land. Portugal, Denmark and Iceland were soon to join as well and by July talks between the WEU and George Marshall were well underway.

That same month, commanders on the ground began planning the defence of the Western zones. Emergency plans were drawn up for a withdrawal of troops to a defensive line utilising the Rhine. Negotiations between the interested states carried on into 1949, and by March it was clear that a draft document could be produced. A final document was signed on 4 April 1949, stating that an attack on Belgium, Canada, Denmark, France, Iceland, Luxembourg, Holland, Italy, Portugal, Norway, the USA or United Kingdom would now be considered as an attack on them all. Stalin had completely misread the situation. All he succeeded in doing was ensuring that the United States remained Europe's protector for the foreseeable future. NATO was formally ratified in the US

The signing of the NATO agreement on 4 April 1949. The United States effectively became the protector of free Europe.

Senate on 21 July 1949; the communisation of Western Germany and eventually Europe was now incredibly unlikely without war.

Creation of the West German State

The struggle for Berlin, or rather the minds of its people, had effectively split the country in two. The Soviets had consistently argued that Germany should be re-united with strong military 'supervision', and by Christmas 1948 it was clear that Moscow would try to control the country once it was united, maybe not militaristically but certainly politically. More influence in the Ruhr and a hand in currency reform were the most likely tactics. To ensure victory the hearts and minds of the population would have to be won. Both sides recognised this, but only one side demonstrated that they meant it. Those in the East had already experienced Soviet reprisals first hand. And since the defeat of the country stories had been filtering out about the 'kidnapping' and 'disappearances' of useful people. The Western zones carried the extra burden of more than 7 million Displaced Persons dislodged from former ethnic German areas, and Stalin had demonstrated his intent by

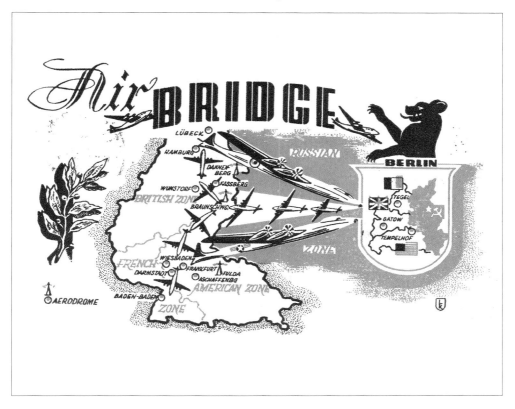

Cards and stamps began to appear for the first anniversary of the lift. At this time the lift was still going flat-out.

trying to starve over 2 million in Berlin. Unpalatable as it was, the only real solution to this was the partition of Germany, and by 12 May, the day the blockade was lifted, Generals Robertson and Clay met in Frankfurt to discuss the issue of the 'Basic Law'. In what appeared to be a double slap in the face the Basic Law was accepted that day by the Allies and the new West German Constitution was adopted on the day the Council of Foreign Ministers met in France. By September 1949 the Federal Republic of Germany had its first parliamentary meeting.

Britain prepares a stand

To those in Britain the blockade of Berlin was seen as another step on the way to war. In the immediate post-war years it had become apparent that Eastern Europe had already fallen and Germany was now likely to be next. Accordingly, a number of civil-orientated organisations were resurrected; some like the Royal Observer Corps had reappeared by 1946 and now covered 1,420 observation posts. Others, however, can be recognised as being a direct consequence of the blockade.

The announcement of the Civil Defence Bill at the opening of Parliament in October 1948 paved the way for protection of the public against attack from overseas. The Act was far reaching, calling for the training of civil defence forces, formation of large equipment stocks, requisition of premises and the formation of a large, voluntary corps. The Civil Defence Corps were formally introduced in April 1949 and the force was to form the backbone of British Cold War civil protection until April 1968. 1949 also saw the formation of the Auxiliary Fire Service, equipped a few years later with the iconic 'Green Goddess'. Similar organisations were to appear across Western Europe.

Cominform

By the beginning of the blockade Soviet domination in the East was effectively the rule of law. After the foundation of the Cominform in September 1947, this domination was tightened to such an extent that it was considered, ominously, 'Stalinist' by the West. Many of the ancient cities of Eastern Europe now fell under this renewed effort to spread the communist ideal, but there were exceptions. Tito had consistently argued that he should be able to remain independent from the Soviet Union, guiding Yugoslavia on the true path of communism. By mid-1948 he was expelled from the Cominform on the pretext that he was trying to build a 'Balkan Federation' with Bulgaria and Albania. Clearly Stalin, who intended to control everything from the centre, was not impressed and started an economic blockade of the country. In 1949 Tito accepted Western aid to help resist the Soviets. Truman must have considered this the perfect antidote! Much worse fell to those who objected in Central Europe; thousands disappeared or were murdered at the hands of

Right: One of the many souvenirs brought back by British servicemen was a plaster wall plate. These were manufactured in local workshops and sold in Malcolm Clubs across the airlift bases.

Opposite: Ernst Reuter became a worldwide figure on account of his stance against the Communists.

the Moscow-orientated police. The only way to combat 'Titoism' was to become rigidly Stalinistic and, accordingly, many local communists were stripped of office.

Eastern Europe now became a mirror image of the Soviet Union. The counter-blockade initiated by the West had mixed results. Initially, the Russian zone and countries immediately around it suffered from a lack of raw materials. However, the blockade actually strengthened Churchill's Iron Curtain as the counter-blockade forced the Soviets to locate alternative resources. By late 1949, industrial output had doubled, as new 'puppet' governments made natural resources available including mass manual labour.

Short odds

On 29 August 1949, 7 a.m. local time, at the Semipalatinsk Test Site, Kazakhstan, the Soviet Union broke the United States' nuclear monopoly when it detonated 'First Lightning' with an estimated yield of 22kT. This came as a shock to the Western governments, as the detonation came two years earlier than the intelligence community had predicted. Now the Soviet Union would have the upper hand. Moscow had manoeuvred itself into a position of strength, one that would prevail for the next four decades. The premise was simple: Russia had before it a shield of puppet states, all full of Soviet troops, aircraft and equipment. It could pierce the Iron Curtain at a moment's notice and cause maximum damage to Western Europe in the process. It has to be remembered that NATO emergency planning intended to allow a Soviet invasion to get as far as the River Rhine before making a stand. Behind this was the opinion that the Red Army could be smashed on the German Plains. Only a few years later this plan was to involve tactical nuclear weapons.

On 10 July 1951 the memorial to those who died was unveiled in front of 80,000 grateful Berliners.

And so, by 1950, it was clear to both superpowers that any conflict directly involving the two would be extremely costly. In late May 1950 Stalin approved the invasion of South Korea by the North. By 25 June Britain, as part of a United Nations force, entered the conflict though many in the Government considered this a prelude to Russian strikes in Western Europe. This set the tone for all future conflicts throughout the Cold War period.

Remembrance

On 10 July 1951, a crowd almost 80,000-strong gathered to witness the unveiling of a monument to those who had lost their lives during the airlift. The square where the monument stood was renamed *Platz der Luftbrücke* as a symbol of freedom. The memorial, designed by Eduard Ludwig, quickly became known as *die Gabel* (the fork) and *die Hunger-Harke* (the hunger rake) by Berliners. The three arching 'prongs' represent the three air corridors pointing towards Frankfurt. A corresponding monument reaches from Frankfurt. The Monument reads:

Sie gaben ihr Leben für die Freiheit Berlins im Dienste der Luftbrücke 1948/49

They lost their lives for the freedom of Berlin in service for the Berlin Airlift 1948/49

In 1989 Chancellor Helmut Kohl of the Federal Republic of Germany commented:

The airlift will not be forgotten. It will always be a token of Anglo-German friendship and partnership for the cause of freedom, human rights and democracy.

Ten years later, the city of Berlin took the opportunity to say thank you formally to those who had taken part. On the morning of 12 May 1999, wreaths were laid by the German Air Force at the monument at the *Platz der Luftbrücke* at a ceremony attended by hundreds of airlift veterans. The veterans travel had been paid for by donations and came from all around the world. Later they were treated to a tattoo at the Olympic Stadium to celebrate their efforts fifty years previously.

Len Guyatt AC1 Radar Fitter at Wunstorf summed up his time on Operation Plainfare:

It was a very rewarding experience, I'm glad I took part.

This modest approach is how a lot of veterans explain their time on the lift. Many see it as a life-changing experience when humanity could raise its head after the horrors of the Second World War. They achieved much more than self respect; they secured through their efforts a peace in Europe that prevails today. Three generations have benefited from the sense of unity born out of the airlift. General Clay wrote in 1950:

Volumes can be written, and perhaps will be written, to cover in detail the work of the airlift, though I doubt if they will do it justice.

Over the years a few volumes have, indeed, been written. Hopefully the General would approve of this one.

Personal Contributions

Any inquiry into history is coloured by personal recollection and this account of the Berlin Airlift is no different. The following list contains those veterans from around the world who have given their time to recollect events from sixty years ago. They are now becoming few in number and it is humbling that they gave freely of their time. They are mentioned here with notes about their status at the time of the blockade.

Guy Kenney, Airman Second Class, aircraft electrician, stationed at Burtonwood throughout 1949.

Allyne Conner, Sergeant, 59th Air Depot Wing, Vehicle Mechanic, stationed at Burtonwood from September 1948 to November 1949.

Heinz Johannsen, lived near Schleswigland airfield during the airlift and made many visits; aged thirteen at the time.

Ernie Jessen, lived 12 miles from Schleswigland Airfield during the airlift. Dated a girl who worked for a transport company on the airbase.

W.C. (Dub) Southers, flight engineer with 41st Troop Carrier Squadron stationed at RAF Celle from 16 December 1948 to late July 1949.

Francis Adam Watt, Aircraftman First Class, Dental Centre orderly at Station Sick Quarters, RAF Fassberg, from June 1948 to August 1949.

John Collier, RAF Regiment based in Germany throughout Operation Plainfare.

John Beavin, posted to 80 Squadron, Wunstorf, just five days before the blockade and operated Spitfires from Gatow during the initial phase of Operation Cater Paterson and Plainfare.

Roy Smith, Aircraftman First Class, signals clerk HQ 48 Group RAF Abingdon. Took the initial signal for Operation Cater Paterson and was involved in the build-up of Avro Yorks on the airlift.

Edward Newman, Aircrew on Lancasters 1656 HCU Lindholme 1942 then 1 group Scampton before moving onto Liberators operating out of Ballykelly, Northern Ireland.

Val Spaven, Aircraftman First Class, Flight Mechanic Engines, 77 Squadron Dakotas. Stationed at Fassberg and later Lübeck.

Joe Gyulavics continued to fly as an enlisted navigator bombardier radar operator with the 28th Bomb Group in B-29s at Rapid City, South Dakota. Served temporary duty in Germany (Giebelstadt) and England (Scampton) during the Berlin Airlift.

Sam Pover, pilot with Air Transport Charter (CI). Operated the company's only Dakota from Lübeck and then Hamburg, carrying predominantly flour.

John Beauchamp, rigger with 99 Squadron RAF Lyneham, then posted to Wunstorf, working the Dakota flight line.

Richard E. Wilson, Corporal, 158th AACS Squadron. Stationed in Berlin from September 1948 to November 1949. Richard worked as an air traffic controller in the Berlin Air Safety Centre and then Tempelhof Tower.

Christine Clarke (*née* Bulmer), a child in post-war Britain. She visited the British zone and remembers some of the devastation caused by the Allies' bombing campaign in the Cologne area.

William Ball. Bill was stationed at Waterbeach on 77 Squadron Dakotas and was due to travel to the Far East before being posted to Wunstorf. From there he moved to Lübeck.

John Dury, flight mechanic with 297 Squadron Hastings. Stationed at Schleswigland, on the line between 1948 and 1949. John worked alongside German ex-servicemen on the ramp.

Neville Cox, RAF National Service aircraft electrician based at RAF Finningley during the Berlin Blockade.

Bella, WAAF Aircraftwoman First Class, Bad Elsen, RAF Signals. Bella was one of eleven girls posted to Lübeck. She operated the telex, forwarding information to Berlin about loads and operation times.

Dieter Hesse, now Pete McCoy, born in Berlin on the night of the first air raid in a bomb shelter on 26 August 1940. Pete was later adopted by an American GI. He actually caught some of the candy that Captain Gail Halverson and his friends dropped and spoke to him on the phone to thank him some years later.

Les Haines, engine fitter at Fassberg and Lübeck. Les was on National Service and was originally based at Upper Heyford when he volunteered for service in Germany.

Len Guyatt, Aircraftman Second Class, air radar fitter. Len was based at Wunstorf for the duration of Operation Plainfare working on 'G' and other flight navigation aids for Yorks. Len found the time to take his Aircraftman First Class whilst on the lift – and passed!

Harlan Senior, instrument fitter on Hastings during 1948 to 1949, based at RAF Topcliffe.

Glossary

AACS	Army Airways Communications System
AATO	Army Air Transport Organisation
AC	Aircraftman (RAF)
ACC	Allied Control Council
AHQ	Allied Headquarters
AOC	Air Officer Commanding
ARB	Air Registration Board
ATC	Air Traffic Control
BAAS	British American Air Services
BABS	Blind Approach Beacon System
BAFO	British Air Forces of Occupation
BAFS	British Armed Forces Special Vouchers
BAIC	British Aviation Insurance Company
BASC	Berlin Air Safety Center
BATF	Berlin Airlift Taskforce
BEA	British European Airways
BOAC	British Overseas Airways Corporation
BSAA	British South American Airways
CACC	Civil Aviation Control Commission
CALTF	Combined Airlift Task Force
CDU	Christian Democratic Union
CFM	Council of Foreign Ministers
CRT	Cathode Ray Tube
DP	Displaced Persons
DP	Deutches Partei
EAC	European Advisory Committee
ETA	Estimated Time of Arrival
FASO	Forward Airfield Supply Organization
FO	Foreign Office
FR	Flight Refueling

GCA	Ground Controlled Approach
GCLO	German Civilian Labour Organisation
HMSO	His Majesties Stationery Office
IAS	Indicated Air Speed
IFR	Instrument Flight Rules
KPD	German Communist Party
LAC	Leading Aircraftman (RAF)
LAC	Lancashire Aircraft Corporation
MAF	Ministry of Agriculture and fisheries
MATS	Military Air Transport Service
MCA	Ministry of Civil Aviation
MOD	Ministry of Defence
MP	Military Police (US)
MRSU	Mobile Repair and Salvage Unit
MT	Mechanical Transport
MU	Maintenance Unit
NAAFI	Navy, Army, Airforce Families Institute
NATO	North Atlantic Treaty Organisation
NCO	Non-Commissioned Officer
NSC	National Security Council
OEEC	Organisation for European Economic Cooperation
OCU	Operational Conversion Unit
PLUTO	Pipeline Under The Ocean
POL	Petrol, Oil, Lubricant
POW	Prisoner of War
PSP	Pierced Steel Planking
QNH	Part of international 'Q' Code, signifying altimeter setting above sea level
RAAF	Royal Australian Air Force
RAF	Royal Air Force
RASC	Royal Army Service Corps
RASO	Rear Airfield Supply Organization
RIAS	Radio In the American Sector
RNZAF	Royal New Zealand Air Force
R/T	Radio Telephony
SAAF	South African Air Force
SAC	Strategic Air Command (US)
SASO	Senior Air Staff Officer
SDP	Social Democratic Party
SED	Socialist Unity Party (Amalgamated Workers' Party)
SHAEF	Supreme Headquarters Allied Expeditionary Forces
SHQ	Station Headquarters
SMA	Soviet Military Authority
SSQ	Station Sick Quarters

TCG	Troop Carrier Group (US)
TEMCO	Texas Engineering and Manufacturing Company
TDY	Temporary Duty (US)
UGO	Railway Worker's Union
UK	United Kingdom
USA	United States of America
USAAF	United States Army Air Force (wartime)
USAF	United States Air Force (post–war)
USAFE	United States Air Force, Europe
USSR	Union of Soviet Socialist Republics
VFR	Visual Flight Rules
VHF	Very High Frequency
Volksturm	People's Army
WAAF	Women's Auxiliary Air Force
ZENTRUM	Centre Party (Germany)

Selective Bibliography

Books

Air Historical Branch, *Britain and the Berlin Airlift*, The Stationery Office, London, 1998

Allied Museum, *Pioneers of the Airlift*, Nishen, Berlin, 1998

Allied Museum, *Past And Present, 50 Mementos recall the Western Allied Presence in Berlin 1945–1994*, 1998

Barker, D., *The Berlin Airlift: An Account of the British Contribution*, His Majesty's Stationery Office, London, 1949

Bennett, L., *Bastion Berlin: Das Epos Eines Freiheitskampfes*, Fredrich Rudl, Verleger-Union, Frankfurt, 1952

Clarke, B., *Four Minute Warning: Britain's Cold War*, Tempus Publishing, Stroud, 2005

Clay, L.D., *Decision in Germany*, Doubleday, New York, 1950

Collier, R., *Bridge Across the Sky: The Berlin Airlift and Blockade, 1948–1949*, Macmillan, London, 1978

Corbett, R.J.S., *Berlin and the British Ally 1945–1990*, Zumm, Druck & Satz KG, Berlin, 1991

Cruddas, C., *In Cobham's Company: Sixty Years of Flight Refuelling*, Cobham plc, Wimborne, 1994

Donovan, F., *Bridge in the Sky: The Story of the Berlin Airlift*, Robert Hale and Company, London, 1970

Erickson, J. & Dilks, D. (eds), *Barbarossa: The Axis and the Allies*, Edinburgh University Press Ltd, Edinburgh, 1994

Haydock, M.D., *City Under Siege: The Berlin Blockade and Airlift 1948–1949*, Brassey's, Washington, 1999

Operation Vittles Cook Book: The American Women in Blockaded Berlin, Deutscher Verlag, 1949

Kidson, P., *Avro on the Airlift*, The Cloister Press Limited, Manchester, 1948

Lee, D., *Eastward: A History of the Royal Air Force in the Far East 1945–1972*, Her Majesty's Stationery Office, London, 1984

Miller, R.G., *To Save a City: The Berlin Airlift 1948–1949*, Air Force History and Museums Program, US Government Printing Office, 1998

Morris, E., *Blockade: Berlin & the Cold War*, Victorian (& Modern History) Book Club, Newton Abbot, 1974

Samuel, W.W.E., *I Always Wanted to Fly: America's Cold War Airmen*, Roundhouse Publishing, 2001

Samuel, W.W.E., *German Boy: A Child in War*, Sceptre, 2002

Tunner W.H., *The Berlin Airlift*, extract from Tunner, W.H., 1964, *Over the Hump*, Duell, Sloan & Pearce, 1985

Tusa, A. & J., *The Berlin Airlift*, Atheneum, New York, 1988

Wynn, H., *Forged in War: A History of Royal Air Force Transport Command 1943–1967*, The Stationery Office, London, 1996

Magazines and periodicals

Jenks, G., 1981, Yeoman York – Part One, *Aeroplane Monthly*, Vol.9, No.12, pages 667–671
Jenks, G., 1982, Yeoman York – Part Two, *Aeroplane Monthly*, Vol.10, No.1, pages 4–9
Jones, T., 1978, Aquila Airways, *Aeroplane Monthly*, Vol.6, No.7, pages 340–348
Riding, R., 1981, Avro's Stopgap Airliner, *Aeroplane Monthly*, Vol.9, No.4, pages 188–198
Riding, R., 1981, Avro's Stopgap Airliner, *Aeroplane Monthly*, Vol.9, No.5, pages 243–249
Seabrook-Smith, H., 1977, Berlin Air Lift, *Aeroplane Monthly*, Vol.5, No.4, pages 200–205
Seabrook-Smith, H., 1977, Berlin Air Lift, *Aeroplane Monthly*, Vol.5, No.5, pages 244–250
Turpin, B., 1977, The Tudor Family, *Aeroplane Monthly*, Vol.5, No.6, pages 299–306

Contemporary articles and magazines

A Special Study of 'Operation Vittles', *Aviation Operations Magazine 1949*, Conover Mast Publications, New York
Bee-Hive, United Aircraft Corporation. 1948 The Berlin Airlift, Vol.XXIII, No.4
Information Services Division, Control Commission for Germany (BE), *British Zone Review*, Vol.2, No.21, Broschek & Co., Hamburg, 19 March 1949
Detzer, K.. 'With the Airlift Boys in Berlin', *The Readers Digest*, pages 16–20, 1949
Fricker, J. With the Airlift Again, *The Aeroplane*, Vol. LXXV, No.1954, pages 643–645
'Airlift to Berlin', *National Geographic Magazine*, Vol. XCV, No.5, pages 595–614
The Great Airlift Sustains Berlin, *Life*, Vol.25, No.6, pages 15–19
Illustrated London News, 27 December, 1947, Vol.211, No.5671
Illustrated London News, 3 April, 1948, Vol.212, No.5685
Illustrated London News, 17 April, 1948, Vol.212, No.5687
Illustrated London News, 3 July, 1948, Vol.213, No.5698
Illustrated London News, 24 July, 1948, Vol.213, No.5701
Illustrated London News, 31 July, 1948, Vol.213, No.5702
Magistrats von Gross Berlin Luftbrucke Berlin, Ein Dokumentarisches Bildbuch, Grunewald, Berlin, 1949
The *Task Force Times*, Thursday, 17 February, 1949
The *Task Force Times*, Saturday, 26 February, 1949

Government papers

Department of the Scientific Adviser to the Army, October 1948, Army Operational Research Group, Report No.8/48, Time and Motions Study of Air Supply (Operation Plainfare)
Department of the Scientific Adviser to the Army, December 1949, Army Operational Research Group, Report No.28/49, Observations on Army Aspects of Operation Plainfare

Public Record Office documents

AIR 20/7808 Operation Plainfare-Operation of Flying Boats
AIR 20/7823 Airlift-Accidents to Civil Aircraft in Germany-Policy
AIR 38/297 Berlin Airlift-Carriage of Liquid Fuels by Air-Tanker Aircraft Capacity
AIR 38/309 The Employment of the Glider Pilot Regiment on Operation Plainfare

BT 217/2270 The Berlin Airlift

F7/304/24 Berlin Air Lift; Loss of York Aircraft G- AHFI Belonging to Skyways Ltd

FO 371/76549 Berlin currency and trade. Russian blockade of West Berlin and Western counter-measures. Berlin railway strike: municipal elections December 1948. Transport situation: Evacuation of Jews. Administration of Western Berlin. Status of Berlin

AIR 38/333 Shuttle service to Berlin: operation 'Knicker' (provision for supply by air to the British zone of Berlin and evacuation of married families by air) April–June 1948

FO 1030/63 Berlin airlift policy: vol.1. 1948 August–December

BT 217/2083 Accident to British European Airways Corporation Viking Aircraft G-AIVP; Berlin (Gatow) Airport, 5 April 1948: report of Court of Enquiry; correspondence 1948

Index

If you are interested in purchasing other books published by Tempus,
or in case you have difficulty finding any Tempus books in your local bookshop,
you can also place orders directly through our website

www.tempus-publishing.com